Cracking the
COOP®/TACHS®
& HSPT®

Second Edition

By the Staff of The Princeton Review

PrincetonReview.com

Penguin Random House

The Princeton Review
24 Prime Parkway, Suite 201
Natick, MA 01760
E-mail: editorialsupport@review.com

Published in the United States by Penguin Random House LLC,
New York, and in Canada by Random House of Canada, a division of Penguin Random House Ltd., Toronto.

The Independent Education Consultants Association
recognizes The Princeton Review as a valuable resource for
high school and college students applying to college and
graduate school.

Terms of Service: The Princeton Review Online Companion
Tools ("Student Tools") for retail books are available for
only the two most recent editions of that book. Student
Tools may be activated only twice per eligible book pur-
chased for two consecutive 12-month periods, for a total
of 24 months of access. Activation of Student Tools more
than twice per book is in direct violation of these Terms
of Service and may result in discontinuation of access to
Student Tools Services.

ISBN: 978-1-101-88215-3
eBook ISBN: 978-1-101-88216-0
ISSN: 2379-6081

The Princeton Review is not affiliated with Princeton University.

Editor: Sarah Litt
Production Editor: Beth Hanson
Production Artist: Deborah A. Silvestrini

Printed in the United States of America on partially recycled
paper.

10   9   8   7   6   5   4   3   2   1

Second Edition

Editorial
Robert Franek, Senior VP, Publisher
Casey Cornelius, VP Content Development
Mary Beth Garrick, Director of Production
Selena Coppock, Managing Editor
Meave Shelton, Senior Editor
Colleen Day, Editor
Aaron Riccio, Editor
Callie McConnico, Editorial Assistant

Random House Publishing Team
Tom Russell, Publisher
Alison Stoltzfus, Publishing Manager
Melinda Ackell, Associate Managing Editor
Ellen Reed, Production Manager
Kristin Lindner, Production Supervisor
Andrea Lau, Designer

Acknowledgments

The Princeton Review would like to give a special thanks to Anne Morrow for her hard work on the revisions for this edition.

Contents

An Introduction for Parents vii

An Introduction for Students ix

Register Your Book Online! xv

1   General Test-Taking Skills 1

2   Vocabulary 5

Part I: Cracking the COOP 11

3   What Is the COOP? 13

4   Sequences 15

5   Analogies 25

6   Quantitative Reasoning 31

7   Verbal Reasoning—Words 43

8   Verbal Reasoning—Context 55

9   Reading and Language Arts 69

10 Mathematics 87

11 Answers to COOP Exercises 119

Part II: Cracking the HSPT 129

12 What Is the HSPT? 131

13 Verbal Skills 135

14 Quantitative Skills 149

15 Reading Comprehension and Vocabulary 177

16 Mathematics 193

17 Language Skills 207

18 Answers to HSPT Exercises 221

Part III: HSPT Practice Tests 229

19 HSPT Practice Test 1 231

20 HSPT Practice Test 1: Answers and Explanations 281

21 HSPT Practice Test 2 299

22 HSPT Practice Test 2: Answers and Explanations 349

An Introduction for Parents

Congratulations on taking the first step in helping your child prepare for the COOP, the TACHS, or the HSPT! There are ways, besides using this book, in which you can increase your child's performance on these tests and improve his or her chances of admission to a given private secondary school. We've compiled a few suggestions that you can follow to help your child have a healthy and productive educational experience during the application and admission process.

THE RIGHT PERSPECTIVE

Many parents and students have the false impression that doing poorly on a standardized test means that the student has not learned mathematics or English. It's important for you and your child to know that standardized tests such as the COOP and the HSPT are not intelligence tests. Nor are they really tests of what your child has learned in primary school. While many of the problems involve mathematics or English language mechanics, what the tests really measure are *extremely narrow* skills, which bear only a passing resemblance to the skills taught in school. Certainly, knowing the basics of mathematics and English language mechanics is important and will be covered in this book, but what is just as important is for students to learn how these basic skills are tested on the COOP and the HSPT. Learning how to do well on standardized tests is a skill unto itself that many students have never learned. This explains why many students who are perfectly capable in math and English still score poorly on these tests.

It's important that your child understand what these tests truly measure. Placing too much emphasis on standardized tests can lead to one stressed-out kid! While a little anxiety can be motivational, too much anxiety can be hurtful to the learning experience.

HOW YOU CAN HELP YOUR CHILD

First and foremost, be supportive and involved. Preparing for these tests and applying to private school can be intimidating. The more you can accompany your child through the process, the more comfortable he or she will feel. Help your child learn vocabulary. Review the practice tests together and help reinforce the basic skills outlined in this book. You'll probably find it an interesting experience, and it will help you to get to know your child better as well as make the educational process fun.

Second, understand that standardized tests are very different than tests that are taken in school. The expected rules that apply to school tests may not apply here. Many students, for instance, actually hurt their scores by trying to answer every question. On timed tests like these, accuracy is much more important than speed. Students should adopt a strategy that will get them the greatest number of points, which usually means slowing down and doing fewer problems.

Finally, be understanding. Your child may not yet have learned how to take standardized tests or how to perform well on them. This is especially intimidating. Imagine how a good student who scores poorly on a standardized test must feel, despite the fact that he or she knew the material tested. Remember that test-taking is a skill that can be learned. It simply takes expert instruction, practice, and time (the first two of which we will provide in this book!).

Of course, a little cajoling is also in order. Make sure that your child is committed to spending the time necessary to work through this book thoroughly and accurately.

Encourage your child to read something every day and to look up the difficult vocabulary words. With a bit of concentrated time and effort—and a lot of support—almost all students can learn to perform well on these tests.

WHAT COUNTS AS A GOOD SCORE? WHAT ABOUT THE ADMISSIONS PROCESS?

The writers of the COOP and the HSPT do not publicly release data on the performance of everyone who takes the test, so there is no way to know how students do in relation to one another. Moreover, each school has its own policies regarding the significance of these tests. Most consider a number of factors, in addition to test scores, when making admissions decisions. There is, therefore, no way to know exactly what score will qualify a student for admission at a particular school. You should simply try to help your child perform his or her best by giving him or her all the support and attention you can. You should, however, contact the schools to which your child is interested in applying to learn more about their admissions criteria.

What Are the SSAT and the ISEE?

The SSAT and the ISEE are two other common tests used by private high schools for admissions purposes. Although this book will provide some overlap in preparation for these tests, we highly recommend that you purchase *Cracking the SSAT & ISEE*, which is specifically designed to prepare students for these tests.

We hope that you find this book to be a useful, accessible, and helpful tool in your preparations, and we wish you the very best of luck in your child's future success.

An Introduction for Students

HOW DO I USE THIS BOOK?

This book will review the basic concepts, question types, and problem-solving techniques you'll need to improve your score on either the COOP or the HSPT. The practice tests will help you get used to the timing and pace of the tests. The more quality time you put into studying this book, the better you'll do. Learning to take standardized tests is like learning to play any sport: The first time you try you may feel clumsy, but with practice you can always improve.

STUDY RULES

Set aside a time when you can concentrate with no distractions. It's a good idea to have a place (such as your room or a library) where you always study. Have a few sharpened pencils and a dictionary handy.

As you read each chapter, try the techniques and do all the exercises. Check your answers against the answer keys, and note any questions you get wrong. Review your errors carefully, and work through them. Remember: Now is the chance to make all the errors you want (and learn from them) so that you won't make them on the actual test!

When Should I Start to Study?

We suggest that you start studying for the test about a month before it's given. If you're starting earlier than that, we suggest that you do two things from now until the test to help improve your score: Read as much as you can and learn new vocabulary words.

Reading

Both the COOP and the HSPT—as well as almost every other standardized test you're ever going to take—place a lot of weight on reading comprehension. How do you get better at reading? By reading. The more you read, the better you'll be at it. Follow these tips to get started:

- Try to find a short article or story every day to read. After you read it, try to explain it to a friend or parent. By trying to explain it to someone else, you'll see how much of it you really understood.

- Pick something to read that is just a bit above your current reading level. It can be an adventure book, a weekly magazine, or a column in a newspaper.

- Mark any words you don't know. Try to figure out what a word means from the context (the sentence and paragraph it's in); if you can't, look up the word. Write down these words and definitions on index cards to help you remember them.

When You Take a Practice Test

The study plan below advises you on when to take the practice tests. Here are some tips for getting the most out of them:

- Time yourself correctly. Use a timer, watch, or stopwatch that will make a noise, or have someone else time you. You want to get a feel for exactly how much time you'll have for each section.

- Take the practice test in one sitting, just like the real thing. It's important to build up your endurance for the actual test.

- Take the practice tests using the answer sheet with bubbles to fill in (you can find this in the back of this book or online), just like on the real test. You should practice filling in your bubbles thoroughly and checking to make sure that you're filling in the correct bubble for a given question.

A STUDY PLAN *

*If you're taking the HSPT, you can find your study guide on page 132!

COOP Study Plan

If you are taking the COOP, follow this nine-session study plan.

Session 1

- Before you do anything else, besides reading this introduction, take the first practice COOP test online. Correct it and pay particularly close attention to your mistakes.

- Write down anything you notice that you had difficulty with, such as "triangle problems." This will help you remember to pay extra attention to those concepts when you study those chapters.

- If you got more than 25 percent incorrect in any section, tell yourself to slow down and do fewer problems. You are much better off doing only 75 percent of the questions and getting more of them correct than doing all of the problems and getting many of them wrong.

Session 2

- Read Chapter 1: General Test-Taking Skills

- Read Chapter 2: Vocabulary

Session 3

- Read Chapter 3: What is the COOP?

- Read Chapter 4: Sequences

Session 4

- Read Chapter 5: Analogies

- Read Chapter 6: Quantitative Reasoning

Session 5

- Read Chapter 7: Verbal Reasoning—Words

Session 6

- Read Chapter 8: Verbal Reasoning—Context

Session 7

- Read Chapter 9: Reading and Language Arts

Session 8

- Read Chapter 10: Mathematics (You may find that you need to spread this chapter over two sessions—and that's okay.)

Session 9:

- Take the second practice COOP test online. Correct the test, ooh and ahh over how much your score improved, and review the concepts in the book for the questions you answered incorrectly.

- Use any additional days before the test to continue to review the concepts and test-taking techniques covered in the book.

THE DAY OF THE EXAM

No matter how much you prepare for the test, if you don't do all of these things the day of the exam, you are likely to run out of steam and do poorly.

- Wake up refreshed from a good night's sleep.

- Eat a good breakfast.

- Arrive early to the testing session.

- Remind yourself that you do not need to solve every problem to get a good score. Pace yourself!

And one more thing: Good luck!

Register Your

1 Go to **PrincetonReview.com/cracking**

2 You'll see a welcome page where you can register your book using the following ISBN: 9781101882153.

3 After placing this free order, you'll either be asked to log in or to answer a few simple questions in order to set up a new Princeton Review account.

4 Finally, click on the "Student Tools" tab located at the top of the screen. It may take an hour or two for your registration to go through, but after that, you're good to go.

If you are experiencing book problems (potential content errors), please contact EditorialSupport@review.com with the full title of the book, its ISBN number (located above), and the page number of the error. Experiencing technical issues? Please e-mail TPRStudentTech@review.com with the following information:

- your full name
- e-mail address used to register the book
- full book title and ISBN
- your computer OS (Mac or PC) and Internet browser (Firefox, Safari, Chrome, etc.)
- description of technical issue

Book Online!

Once you've registered, you can...

- Find any late-breaking information released about the COOP, the TACHS or the HSPT

- Take a full-length practice PSAT, SAT, and ACT

- Get valuable advice about the college application process, including tips for writing a great essay and where to apply for financial aid

- Sort colleges by whatever you're looking for (such as Best Theater or Dorm), learn more about your top choices, and see how they all rank according to *The Best 380 Colleges*

- Access comprehensive study guides and a variety of printable resources, including practice COOP and TACHS exams, bubble sheets, and more

- Check to see if there have been any corrections or updates to this edition

Look For These Icons Throughout The Book

 Online Practice Tests

 Applied Strategies

 Proven Techniques

 Study Break

The Princeton Review®

Chapter 1
General Test-Taking Skills

Whether you are taking the COOP or the HSPT, there are certain test-taking skills that you should learn and follow. These alone, without other review, will already improve your score on any standardized test.

PACING

One of the most important test-taking skills is pacing, or how you spend your time. Of course, you want to do as many problems as you can so that you can get as high a score as possible. But on standardized tests, accuracy is more important than speed.

This may sound a little confusing: Although you should fill in every single bubble on the answer sheet, you shouldn't feel that you have to work every single problem on the test. You're better off if you slow down and work at a steady pace to make sure that you get as many problems correct as you can. Most "dumb mistakes" are caused by working too quickly, so make sure that you aren't rushing and doing sloppy work. When you have only a few minutes left, quickly fill in the remaining bubbles with your Letter Of The Day (LOTD). Why? Read on and we'll explain.

Most students think that they need to get every problem on the test to get a great score, and most students hurt their score because they try to do too many problems. There are two reasons why you shouldn't try to do every single problem.

First, it's very hard to find time to answer every question correctly. So, naturally, people rush, then make careless errors and lose points. Almost everyone is better off *slowing down,* using the whole time to work on fewer problems and answering more of those problems correctly. Think about it this way: You'll get a higher score if you do *only 75 percent* of the problems on this test and answer them correctly than if you do all of the problems and answer about half correctly. Weird, huh?

Second, some questions are easier than others, but they're all worth the same number of points. So why waste time working on hard problems when there are easier ones you can do?

In short, if you follow this advice, your score will improve:

- **Slow down.** Make sure you work slowly and carefully enough to make sure that you get most of the problems correct. If you find that you are making lots of mistakes, slow down even more. It may feel funny, but it will help your score.
- Guess at any problems that you don't have time to try. This means that you should **absolutely fill in every bubble on your answer sheet.** Choose a LOTD. You are not penalized for wrong choices, and you will probably get a few extra points by random chance.
- If you find that a problem is too hard or isn't making sense, **skip it and go on to an easier one.** You can always go back if you have time. If you don't, you're better off making your best guess.

PROCESS OF ELIMINATION

Another very important test-taking skill is Process of Elimination. This is a strategy in which you don't have to know the answer to the question to get the correct answer. Have a look at the following problem.

 What is the capital of Malawi?

    A Washington

    B Paris

    C Tokyo

    D London

    E Lilongwe

(Don't worry—you won't see any questions like this on your test. It's just an example.)

How did you know the answer was (E)? Because you knew that it couldn't be (A), (B), (C), or (D). That's Process of Elimination. When you are solving a problem, always cross off the choices you know are wrong, for whatever reason. Especially on the English and reading comprehension sections of the test, you'll often find that you can cross off every answer except one—the right one! Even if you can't always narrow the choices down to only one, you will certainly cross off a few choices and improve your chances of guessing correctly. **Using Process of Elimination whenever you need to will improve your chances of getting the answer correct.**

BALLPARKING

In mathematics sections, another great tool is Ballparking. This means "take a guess and see which answers are in the ballpark." This can help you save time and make a good guess when you don't know or don't have time to figure out the correct answer.

Have a look at the following problem:

2 What is $\frac{1}{2}$ of 1022?

A 51

B 52

C 511

D 512

Before you try to solve this, look at the answer choices. Which ones are in the ballpark? Certainly not (A) and (B). These can be eliminated. If you're out of time or have a hard time solving the problem, you can now guess between (C) and (D).

If you can eliminate choices for any reason, you improve your odds by making a correct guess, and you will improve your chances of getting the right answer.

Chapter 2
Vocabulary

VOCABULARY

Having a good vocabulary will not only help you better understand what you read, but it will help you understand the world around you. As you get older, a broad vocabulary will help you prepare for college and beyond. You should also learn the meanings of words that you come across in school or in your readings that you don't know. Here are some pointers for using vocabulary.

- Every time you find an unfamiliar word, write the word on the front of an index card and write its definition and a sample sentence on the back. Then quiz yourself to practice memorizing the meanings of your words. Remember to include a sample sentence—it's easier to learn words in context.
- Pick five words each day and use them every chance you get. Your friends may think you are a little strange when you walk around saying things like, "*Pretty Little Liars* was an unusually mediocre episode last night." But you'll certainly learn those words. (By the way, mediocre means "of moderate or low quality.")

HIT PARADE

Ab through An

Abandon
Abbreviation
Abdicate
Abhor
Abrupt
Abundant
Abyss
Acclaimed
Accord
Acknowledge
Acute
Adamant
Adapt
Adept
Adhesive
Admire
Admonish
Adversary
Affiliation
Agenda
Aggrandize
Aggravate
Aggregate
Agile
Ail
Aimless
Akin
Alarmed
Allege
Aloof
Alter
Altruism
Ambiguous
Ambivalent
Ameliorate
Amiable
Amorphous
Analyze
Ancient
Androgynous
Anguish
Animosity
Annex

An through Ca

Antagonistic
Antipathy
Anxious
Apprehension
Approximate
Arbitrary
Arid
Ascertain
Aspect
Aspiration
Assail
Assent
Assert
Assess
Assured
Astonish
Astute
Audible
Auspicious
Austere
Authentic
Authoritative
Banal
Barrage
Barren
Barrier
Bashful
Bastion
Belligerent
Bemoan
Benevolent
Benign
Bequest
Betray
Bewilder
Biased
Blatant
Blunt
Bombastic
Brash
Brazen
Brittle
Candid
Capricious

Ca through Cu

Cascade
Cater
Cautious
Censor
Chagrin
Chasm
Chronic
Chronicle
Coalesce
Coerce
Commodities
Compassion
Compel
Competent
Composure
Comprehensive
Conceal
Concise
Condemn
Condescending
Condone
Confer
Confine
Conform
Confound
Congenial
Conniving
Consensus
Conspicuous
Consume
Contemplation
Contented
Contradiction
Contrite
Controversial
Conventional
Cordial
Corpulent
Counsel
Counterfeit
Credible
Creed
Crucial
Cunning

Da through Dr	Du through Fl	Fl through Hi
Dawdle	Dubious	Fleeting
Debate	Duration	Flotsam
Debt	Eager	Flourish
Deceive	Economize	Fluctuate
Decline	Egotist	Foolhardy
Decree	Egress	Foreseen
Defensive	Elegant	Forge
Defiant	Elegy	Formulate
Deficient	Elongate	Fortunate
Deft	Eloquent	Foster
Dejection	Embodiment	Fragile
Deliberate	Embryonic	Frank
Delicate	Emphasize	Frugal
Depict	Endeavor	Fundamental
Despair	Enigma	Furious
Desolate	Entrust	Gap
Detest	Envy	Genial
Detrimental	Ephemeral	Generous
Deviate	Epitome	Genuine
Devotion	Equity	Germane
Dignity	Equivalent	Glean
Dilute	Eradicate	Glint
Differentiate	Erratic	Graceful
Disavow	Esoteric	Gratified
Discreet	Essential	Grievances
Disgraced	Esteem	Gullible
Dismayed	Euphemism	Haphazard
Dispel	Evacuate	Hardship
Disparage	Exalt	Extend
Disperse	Evade	Extent
Display	Exasperate	Extinct
Disputed	Excavate	Extol
Dissect	Excel	Extravagant
Distasteful	Exemplify	Facet
Distort	Exhilarating	Fallacy
Diversity	Exile	Fallow
Docile	Exquisite	Falter
Domestic	Fatigue	Fathom
Dominate	Feasible	Feisty
Dormant	Feeble	Hasten
Doubtful	Feign	Haughty
Drastic	Fickle	Hazard
Dread	Flaccid	Hesitate
Drenched	Flatter	Hideous

Hi through La	Le through Om	Om through Re
Hinder	Legend	Omit
Hoard	Legitimate	Opaque
Homely	Lenient	Optimistic
Ignoble	Liberate	Opulent
Illuminate	Limber	Ostentatious
Illustrate	Linger	Overbearing
Immaculate	Lofty	Overt
Impasse	Lucrative	Pacify
Imply	Luminous	Pact
Impulsive	Lure	Palpable
Inane	Malicious	Paltry
Incident	Meager	Parody
Incidental	Meander	Parsimonious
Incision	Meddle	Particle
Incisive	Menace	Partisan
Incite	Mentor	Patron
Indifferent	Merge	Peak
Indignant	Meticulous	Permeate
Infiltrate	Mimic	Perpetuate
Ingenuity	Mirage	Perplexed
Ingress	Misery	Persevere
Inhabit	Model (adjective)	Persist
Initial	Modify	Pragmatic
Innate	Molten	Precise
Innocuous	Moral	Predicament
Innovate	Morose	Prediction
Inquiry	Muddled	Predominate
Insight	Mundane	Prejudiced
Insinuate	Mystify	Presume
Insipid	Myth	Pretentious
Insolent	Nag	Prevalent
Integrity	Navigate	Primary
Intermission	Negate	Pristine
Integrate	Neglect	Prominent
Intricate	Noncommittal	Prone
Inundate	Nostalgic	Prophesy
Invoke	Notorious	Prototype
Irate	Novel	Provoke
Jeer	Novice	Prudent
Jest	Noxious	Pungent
Jubilant	Null	Puny
Justify	Obscure	Puzzled
Keen	Obstacle	Ratify
Kinetic	Obstinate	Ravenous
Lament	Obstruct	Recalcitrant
Laudatory	Obtuse	Reckless
Lavish	Occupy	Refute
Legacy	Ominous	Reject

Re through Ro	Ru through Ta	Ta through Za
Reluctant	Rue	Task
Reminisce	Ruminate	Taunt
Remote	Ruse	Tenacious
Rendezvous	Rustic	Terse
Renounce	Ruthless	Testify to
Renown	Salvage	Thrive
Personify	Satire	Thwart
Pervasive	Savor	Timid
Pessimistic	Sedate	Tiresome
Petty	Scant	Toil
Pigment	Scarce	Torment
Pilfer	Scorn	Tragedy
Pinnacle	Seclude	Trifle
Pious	Seldom	Trite
Placate	Sequence	Ultimate
Plausible	Shrewd	Uncouth
Plea	Simulate	Undermine
Plight	Sincere	Unique
Plunder	Sinister	Unruly
Pompous	Solemn	Uproot
Porous	Solitary	Utilitarian
Replete	Somber	Utilize
Replenish	Soothe	Vacillate
Replica	Specific	Vend
Reprehensible	Sporadic	Veneration
Repress	Speck	Versatile
Reprimand	Spirited	Vibrant
Reproach	Spontaneous	Viewpoint
Repudiate	Stagnate	Vigorous
Repugnant	Stature	Vigilant
Reservations	Steadfast	Vivacious
(about something)	Stringent	Vivid
Residual	Subside	Voracious
Resilience	Succinct	Vow
Restore	Sullied	Voyage
Resume	Superb	Wane
Reticent	Superfluous	Wax (verb)
Reveal	Suppose	Weary
Revere	Surrogate	Wily
Reverent	Tact	Wrath
Robust	Tangible	Writhe
Rouse	Taper	Zany
Routine		

Part I
Cracking the
COOP

Chapter 3
What is the COOP?

The Cooperative Admissions Examination Program, or COOP, is given to students in certain New York and New Jersey counties who are planning to go to Catholic high schools. It is given to students in late October; check with your local diocese the summer before you plan to test for more precise information on the date of the test. Keep in mind, there is a 30% content change every year, so make sure to visit the site for the most updated information.

The TACHS (Test for Admission into Catholic High Schools) is similar to the COOP, but will test a few different skills. The TACHS is given to students in New York who plan to attend Catholic high school.

In this book, we will review COOP material, and we will indicate what you might see on the TACHS.

Below is the format of the test at the time this book was published. The test does undergo changes from one year to the next, so your test may vary from the model you see here. To learn more about the most recent updates to the exam, go to **www.tachsinfo.com** or **coopexam.org**, depending on which test you're planning to take.

- Sequences
- Analogies
- Quantitative Reasoning
- Verbal Reasoning—Words
- Verbal Reasoning—Context
- Reading and Language Arts
- Mathematics

On the TACHS you will find:

- Reading: including Vocabulary and Language Arts
- Language Skills: including Spelling, Capitalization, Punctuation, and Usage
- Math:
  Ability (this tests your abject reasoning ability, and presents you with things like visual tasks and identifying patterns)

The following chapters cover the broad range of material found on both exams and review the types of problems you are likely to see.

Before you begin, go online and take the COOP Practice Test 1 and see how you do! You might surprise yourself.

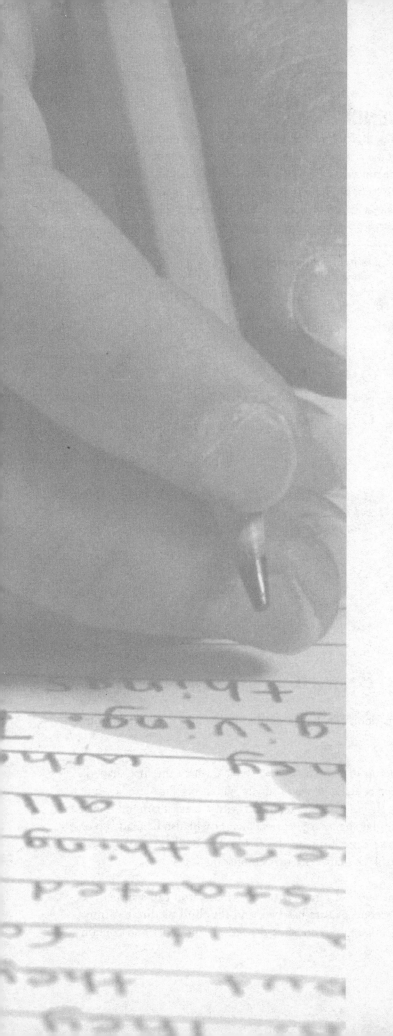

Chapter 4
Sequences

WHAT IS A SEQUENCE?

A sequence is a list of items that follows a pattern. In this section of the COOP, the questions will show you a sequence made up of pictures, numbers, or letters. You will be asked to figure out what picture(s) or number(s) should fill the blank in the sequence. Your job is to figure out the pattern in the sequence. For instance, the numbers 2, 4, 6, 8 make a sequence because each number is 2 more than the number before it.

First, let's look at the sequences made of pictures:

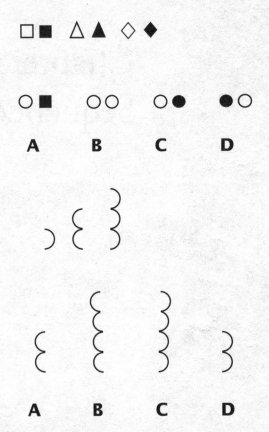

To answer these questions, look at what is similar and what changes from one picture to the next.

The first sequence is made up of pairs of similar shapes, where the first shape is white and the second shape is black: A white square with a black square, a white triangle with a black triangle, and a white diamond with a black diamond. Since all three pairs have two similar shapes, the correct answer will also be made up of similar shapes. Therefore we can eliminate choice (A). Since all three pairs have the white shape before the black shape, the answer must be (C).

The second sequence is made up of numbers of half-circles. You can see that the first picture has one, the second picture has two, and the third picture has three half-circles. Therefore the missing picture should continue the series and contain four half-circles. So we know that (A) and (D) can be eliminated. How can we decide between (B) and (C)? In the first picture, the half-circles are open on the left, in the second picture they are open on the right, and in the third picture they are open on the left. Since they change direction from one picture to the next, the missing picture will have half-circles that are open to the right. Therefore the answer is (B).

Other sequences will be made up entirely of numbers. In these examples there are three numbers in each grouping. All three groupings follow a pattern. You have to figure out what the pattern is in order to choose the correct number.

1

1 5 9 | 3 7 11 | 8 12 __

10	14	16	17
A	**B**	**C**	**D**

Here's How to Crack It
Between the first and second and the second and third numbers in each group, write the number that—by performing an operation like adding, subtracting, multiplying, or dividing—takes you from the first number to the next.

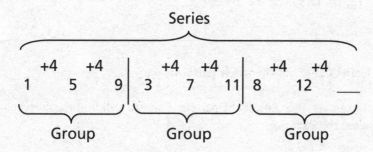

Because in the three groups each number is 4 more (+ 4) than the previous number, the next number in the series must be 16: 8 (+ 4) = 12 (+ 4) = 16. The answer is (C).

On more complicated problems, you'll need to use more than one kind of operation (multiplication, addition, division, subtraction) between each pair of numbers to figure out how the pattern works. You might have to subtract the first and second numbers in each group and then multiply to get the third. Here's an example.

7 5 12 | 19 17 24 | 12 10 __

8	14	17	18
F	**G**	**H**	**J**

$$\begin{array}{ccccccccc} & -2 & +7 & & -2 & +7 & & -2 & +7 \\ 7 & 5 & 12 & | & 19 & 17 & 24 & | & 12 & 10 & \underline{} \end{array}$$

Here's How to Crack It

In this sequence problem, you have to *subtract* 2 from the first number to get the second number and then *add* 7 to the second number to get the third number. Look at the last group to see how easy it can be: 12 − 2 = 10 and 10 + 7 = 17. The pattern is 12, 10, 17, so (H) is correct.

What if I can't figure out the whole pattern?

Even if you can get only *part* of the pattern, you can still find the correct answer. Take a look at this example.

3 _____

2 4 5 | 10 20 21 | 8 16 __

8	14	17	18
A	**B**	**C**	**D**

Here's How to Crack It

Suppose you have a hard time figuring out what operation you need to use to get from the first to the second number. In this problem, as long as you can figure out that you add 1 to the second number to get the third number, you can get the answer. (By the way, the first operation in this sequence was to multiply by 2.)

$$2 \quad 4 \quad \overset{+1}{5} \mid 10 \quad 20 \quad \overset{+1}{21} \mid 8 \quad 16 \quad \overset{+1}{\underline{}}$$

Since 16 + 1 = 17, the answer is (C).

Sometimes the blank will be in the middle of the series rather than at the end. Follow the same technique, and double-check your answer by making sure that the number you put in the blank works with the number that follows.

4 _____

3 5 10 | 9 11 22 | 12 __ 28

14	16	18	24
F	**G**	**H**	**J**

$$\begin{array}{ccccccccc} & \overset{+2}{} & \overset{\times 2}{} & & \overset{+2}{} & \overset{\times 2}{} & & \overset{+2}{} & \overset{\times 2}{} \\ 3 & & 5 & 10 \mid 9 & & 11 & 22 \mid 12 & \underline{} & 28 \end{array}$$

Here's How to Crack It

In this example, the first operation is to add 2, and the second operation is to multiply by 2: 12 + 2 = 14 and 14 × 2 = 28. The answer is (F).

SUBSTITUTE NUMBERS FOR LETTERS TO CRACK LETTER SEQUENCES

The sequence problems toward the end of the section will probably combine letters and numbers or use all letters. These tend to be the most difficult problems on the test. If one of them stumps you, move on to the next one and go back. Try to do as many as you can. Don't forget that you can often solve the problem (or eliminate a few choices) by figuring out just one part of each group in the sequence. You don't always have to figure out the entire sequence. If you're completely stumped, don't forget to guess so that you haven't left anything blank.

One way to make the sequences that use letters easier to solve is to substitute the letters with numbers according to the location of each letter in the alphabet. This often helps you see the pattern of the sequences more easily. The first step is to write the following on your test booklet.

A	B	C	D	E	F	G	H	I	J	K	L	M	N	O	P	Q	R	S	T	U	V	W	X	Y	Z
1	2	3	4	5	6	7	8	9	10	11	12	13	14	15	16	17	18	19	20	21	22	23	24	25	26

This will help you change letters into numbers easily. Now look at the following problem.

5

BDF | HJL | NPR | _____

SUW   TVX   RST   UWY

A   **B**   **C**   **D**

Here's How to Crack It

Look at the chart of numbers and letters above. B is 2, D is 4, F is 6, H is 8, and so on. By using numbers instead of letters, you should be able to figure out the pattern much more easily.

2 4 6 | 8 10 12 | 14 16 18 | _____

Now we can see the pattern. The numbers are all even and increase by 2: 2 + 2 = 4 and 4 + 2 = 6. The original question, before we made the substitution, would look like this:

$$\text{B} \overset{+2}{} \text{D} \overset{+2}{} \text{F} \ \Big| \ \text{H} \overset{+2}{} \text{J} \overset{+2}{} \text{L} \ \Big| \ \text{N} \overset{+2}{} \text{P} \overset{+2}{} \text{R}$$

The correct answer will also have even numbers that increase by 2. Substitute numbers for letters in the answer choices.

A SUW		**A**	19 21 23
B TVX		**B**	20 22 24
C RST		**C**	18 19 20
D UWY		**D**	21 23 25

Only (B) follows the pattern: 20 + 2 = 22 and 22 + 2 = 24. On our number and alphabet chart, 20 is T, 22 is V, and 24 is X, so you know the answer has to be TVX.

COOP Sequence Exercise

(Answers are on page 120)

For Numbers 1 through 3, choose the response that continues the pattern or sequence.

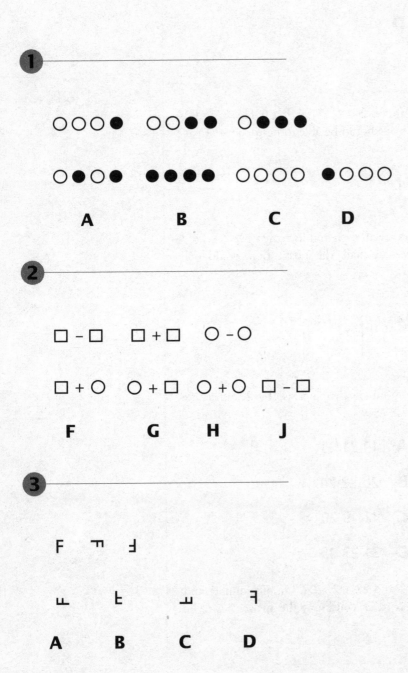

For Numbers 4 through 11, choose the response that continues the pattern or sequence.

4

4 8 12 | 11 15 19 | 21 25 ____

22	23	27	29
F	G	H	J

5

38 32 26 | 17 11 5 | 42 ____ 30

36	34	32	24
A	B	C	D

6

6 12 16 | 4 8 12 | 5 10 ____

8	14	15	20
F	G	H	J

7

10 5 15 | 13 8 18 | 22 ____ 27

15	17	22	25
A	B	C	D

8

8 16 20 | 4 8 12 | 20 ____ 44

24	28	35	40
F	G	H	J

9

20 18 25 | 23 21 28 | 30 28 ____

25	26	35	38
A	B	C	D

10

HFD | LJH | PNL | TRP | ____

RQP	XVT	VUT	YWV
F	G	H	J

11

A1FK | D2IN | G3LQ | J4OT | ____

M5RW	N5QS	N5ST	U6VW
A	B	C	D

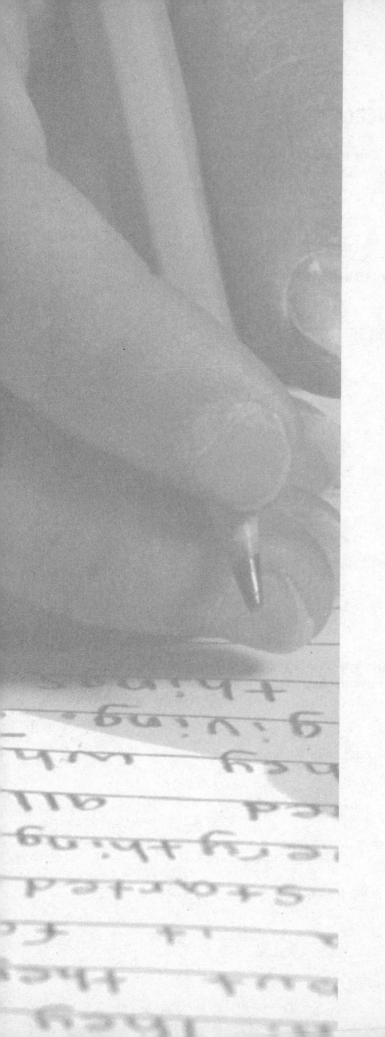

Chapter 5
Analogies

WHAT IS AN ANALOGY?

An analogy is just a fancy word that means two pairs of objects have the same relationship. For instance, kittens/cats and puppies/dogs are analogies. Each pair of words has the same relationship: Kittens are baby cats, just as puppies are baby dogs. On the COOP, instead of making analogies with words, you will be asked to make them with pictures.

How to Approach Analogies

Here is what an analogy question will look like on the COOP:

1

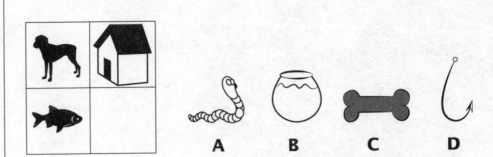

Here's How to Crack It

Even though the COOP asks you to make analogies with pictures, the best way to solve them is to turn those pictures into words. To figure out the relationship between two words, make a sentence using the words. Finally, use that *same sentence* for each of the answer choices, and see which one fits best.

The top two pictures show a dog and a doghouse. What sentence could we make with these two words?

A dog **lives in** a doghouse.

Now let's use that same sentence with the remaining picture and each of the answer choices.

A fish **lives in** a _____.

Does a fish live in a worm? No. Cross off (A). Does a fish live in a fish bowl? Yes. Let's leave (B) in the running. Does a fish live in a dog bone? No. Cross off (C). Does a fish live in a hook? No. Cross off (D). Since we have crossed off (A), (C), and (D), the best answer must be (B).

Let's try one more:

2

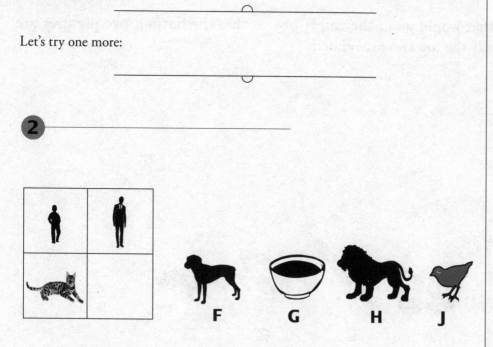

What kind of sentence could we make using the words boy and man?

A boy **is a small** man.

Here's How to Crack It

Now let's try that same sentence with the answer choices. Is a cat a small dog? No. Cross off (F). Is a cat a small bowl of milk? No. Cross off (G). Is a cat a small lion? Maybe. Let's leave H in the running. Is a cat a small bird? No. Cross off (J). This makes (H) the best choice.

As you can see, you should expect to use Process of Elimination on these questions. The one that fits best is the one you should pick.

Now let's put it all together.

COOP Analogy Exercise 1

(Answers are on page 121)

Choose the picture that would go in the empty box so that the bottom two pictures are related in the same way the top two are related.

1

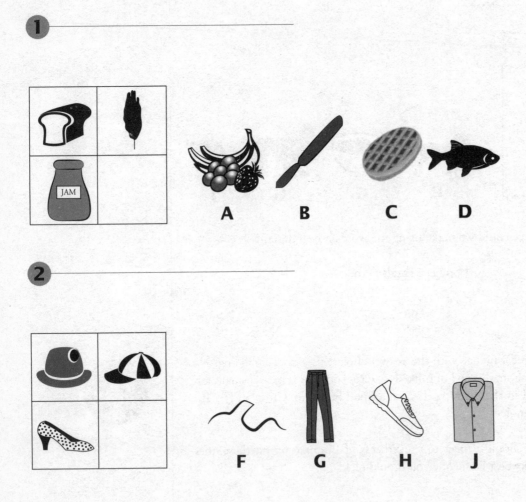

3

A   B   C   D

4

F   G   H   J

5

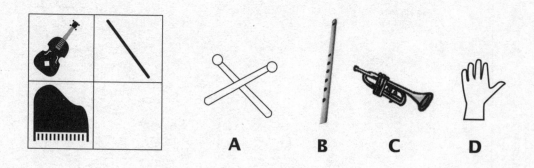

A   B   C   D

Timing

On the COOP, you have seven minutes to complete twenty analogies. This means that you have to move along fairly quickly. If you get stuck on one problem, move on to the next. There are probably easier ones later in the section, and you can always come back to a difficult problem if you have time left at the end. Now that you understand how to crack these questions, go back to the first online practice test and rework any of the analogy problems that you found difficult.

Time to take a walk
and let all that info sink in!

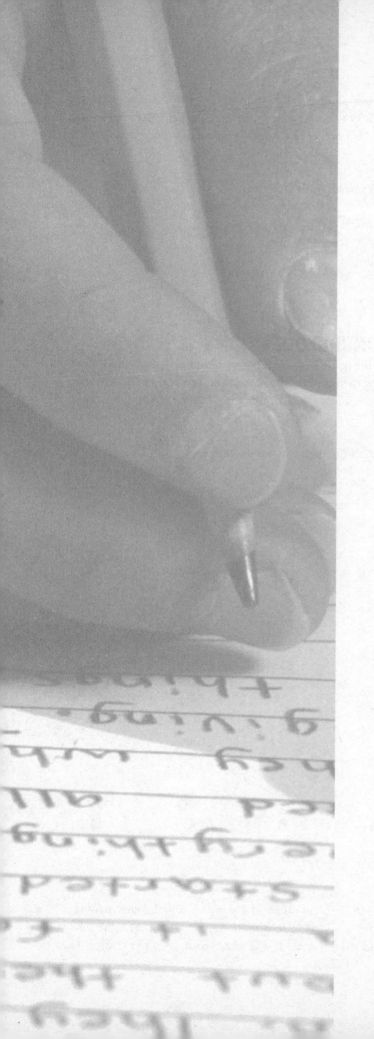

Chapter 6
Quantitative Reasoning

The quantitative reasoning section of the COOP is designed to assess your ability to identify relationships. It is **not** testing your knowledge of mathematics! Rather, like the Sequences section, this portion of the COOP is measuring your ability to recognize relationships.

This section has several different kinds of questions:

- Number relationships
- Visual relationships
- Symbol relationships

NUMBER RELATIONSHIP QUESTIONS

The first set of questions in the quantitative reasoning section will ask you to identify the relationship between the numbers in the first column and the numbers in the second column. Then you must select the missing number from the answer choices.

Here is what a number relationship question will look like:

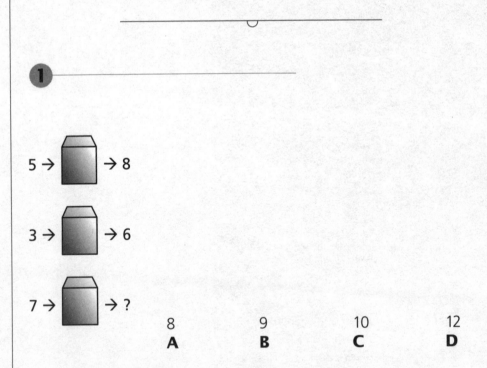

8	9	10	12
A	**B**	**C**	**D**

Here's How to Crack It

Look at the first row: 5 is in the first column and 8 is in the second column. What is the relationship? Well, if 3 is added to 5, 8 is the result. Does that same relationship apply to the second row? It does! If 3 is added to 3, then the result is 6.

Therefore, the relationship between the columns is to add 3 to the first column to produce the second column. Thus, the correct answer is 10, or choice (D), since 7 plus 3 equals 10.

Let's take a look at a second example:

2

 4 → → 8

 3 → → 6

 7 → → ?

10	11	12	14
F	**G**	**H**	**J**

Here's How to Crack It

Notice how, in this example, adding the same number to the first column each time isn't the correct relationship. In this case, the two columns have a different kind of relationship. So what kind is it? Well, if 4 is multiplied by 2, 8 is the result. Does that same relationship apply to the second row? It does! If 3 is multiplied by 2, then the result is 6. Therefore, the relationship between the columns is to multiply the first column by two to get the value in the second column. Thus, the correct answer is 14, or choice (J), since 7 times 2 equals 14.

VISUAL RELATIONSHIP QUESTIONS

In the second set of questions on the quantitative reasoning section, you will be provided with a figure that is divided up into sections, some of which are shaded. You will be asked to choose the answer that represents the shaded region.

Here is what a visual relationship question will look like:

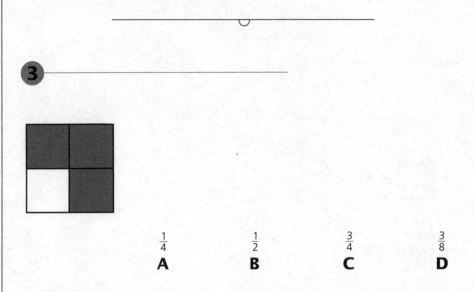

$$\frac{1}{4} \qquad \frac{1}{2} \qquad \frac{3}{4} \qquad \frac{3}{8}$$
A   **B**   **C**   **D**

Here's How to Crack It

Remember that you're looking for the part of the figure that is shaded. The whole figure is divided into four smaller squares, so count up the number of smaller squares shaded. 3 of the 4 smaller squares are shaded, so that means 3 out of 4 (or $\frac{3}{4}$) is the answer, which is choice (C). If you picked choice (A), $\left(\frac{1}{4}\right)$, remember that on these problems, you are finding the shaded portion of the figure, not the unshaded portion.

Here's another example:

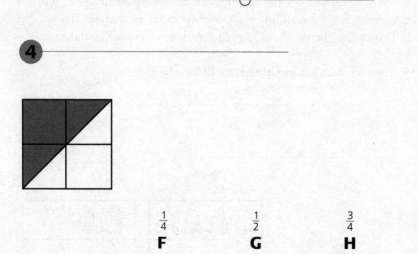

$\frac{1}{4}$ $\frac{1}{2}$ $\frac{3}{4}$ $\frac{3}{8}$

F   **G**   **H**   **J**

Here's How to Crack It

Remember that you're looking for the part of the figure that is shaded. The whole figure is divided into four smaller squares, but in this example two of the smaller squares are only half-shaded. Imagine if those two shaded pieces were put together. What do they make? Together they make a fully shaded smaller square. Therefore, there is a total of two smaller squares shaded. Since 2 of the 4 smaller squares are shaded, that means one half of the figure is shaded, which is choice (G).

SYMBOL RELATIONSHIP QUESTIONS

For the last set of questions on the quantitative reasoning section you will see a scale which shows the relationship between two types of shapes. The scale is balanced, and you must choose the answer that will *keep* the scales balanced.

Here is what a symbol relationship question will look like:

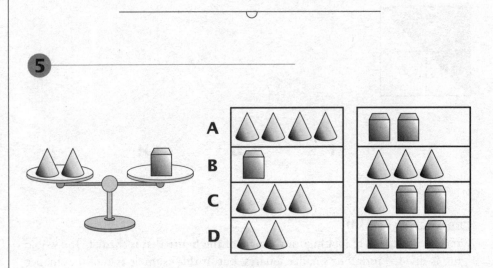

Here's How to Crack It

The goal of these questions is to find a balanced scale—one that uses the same relationship as the original set—so pay attention to how the shapes relate to each other. The correct answer won't necessarily have the same number of shapes as the original. For this example, the original scale shows that 2 cones are equal in weight to 1 cube. Thus, there is a 2:1 relationship between the shapes. The correct answer will also have a 2:1 relationship between cones and cubes. The scale in choice (A) has 4 cones on the left side and 2 cubes on the right side, which is equal to 2 cones to 1 cube, and is therefore the correct answer. The remaining choices would not result in a balanced scale. Remember: 1 cube is equal in weight to 2 cones.

Sometimes you may see two different shapes on one side of the scale in the answer choices. Remember to keep the original relationship in mind and look for a choice that maintains that relationship. Let's look at an example:

6 ————————————

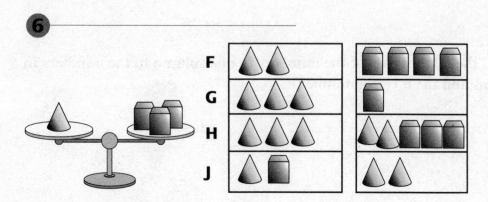

F

G

H

J

Here's How to Crack It

This question is a little trickier since the correct answer combines the two shapes on one side of the scale. In this example, one cone is equal in weight to 3 cubes. Thus, a cone could be substituted for 3 cubes on the right side of the scale. The scale in choice (H) has 3 cones on the left side of the scale, which is equivalent to 9 cubes. The right side of the scale in choice (H) has 2 cones and 3 cubes. Remember that 1 cone equals 3 cubes, so that means 2 cones are equal to 6 cubes. Add those 6 cubes to the other 3 cubes and that makes a total of 9 cubes. Since the two sides of the scale balance, choice (H) is the correct answer. The remaining choices would not result in a balanced scale.

COOP Quantitative Reasoning Exercise

(Answers are on page 121)

For Numbers 1-3, find the relationship of the numbers in one column to the numbers in the other column. Then find the missing number.

4 → ▢ → 1

7 → ▢ → 4

11 → ▢ → ?

1	7	8	14
A	**B**	**C**	**D**

4 → ▢ → 16

1 → ▢ → 4

5 → ▢ → ?

8	9	16	20
F	**G**	**H**	**J**

6 → ▢ → 2

12 → ▢ → 4

9 → ▢ → ?

2	3	6	8
A	**B**	**C**	**D**

For Numbers 4–7, find the portion of the figure that is shaded.

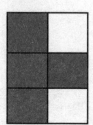

$\frac{1}{2}$	$\frac{1}{3}$	$\frac{2}{3}$	$\frac{4}{5}$
F	**G**	**H**	**J**

5

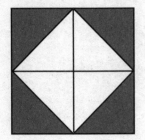

$\frac{1}{2}$ $\frac{1}{4}$ $\frac{3}{4}$ $\frac{5}{8}$
A   **B**   **C**   **D**

6

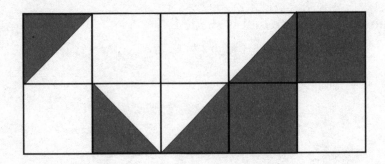

$\frac{3}{10}$ $\frac{4}{10}$ $\frac{5}{10}$ $\frac{6}{10}$
F   **G**   **H**   **J**

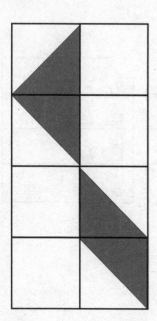

$$\frac{2}{4}$$ $$\frac{2}{8}$$ $$\frac{4}{8}$$ $$\frac{6}{8}$$
A   **B**   **C**   **D**

For Numbers 8–11, look at the scale showing sets of shapes of equal weight. Find an equivalent pair of sets that would also balance the scale.

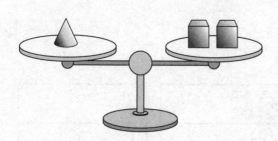

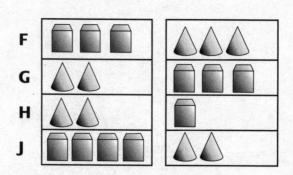

F
G
H
J

9

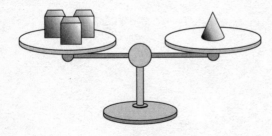

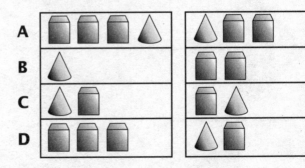

A

B

C

D

10

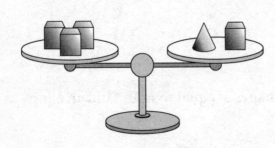

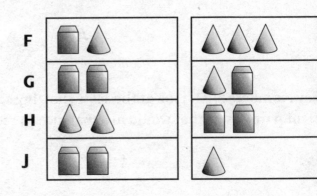

F

G

H

J

11

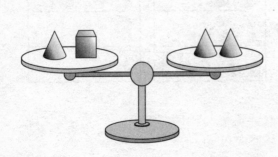

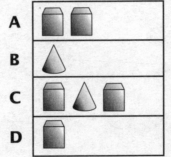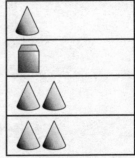

A

B

C

D

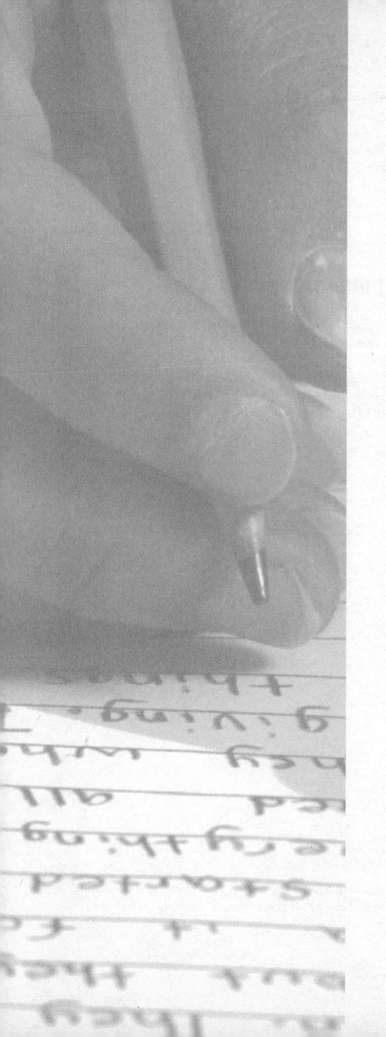

Chapter 7
Verbal
Reasoning—Words

The verbal reasoning—words section of the COOP has several different kinds of questions:

- Necessary part
- Two-story analogies
- Must be true
- Mystery language

NECESSARY PART QUESTIONS

The first of the questions in the verbal reasoning section will ask you to think carefully about the meaning of a word and to find the answer choice that is a necessary part of the meaning of that word.

What does *necessary* mean? It means that you're looking for a choice that describes something that the word *cannot do without*. For instance, could you have an apple that was not red? Yes. Could you have an apple that did not have a stem? Yes. Could you have an apple that was not a piece of fruit? No. This means that the word *fruit* is something that is necessary to the idea of the word apple. You can't do without the word *fruit*.

Here is what a necessary part question will look like:

apple

A   red

B   fruit

C   store

D   stem

Here's How to Crack It

The best way to approach this is to look at the answer choices one at a time, and ask yourself, "Could you do without it?" If the answer is "No," you've found the correct choice. You could have an apple that wasn't red, that wasn't in a store, or that didn't have a stem. Therefore you can eliminate these choices. But you can't have an apple that is not a piece of fruit. You can't do without (B). Therefore (B) is the best answer.

Let's try another example:

2

shirt

F button

G blue

H chest

J sleeve

Here's How to Crack It
Does a shirt have to have a button? No. Cross off (F). Does a shirt have to be blue? No. Cross off (G). Does it have to cover your chest? Probably. Let's leave choice (H). Does it have to have sleeves? Well, most shirts do, but they don't have to. Therefore we can cross off (J). The best answer is (H).

Whenever you find a choice that you're sure is incorrect, cross it off. On more difficult problems, you may find that there are two choices, both of which seem necessary. If you're stuck, take your best guess and move on.

TWO-STORY ANALOGY QUESTIONS

Remember the analogy questions from Chapter 5? The next questions you will see are a bit more complicated. We'll call them two-story analogies.

These problems are trickier because the analogies may go in two directions. The words may relate to each other left to right (horizontally) or up and down (vertically). Let's look at an example of an analogy that relates left to right:

inch	foot	yard
ounce	pound	_____

A gallon

B ton

C ruler

D mile

Here's How to Crack It

As with the ordinary analogies, the best way to solve this type of problem is to make a sentence. In this case, we can make sentences with the words on top of the line.

> An **inch** is a smaller distance than a **foot**, and a **foot** is a smaller distance than a **yard**.

In this case, the words on top of the line represent sizes that go from smaller to larger. Now let's use that same idea with the words below the line.

> An **ounce** is a smaller amount than a **pound**, and a **pound** is a smaller amount than a _____?

Is a pound a smaller amount than a gallon? Not really. A pound measures solid things, and a gallon measures liquids. Cross off (A). Is a pound smaller than a ton? Yes. Is a pound smaller than a ruler? This doesn't make any sense. Cross off (C). Is a pound smaller than a mile? This doesn't make sense, either. It's talking about distance, not weight. Cross off (D). The best answer is (B).

———————○———————

Here's an example of a two-story analogy that goes up and down:

———————○———————

4 ————————————————

dog	pig	horse
kennel	sty	____

F saddle

G hoof

H gallop

J stable

Here's How to Crack It

You can tell this analogy goes up and down, because there's no relation among the words above the line. We can make a sentence only between a word above the line and a word below the line.

A group of **dogs** lives in a **kennel**.

A group of **pigs** lives in a **sty**.

Now let's use that same sentence with the last pair. Does a group of horses live in a saddle? No. Does a group of horses live in a hoof? Definitely not. Does a group of horses live in a gallop? No. Does a group of horses live in a stable? Yes. This makes (J) the best answer. Neat, huh?

———————○———————

MUST-BE-TRUE QUESTIONS

For a must-be-true question, you will be asked to read a few sentences that describe people, places, or things. These sentences will be followed by four short statements. Your job is to find the choice that *must be true* based on the sentences you read.

What Does "Must Be True" Mean?

Look at these two statements.

Jason scored a 92 on his math test.

Lisa scored a 96 on her math test.

There are many things you might assume to be true, given these two statements. Here are some of them.

Lisa is a better student than Jason.

Lisa knows math better than Jason.

Lisa and Jason are in the same math class.

However, none of these choices **must** be true. Sure, they might be true, but we don't really know. Lisa might not be a better student than Jason—maybe she just got lucky on this test, or maybe in most other subjects she scores much worse than Jason. Lisa might not be better at math—maybe she's just taking an easier math class than Jason is taking. We don't know whether or not they're in the same math class. We don't even know whether they're in the same grade or the same school! Don't make any assumptions on must-be-true questions.

What is something that *must* be true given the information above? Only this:

Lisa scored higher on her math test than Jason scored on his math test.

That's the only statement that really *must* be true. It's something that we *know* for certain is true given the facts.

Must-Be-True Questions on the COOP

Here is an example of the way the COOP will give you a must-be-true problem.

———————◯———————

Jason goes to math class for exactly two hours per day, English class for exactly one hour per day, and Science class for exactly three hours per day. Jason never takes math and science at the same time. If all of the information above is true, which of the following must also be true?

A Jason likes science class better than he likes math class.

B Jason never goes to history class.

C Jason spends more time in science class per day than in math class.

D For exactly two hours per day, Jason does not take math or science.

Here's How to Crack It

Take each choice one at a time, and ask yourself, "Does this *really* have to be true based on the information in the passage?"

Do we know anything about what Jason likes or does not like? The passage says nothing about this. Therefore we can cross off (A). Do we know that Jason never goes to history class? The passage doesn't say this. Cross off (B). Do we know that he spends more time each day in science class than in math class? Yes, since he spends three hours in science class and two hours in math class. Leave (C) in. Do we know Jason does not take math or science for exactly two hours per day? If we knew how many total hours were in Jason's school day, we might be able to figure it out. But as it stands, we can't know whether this is true or not, so we can cross off (D). The best answer is (C).

———————◯———————

MYSTERY LANGUAGE QUESTIONS

Finally, you will see a couple questions that we call mystery language questions. These questions ask you to figure out the way to say something in an imaginary foreign language.

The following is an example of a mystery language question.

maxelipoti means science book
yipipoti means history book.
maxeligolub means science teacher

Which of the following could mean history teacher?

A *yipigolub*

B *maxeliyipi*

C *maxeligolub*

D *yipipoti*

Here's How to Crack It

Step 1: Find two mystery words that have one set of letters that are the same, and then see what English word they have in common. This is what that set of letters must mean.

In this case, we can see that the first two mystery words both have "poti" in them. These two words share the English word "book," so "poti" must mean "book."

We can also see that the first and third mystery words have the letters "maxeli" in them. These two words share the English word "science," so "maxeli" must mean "science."

Step 2: Use Process of Elimination to eliminate those parts of the mystery words that do not correspond with the English word you are asked for.

In this case, we are asked for the word that means "history teacher." We know that "poti" means "book" and that "maxeli" means "science." Therefore we can cross off any choice with "poti" or "maxeli" in it. This will allow us to cross off (B), (C), and (D). The correct answer is (A): "Yipi" means history and "golub" means teacher.

COOP Verbal Reasoning—Words Exercise

(Answers are on page 122)

For Numbers 1-2, find the word that names a necessary part of the underlined word.

 1

<u>pen</u>

A letter

B ink

C hand

D black

 2

<u>book</u>

F picture

G history

H page

J introduction

For Numbers 3-4, the words in the top row are related in a certain way. The words in the bottom row are related in the same way. Find the word that completes the bottom row of words.

 3

walk	skip	run
tug	pull	____

A yank

B draw

C lift

D push

 4

tie	bracelet	belt
neck	wrist	____

F watch

G waist

H joint

J jewelry

At a track meet, Irene ran in 8 races. She won one gold medal, two silver medals, and three bronze medals. After the track meet she saw a movie and had dinner with her parents.

According to the information above, which of the following must be true?

A   Irene's family watched her win her medals at the track meet.

B   Irene's favorite activity is running races.

C   Irene set a record in one of the events.

D   Irene won a greater number of silver medals than gold medals.

Paul can jump farther than David and Jeff. Jeff and Edwin can both jump farther than Larry.

Based on the information above, which of the following must be true?

F   Larry cannot jump as far as Paul can.

G   Paul can jump farther than anyone else at school.

H   Larry does not practice jumping very often.

J   Jeff jumps father than David.

Which of the following could mean orange juice?

uticitho means pear tree
oopicitho means pear juice
utilanno means orange tree

A   *utioopi*

B   *oopilanno*

C   *oopicitho*

D   *uticitho*

Which of the following could mean back door?

tolomaguni means front window
tolokala means back window
werimaguni means front door

F   *werikala*

G   *weritolo*

H   *tolomaguni*

J   *kalamaguni*

Chapter 8
Verbal
Reasoning—
Context

HOW TO THINK ABOUT VERBAL REASONING—CONTEXT

Reading the passages on the COOP is different from most other kinds of reading that you will do in school. You might think that you have to read slowly enough to learn all the information in the passage. But there is much more information in the passage than you can learn in a short time, and you will be asked about only a few facts from the passage. So trying to understand all of the facts in the passage is not the best use of your time.

Most importantly, you don't get points for understanding everything in the passage. You only get points for answering questions correctly. Therefore, we're going to teach you the best strategy to get the most correct answers.

There is one more important thing to know, which works to your advantage: The answer to every question can be found somewhere in the passage. All you've got to do is find it. This means that you should think of verbal reasoning—context like a treasure hunt: You need to use clues in the questions to find the answers in the passage and earn your points.

Strategy for Attacking Verbal Reasoning—Context

Step 1: Read the passage and label each paragraph. Don't try to learn every single fact in the passage; you can always go back later. It is important only to get a general idea of what each paragraph talks about.

Step 2: Answer the general questions based on your paragraph labels.

Step 3: Answer the specific questions by looking back at the passage and finding the answer.

Important! In steps 2 and 3, answer your questions by using Process of Elimination. The test-writers will often try to disguise the correct answer by using different words that mean basically the same thing as the words used in the passage. You might not recognize these words right away as the ones used in the passage. Why do the test-writers do this? If they gave you the exact same words straight out of the passage, that would be too easy. Your best bet is to cross off the choices that you know are wrong and pick from the choices that are left.

Now let's look at each step in more detail.

Step 1: Label Your Paragraphs

Every good treasure hunt needs a map, which will help you locate the answers in the passage. The best way to make a map is to label your paragraphs as you read. This will help you understand the main idea of the passage and at the same time make it easier to locate facts in the passage while you're reading.

After you finish each paragraph, stop for a moment and ask yourself, "What is this paragraph about?" Try to summarize the idea of this paragraph in seven or eight words, and quickly write this summary in the margin. This way you'll have a guide to important parts of the passage when you have to answer a question.

After you have read the entire passage, take a moment and ask yourself, "What is this whole passage about?" Write a one-sentence summary at the bottom of the page. This will help you answer any main-idea questions you may see. Try doing Step 1 for the following passage:

Contrary to popular belief, the first European known to lay eyes on America was not Christopher Columbus or Amerigo Vespucci, but a little-known Viking named Bjarni Herjolfsson. In the summer of 986, Bjarni sailed from Norway to Iceland, heading for the Viking settlement where his father Heriulf resided.

When he arrived in Iceland, Bjarni discovered that his father had already sold his land and estates and set out for the latest Viking settlement on the subarctic island called Greenland. Discovered by an infamous murderer and criminal named Erik the Red, Greenland lay at the limit of the known world. Dismayed, Bjarni set out for this new colony.

Since the Vikings traveled without a chart or compass, it was not uncommon for them to lose their way in the unpredictable northern seas. Beset by fog, the crew lost their bearings. When the fog finally cleared, they found themselves before a land that was level and covered with woods. They traveled farther up the coast, finding more flat, wooded country. Farther north, the landscape revealed glaciers and rocky mountains. Without knowing it, Bjarni had arrived in North America.

Though Bjarni realized this was an unknown land, he was no intrepid explorer. Rather, he was a practical man who had simply set out to find his father. Refusing his crew's request to go ashore, he promptly turned his bow back to sea. After four days' sailing, Bjarni landed at Herjolfsnes on the southwestern tip of Greenland, the exact place he had been seeking all along.

What is this whole passage about? _____

Your labels and passage summary should look something like this:

Paragraph 1: America was first visited by Bjarni Herjolfsson.

Paragraph 2: Herjolfsson wanted to follow his father to Greenland.

Paragraph 3: He got lost and ended up at America.

Paragraph 4: He turned around and finally reached Greenland.

Summary: How Bjarni Herjolfsson got lost and saw America before anyone else.

Now we have a good picture of the overall point of the passage, and we should be able to look back and find any details we need. So let's turn to the questions.

Step 2: Answer the General Questions

It's usually best to answer the general questions first. These questions ask you about the passage as a whole. There are several types of general questions, and they look like this.

Main Idea/Purpose

- The passage is mostly about
- The main idea of this passage is
- The best title for this passage would be
- The purpose of this passage is to
- The author wrote this passage in order to

Tone/Attitude

- The author's tone is best described as
- The attitude of the author is one of

General Interpretation

- The author would most likely agree that
- It can be inferred from the passage that
- The passage implies that
- You would probably find this passage in a
- This passage is best described as

To answer a main idea/purpose question, ask yourself, "What did the passage talk about most?" Look at the choices and cross off anything that was not discussed or that was only a detail of the passage.

To answer a tone/attitude question, ask yourself, "How does the author feel about the subject?" Cross off anything that doesn't agree with the author's view.

To answer a general interpretation question, ask yourself, "Which answer sounds most like what the author said?" Cross off anything that was not discussed in the paragraph or that does not agree with the author's view.

Let's take a look at some general questions for this passage:

---

1 **The passage is mostly about**

    A the Vikings and their civilization

    B the waves of Viking immigration

    C sailing techniques of Bjarni Herjolfsson

    D one Viking's glimpse of America

Here's How to Crack It

To answer this question, let's look back at our labels and our summary of the passage. We said that the main idea of the passage was how Bjarni Herjolfsson got lost and saw America before anyone else. Choices (A) and (B) are about the Vikings in general and not about Herjolfsson, so they can be eliminated. Choice (C) is about Herjolfsson, but his sailing techniques are not really discussed. This makes (D) the best choice.

---

2 **Which of the following can be inferred from the passage?**

    F The word America was first used by Herjolfsson.

    G Herjolfsson's discovery of America was an accident.

    H Herjolfsson was helped by Native Americans.

    J Greenland and Iceland were the Vikings' most important discoveries.

Here's How to Crack It

You should be able to make quick work of this problem by using Process of Elimination. The passage never says anything about Native Americans, so (H) can be eliminated. Also, it doesn't say that Herjolfsson ever used the word *America*, so you can cross off (F). (If you're not positive whether this is true or not, quickly skim back and double-check this in the passage.) We're already down to two choices. Choice (J) is an extreme choice—meaning it uses strong language that makes something absolutely true or false—due to the word most, so it probably is not the answer. If you check the passage, you can see that (J) is never stated. Therefore (G) is the best choice.

Step 3: Answer the Specific Questions

Specific questions ask you about a fact or detail mentioned in the passage. For these questions, look back at the passage to find your answer. These are the different kinds of specific questions.

Fact

- According to the passage
- According to the author
- Which of these questions is answered by the passage?

Vocabulary in Context

- The word <u>pilfer</u> probably means
- What does the passage mean by <u>pilfer</u>?

Specific Interpretation/ Purpose

- The author mentions Mother Goose in order to
- From the information in the passage, Mother Goose would probably

To answer a **Fact** question, look back at the passage and find the lines that mention the thing you are asked about. Use your passage labels to find the information quickly, or simply skim until you find it. Reread those lines to see exactly what the passage says. Then look for a choice that best restates what the passage says. Cross off anything that is never stated or that says the opposite of the information in the passage.

To answer a **Vocabulary in Context** question, look back at the passage and find the underlined word. It will probably be a word that you don't know. Cover the word with your finger. Reread the lines around that word, and think of the word that you would put there. Then look at the answer choices and see which comes closest to the word that you think should go there. If you can't think of the exact word, it's okay to simply note that the word should be a "positive word" or a "negative word."

To answer a **Specific Interpretation/ Purpose** question, look back at the passage and find the lines that discuss the thing you are asked about. Use your passage labels or skim the passage. Reread those lines to see exactly what the passage says. The correct answer will always be very closely based on the information in the passage. For instance, if a passage tells us that John likes to play tennis, we can infer that he will probably play tennis if he is given the chance. Cross off any choices that are not stated in the passage or sound very far off from what the passage says.

---

3   **According to the passage, Greenland was discovered by**

   A   Amerigo Vespucci

   B   Bjarni Herjolfsson's father

   C   Bjarni Herjolfsson

   D   Erik the Red

Here's How to Crack It

To answer this question, we should look back at the passage and find the line that talks about the discovery of Greenland. If you skim for the word *Greenland*, you'll find it in the second paragraph: "Discovered by an <u>infamous</u> murderer and criminal named Erik the Red, Greenland lay at the limit of the known world." Therefore the answer is (D).

---

4   **The word infamous probably means**

   F   lazy

   G   strong

   H   wicked

   J   intelligent

Here's How to Crack It

Let's reread the line that mentions the word *infamous*: "Discovered by an infamous murderer and criminal named Erik the Red…." Since the word *infamous* describes a *murderer* and *criminal*, it must be a word that describes someone who is bad. Choices (G) and (J) are positive words, so you can eliminate them. Choice (H) sounds much more like a description of a bad person than (F), so the best choice is (H).

---

5 **According to the passage, Bjarni Herjolfsson left Norway to**

A start a new colony

B open a trade route to America

C visit his relatives

D map the North Sea

Here's How to Crack It

The end of the first paragraph discusses Herjolfsson's departure. There it states, "Bjarni sailed from Norway to Iceland, heading for the Viking settlement where his father Heriulf resided." The correct answer will use different words, but it should restate the same idea. Can we find anything here about starting a colony? No, so (A) can be eliminated. Does it mention opening a trade route to America? No, so (B) can also be eliminated. (It's true that he does eventually reach America, but that isn't the reason why he left.) Does it mention visiting his relatives? Well, it does say that he wanted to find his father. So let's leave (C). Does this sentence mention mapping the North Sea? No. Choice (D) is wrong, and (C) is the answer.

---

6 Bjarni's reaction upon landing in Iceland can best be described as

F disappointed

G satisfied

H amused

J fascinated

Here's How to Crack It

Where can we find a description of Bjarni Herjolfsson's arrival in Iceland? At the beginning of the second paragraph. There it states, "When he arrived in Iceland, Bjarni discovered that his father had already sold his land and estates and set out for the latest Viking settlement on the subarctic island called Greenland." Feeling "dismayed," Bjarni left to look for the new colony. Since he had missed his father, he was unhappy. Which word best states this idea? Choice (F).

7 When the author says, "The crew lost their bearings," this probably means that

A the ship was damaged beyond repair

B the sailors did not know which way they were going

C the sailors were very angry

D the sailors misplaced their clothes

Here's How to Crack It

Let's reread the lines around "the crew lost their bearings": "since the Vikings traveled without a chart or compass, it was not uncommon for them to lose their way in the unpredictable northern seas. Beset by fog, the crew lost their bearings." Since the story says that the crew would often "lose their way," the best answer is (B).

PROCESS OF ELIMINATION

If you're stuck on which answer is correct, remember to use Process of Elimination to cross off answers you know are wrong. On *general* questions, you'll usually want to cross off answers that

- are not mentioned in the passage
- are too detailed—if the passage mentions something in only one line, it is a detail, not a main idea
- go against, or say the opposite of, information in the passage
- are too big—you can't say much in four or five paragraphs; any answer that says something like, "The passage proves that the theory Einstein spent his entire life creating was right" is probably a wrong answer
- are too extreme—if a choice uses absolute terms such as "all," "every," "never," or "always," it's probably a wrong answer
- go against common sense

On *specific* questions, you should probably cross off answers that

- are extreme
- go against information in the passage
- are not mentioned in the passage
- go against common sense

If you look back at the questions in the sample reading comprehension passage above, you'll see that following these guidelines eliminates many of the wrong answer choices. Use these guidelines when you take the COOP!

What Kind of Answers Do I Keep?

Correct answers tend to be

- restatements or paraphrases of what is said in the passage
- traditional and conservative
- moderate, using words such as "may," "can," and "often."

COOP Verbal Reasoning—Context Exercise

(Answers are on page 123)

Try the following reading comprehension passage. Don't forget to label your paragraphs!

Although many people associate indoor lighting with modern electrical wiring, practical indoor lighting existed thousands of years before Thomas Edison invented the light bulb. <u>Rudimentary</u> oil lamps, a primitive ancestor of the gaslight, were used in the caves in which prehistoric humans lived.

Approximately 50,000 years ago, cave-dwelling humanoids fashioned a basic oil-based lamp out of animal fat that was kept inside a stone base as well as a wick made out of a cloth-like material. Due to the fact that animal fat smells awful when burned, the lamp gave off a terrible odor.

Thousands of years later, during the Egyptian era (around 1300 B.C.E.) the structure and design of the lamp changed. Instead of using only stone, the Egyptians used a form of decorated pottery with a papyrus-based wick and vegetable oil instead of the foul-smelling animal fat.

In times of need people burned whatever oil was plentiful. Because vegetable oil and animal fat are both edible, in times of hunger people did not burn lamps; they used the oil for food. But oil lamps brought with them other problems. Wicks for the lamps did not always burn away and had to be changed periodically. Soon the oil lamp gave way to the candle, which became a popular source of light in Rome during the first century B.C.E.

1   What is this passage mostly about?

     A   how Egyptians lit their homes

     B   why the candle is better than the oil lamp

     C   the history of indoor lighting

     D   why vegetable oil replaced animal fat in oil lamps

2   It can be inferred that the author views the change from oil lamps to candles as

     F   the most important discovery of human history

     G   a mistake made by the Romans

     H   important to the discovery of electricity

     J   a step in the development of indoor lighting

3   The word rudimentary most likely means

     A   expensive

     B   basic

     C   colorful

     D   handy

4   The author mentions Thomas Edison in the passage in order to

     F   explain his discoveries

     G   compare him with other modern inventors

     H   introduce someone that the author will discuss later

     J   show that Edison was not the first to discover indoor lighting

5   The word foul probably means

     A   awful

     B   sweet

     C   fruity

     D   clean

6   People probably stopped burning animal fat in lamps because

     F   vegetable oil was more plentiful

     G   they needed the animal fat for cooking

     H   animal fat smelled bad

     J   burning animal fat was against the law

7 The author's tone can best be described as

A angry

B unconcerned

C instructive

D critical

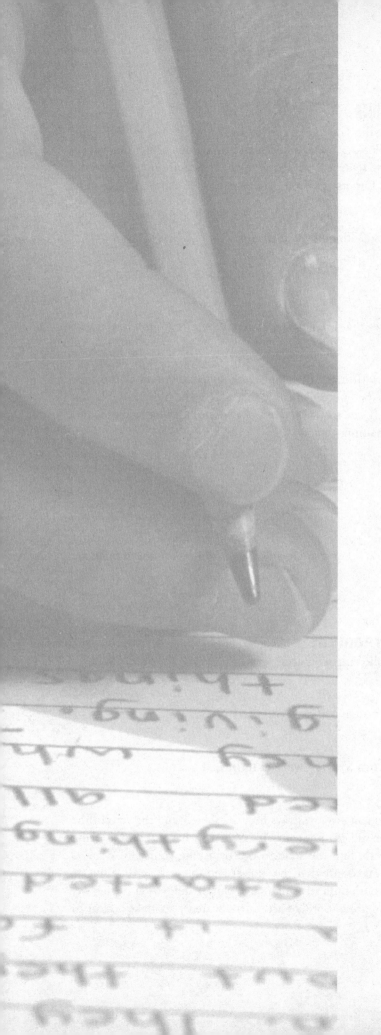

Chapter 9
Reading and
Language Arts

Taking the TACHS?
Then pay close attention
to this section!

USAGE QUESTIONS

Most of the questions in the language expressions section of the COOP (and TACHS) will ask you to look at five sentences and figure out which one is correctly written. Some of the sentences can be eliminated because they violate the rules of English grammar. Others are wrong because they are awkward or hard to understand.

Follow this procedure for attacking usage questions.

Step 1: Read all five sentences, and eliminate any choice that breaks a rule of grammar.

Step 2: Reread the choices that are left, and cross off any that are awkward or don't make sense.

The sentence you are left with may not sound great, but you should always pick the one that is the best of the bunch—the one that makes the most sense. If you can't narrow it down to only one sentence, that's okay. Cross off what you can, and guess from among the remaining choices.

ERRORS

What kind of errors should you look for? The COOP tests only a few kinds of errors. Learn them, and you'll know what to look for, which can greatly increase your score.

Subject/ Verb Agreement

What is wrong with the following sentences?

1 **The cats in the house watches the bird.**

2 **A wild dingo from Sydney were caught last year.**

To spot subject/verb agreement errors, always find the subject and the verb in the given sentence. To find the subject, ask yourself, "Who or what is acting or being described?" To find the verb, find the action word by asking yourself, "What is the subject doing?" Then make sure that the subject and the verb agree. Subjects and verbs have to agree in both number (singular or plural) and person (I, she, we, you). You may have to read around other parts of the sentence to make it clear to yourself.

What is the subject in sentence 1? It's the cats who are watching the bird. Can you say, "The cats **watches** the bird?" No. *Cats*, in this case, is plural—more than one cat—so the verb has to agree. It should be: "The cats **watch** the bird."

What is the subject in sentence 2? A wild dingo is the thing being described. Can you say, "A wild dingo **were** caught last year"? No; in this case *dingo* is singular, and the verb has to agree with a singular subject. It should be "A wild dingo **was** caught last year."

Verb Form and Tense

What is wrong with the following sentences?

3   **Yesterday, John is going to the playground.**

4   **Patricia has took her hamster to the vet.**

Verb Tense

The word yesterday in sentence 3 tells us that the verb should be in the past tense. You can see that this sentence has an error because it clearly says that the action happened yesterday, but the verb "is going" is in the present tense. The sentence should read "Yesterday, John **went** to the playground." *Went* is the past tense of the infinitive verb *to go*. To spot tense problems, look for words and phrases that indicate present or past, such as

- today (present)
- now (present)
- yesterday (past)
- last week (past)
- in 1956 (past)
- once (past)
- a long time ago (past)
- during the Second World War (past)

Verb Form

Sometimes the error will be in the verb form, such as in sentence 4. Recognizing correct verb form is as simple as knowing the proper present, past, and future forms of verbs. The COOP will ask you not to identify and name verb forms, just to choose the correct version of the sentence. Usually, it should be obvious to you when a verb form is wrong because the sentence just won't make sense. The past tense form of the verb *to take* would be either *took* or *has taken*. You could say, "Patricia **took** her hamster to the vet" or "Patricia **has taken** her hamster to the vet." But *has took* is not a possible form. Make sure that you review proper verb forms as part of your preparation for the COOP.

Adjective/ Adverbs

What is wrong with the following sentence?

5   **Kim ran quick around the track.**

What is the word *quick* describing? The way that Kim ran around the track. If a word describes a person or a thing, it should be an adjective like *quick*. But if a word describes an action (verb), it should be an adverb like *quickly*. Don't forget: Most adverbs end in *-ly*.

Remember this rule: Adjectives modify nouns; adverbs modify everything else.

Comparison Words

What is wrong with the following sentences?

6   **He was one of the most greatest authors of his time.**

7   **She is intelligenter than he is.**

Some questions on the COOP will ask you to determine the correct form of a comparison word. In the sentences above, *greatest* and *more intelligent* are the correct forms of the comparison words. For most adjectives that have only one syllable, we make them into comparison words by adding *–er* and *–est* to the end of the word, such as big, bigger, biggest and great, greater, greatest.

For most adjectives with more than one syllable, we make the comparison using the words more and most, as with intelligent, more intelligent, most intelligent, and interesting, more interesting, most interesting.

Pronoun Agreement and Case

8   **The dog ran away, but they came back soon.**

9   **Murray is a man which loves to play the piano.**

10   **Olivia gave the assignment to Peter and I.**

Pronouns are words such as *I, it, they, me,* and *she* that take the place of nouns. Whenever you see pronouns in a sentence, check to make sure that they agree with the nouns they stand for and that they are in the proper case. Pronoun *agreement* means that singular pronouns stand in for singular nouns, and plural pronouns stand in for plural nouns. In sentence 8, the subject is "the dog," which is singular, but the pronoun "they" is plural. The sentence should read "The dog ran away, but it came back soon."

Another important rule to remember is to use the pronoun *who* for people and *which* or *that* for things. Therefore sentence 9 should read "Murray is a man who loves to play the piano."

Pronoun *case* means that the subject of the sentence (the thing doing the acting) needs a subject pronoun, and the object of a sentence (the thing receiving the action) needs an object pronoun. In the sentence "Mary threw the ball to John." Mary is the subject and John is the object. Below is a chart that tells you how to use a pronoun, whether it is the subject or the object.

Subject	Example
I	I left the office.
You	You should get some rest.
He/she/it	He knew the best route to take.
We	We love to visit our grandparents.
They	They live in California.
Object	**Example**
Me	My boss told me to go home.
You	A good night's sleep would do you some good.
Him/her/it	Jenny refused to tell him the best route to take.
Us	Our grandparents love us.
Them	We visited them in California.

In sentence 10, does the word *I* describe someone who is giving the book (a subject) or someone to whom the book was given (an object)? Think about it this way: We say *I* gave it to *him*, but *he* gave it to *me*. In the example sentence, the word *I* describes someone who received the action, not someone who was doing the action. So the pronoun used should be the object pronoun, and the sentence should read "Olivia gave the assignment to Peter and **me**." If you are confused about the correct answer, try this trick: Take away the word *Peter* and see what is left. You wouldn't say, "Olivia gave the assignment to I," but you would say, "Olivia gave the assignment to me."

Important note: Whenever a pronoun follows a proposition (such as *to, of, in, at, around, between,* and *from*) the pronouns are *always* in the object case.

Here are some common pronoun mix-ups. Don't forget them! Recognizing pronouns is a simple way to rack up points on the COOP.

It's = it is	It's raining outside.
Its = belongs to it	The dog eats its bone.
You're = you are	You're a great friend.
Your = belongs to you	I love your shoes.
Who's = who is	Who's at the door?
Whose = belongs to who	Whose car is this?

Sentence Fragments

What is wrong with the following sentences?

11   **Told me that I would have to see the dentist.**

12   **The elephant, after eating dinner, walking around the zoo.**

Every sentence has to express a complete thought and have both a subject and a verb. What is the subject in sentence 11? Who or what told me to go to the dentist? There is no subject in this sentence, and therefore it is only a sentence fragment. Sentence fragments are not complete sentences and are never the correct answer on the COOP.

Sentence 12 has a subject—the elephant—but it has no true verb. It is also a fragment so we know it's an error!

Parallelism

What is wrong with the following sentences?

13   **Lawrence left the house and going to school.**

14   **Erica wanted to eat lunch, visit her friend, and to play soccer.**

Whenever you read a sentence that contains a list of actions or objects, check to make sure that the items in the list are all in the same form. For instance, in sentence 13 there are two actions. The first action is that Lawrence left the house. So the second action must be in the same form; however, *left* and *going* aren't in the same form. The second part of the sentence should read "Lawrence went to school" to make this a parallel sentence.

In sentence 14, there are three items that Erica wanted: to *eat* lunch, *visit* her friend, and to *play* soccer. Are these three items in the same form? No. The first and the third items in the list use the infinitive verb forms—*to eat* and *to play*—but the second does not. To be parallel and correct, the sentence should read "Erica wanted to eat lunch, to visit her friend, and to play soccer." You could also say, "Erica wanted to eat lunch, visit her friend, and play soccer." Make sure you check to see what your answer choices are.

Double Negative
What is wrong with the following sentence?

15   **Paul has hardly seen no birds today.**

In English, you should have only one negative word in the same phrase. When a sentence has two, it is called a double negative. All of the following are double negatives, and are always considered incorrect.

- can't hardly
- can't never
- barely none
- barely never
- won't never
- won't hardly
- hardly never
- hardly none
- hasn't got none

Errors Exercise

(Answers are on page 124)

1 There is already many people in the auditorium.

2 Since my father's company has so much business, they are very busy.

3 My uncle often help my parents to make dinner.

4 Henry going to school, runs into his friend.

5 The giant mouse ran through the house and escaping from the cat.

6 Last year, Ines won the first prize and receives a beautiful trophy.

7 Roger finished his most biggest assignment.

8 Colin cleaned the bowl and gives it to his mother.

SENTENCE COMPLETIONS

A few questions in the language expression section will ask you to complete a sentence by filling in a blank.

Some of the questions in this section of the TACHS will test how well you can pick the correct word based on the "direction" of the sentence.

How would you fill in the blanks in the following sentences.

Check it out, TACHS takers! This one's for you!

1   **I really like you _____ you are very friendly.**

2   **I really like you _____ you are a very nasty person.**

In sentence 1, you probably picked a word like "because." How did you know that this word was the right one to choose? Because the idea after the blank ("are very friendly") kept going in the *same direction* as the idea before the blank ("I really like you"). The sentence started out with a positive idea and continued with a positive idea.

In sentence 2, you probably picked something like "but," "although," or "even though." Why? Because the idea after the blank ("you are a very nasty person") went in the *opposite direction* from the idea before the blank ("I really like you"). The sentence started out with a positive idea and then changed to a negative idea.

Here are lists of same-direction and opposite-direction words:

Same-Direction
- and
- moreover
- in fact
- for instance
- for example
- so
- therefore
- because
- since

Opposite-Direction
- however
- but
- yet

- although
- though
- nevertheless
- nonetheless
- despite
- rather
- instead
- in contrast

Try the following example:

---○---

3 **Susie's mother wanted her to be a dancer; _____ Susie felt like becoming a doctor.**

   A because,

   B however,

   C in fact,

   D rather,

   E in general,

Here's How to Crack It

In this case, the idea after the blank ("becoming a doctor") goes in the opposite direction from the idea before the blank ("be a dancer"). Therefore we can eliminate (A), (C), and (E). If you get no further, you have a great guess. The best choice is (B).

Other questions will test the same rules of grammar you have already learned earlier in this chapter—especially the rules of comparison words and double negatives.

---○---

Here is a sample problem.

---

4 **John is the _____ player on our soccer team.**

    F   more important

    G   most important

    H   much important

    J   importanter

    K   importantest

Here's How to Crack It

We've already learned that with comparison words that have more than one syllable we can only use more or most. Choices (H), (J), and (K) are not grammatically correct and can be eliminated. Since we are comparing John with all the other players on the team, we want to use most important, (G).

FIND THE SUBJECT/PREDICATE

You'll also see a set of questions that asks you for the simple subject of the sentence, while some questions will ask you for simple predicate (verb) of the sentence.

What is a simple subject? The simple subject is always the noun that is performing the action or being described in a sentence. This means that the simple subject

- must be a noun (person, place or thing) and
- is not describing something else

The latter part is tricky. Nouns can be used to describe things when they are used after words such as *in, on, at, around, under, after, when,* and *that.*

Look at the following sentences:

5   The cat is on the mat.

6   The cat that belongs to John is on the mat.

7   After eating lunch in the kitchen, the cat took a bath.

8   When John came home, the cat began to run around the house.

Here's How to Crack It

In sentence 5, the word *mat* is a noun, but it is part of the phrase "on the mat," which describes where the cat is sitting. Therefore *mat* cannot be the simple subject. In sentence 6, the word *John* is a noun, but it is part of the phrase "that belongs to John," which describes the cat. Therefore *John* cannot be the simple subject. In sentence 7, the words *lunch* and *kitchen* are nouns, but they are part of the phrase "After eating lunch in the kitchen," which describes what the cat did earlier in the day. In sentence 8, the words *John*, *home*, and *house* are nouns, but they are part of phrases that describe the cat.

In all four sentences, "the cat" is the simple subject.

Follow these steps to answer questions that ask you for the simple subject.

Step 1: Cross off any words that you know are not nouns—verbs, adjectives, and adverbs.

Step 2: Cross off any words that are not the simple subject—any noun that follows a preposition such as *in, at, of,* or *to* and any noun that appears in a phrase that begins with *if, when, since, after,* or *that.*

What is a simple predicate (verb)? The simple predicate is always the main verb in the sentence. This means that the simple predicate

- must be a verb (an action word) and
- is not describing something else

Again, the latter part is tricky. Just like nouns, verbs can be used to describe other things when they appear in phrases that begin with words such as *if, when, after,* and *that.*

9   The cat slept on the mat that John made at school.

10   Since she was tired from running in the park, the cat slept on the mat.

11   While John cooked dinner, the cat slept on the mat.

Here's How to Crack It

In sentence 9, the word *made* is a verb, but it is part of the phrase "that John made," which describes who made the mat. Therefore *made* cannot be the simple verb. In sentence 10, the word *was* is a verb, but it is part of the phrase "Since she was tired," which describes the cat. Therefore *was* cannot be the simple verb. In sentence 11, the word *cooked* is a verb, but it is part of the phrase "While John cooked dinner," which describes what John did while the cat was asleep.

In all three sentences, "slept" is the simple predicate.

Follow these steps to answer questions that ask you for the simple predicate.

Step 1: Cross off any words that you know are not verbs—nouns, adjectives, and adverbs.

Step 2: Cross off any words that are not simple verbs—any verb that follows a word such as *if, when, since, after,* or *that.*

Simple Subject Exercise

(Answers are on page 124)

1 After many years, Jonathan finally found his favorite cat.

2 The most important part was probably the discovery of the Northwest Passage.

3 When she figured out the answer, her teacher was very pleased with her.

4 If he had known about his neighbor's collie, he never would have said that his dog was the fastest.

Simple Predicate Exercise

(Answers are on page 125)

1 Since his sister had already washed the dishes, Jonas volunteered to dry them.

2 In order to finish the race without falling down, Alexander drank a great deal of water.

3 Adrienne never imagined that she would be chosen to play the leading role in the production.

4 Because Laurie ate too much, she felt too sick to play soccer.

STRUCTURE QUESTIONS

A few questions in this section will ask you to choose which sentences fit best with our other sentences in a paragraph. You may be asked to find

- the best topic sentence
- the sentences that best follow a topic sentence
- which sentence belongs in the paragraph
- which sentence does not belong in the paragraph

To answer all of these questions, make sure that the ideas are in a logical order from one sentence to the next.

What is a topic sentence? A topic sentence is the first sentence in a paragraph, and it is supposed to introduce the idea that will follow. The sentences that follow the topic sentence should talk more about the subject that is mentioned in the topic sentence. To answer a question that asks you to find the best topic sentence, you should read the sentences in the paragraph and ask yourself, "What are these sentences talking about?" Then look at the answer choices and find the one that best fits the idea.

To answer a question that asks you to find the sentences that should follow a topic sentence, read the topic sentence and ask yourself, "What is the main idea in this topic sentence?" Then find the sentences that describe this idea in more detail.

To answer a question that asks you which sentence belongs in the paragraph, read the sentences before and after the blank. You should find a sentence that discusses the same ideas as the sentences before and after it, while watching out for same-direction or opposite-direction words.

To answer a question that asks you which sentence does not belong, read the paragraph and ask yourself what the paragraph is about. Then reread it, and find the sentence that does not discuss this same idea or suddenly changes the topic.

Take a look at the following examples.

19   Which of the following is the best topic sentence for this paragraph?

_____. It was first made in China around 100 B.C.E. from bits of plants and tree bark. At first it was rough, and not very suitable for official documents. Soon, however, people found ways to make it flat and even. Over the next few hundred years, paper was introduced to the rest of Asia, where it was used to keep government documents and religious inscriptions.

A Today, many documents are stored electronically instead of on paper.

B The ancient Chinese discovered many useful things.

C Paper has a long and interesting history.

D Modern governments would not be able to survive without paper.

E One interesting kind of art is the making of beautiful paper.

Here's How to Crack It

If we read the paragraph, we see that it is mostly about the history of paper. Therefore, the topic sentence should introduce the idea. Choice (B) is not specifically about paper at all, and (A), (D), and (E) are not about the history of paper. Therefore, (C) is the best choice.

20 Which of the following sentences does not belong in the paragraph?

1) One of the most loved musical styles today is blues. 2) Blues originated in the early 1900s in America. 3) It was born from a combination of African-American work chants and gospel songs. 4) The blues got its name from the introduction of special "blue notes," which are created by "bending" normal notes up or down. 5) These blue notes give the song a certain sad sound that people recognize as part of the blues. 6) While some people like sad music, other people prefer happier songs. 7) In the 1920s, blues began to incorporate elements from jazz, dance music, and show tunes. 8) Today, blues has spread to many different countries and is one of the most popular types of music in the world.

F sentence 2

G sentence 3

H sentence 4

J sentence 5

K sentence 6

Here's How to Crack It

If we read the paragraph, we see that it is about the musical style called blues. Each sentence talks about this idea except for sentence 6, which talks about whether people like happy or sad music. This makes (K) the best choice.

You've absorbed a lot of information! Now get outside and absorb some sun! (But be sure to wear sunscreen.)

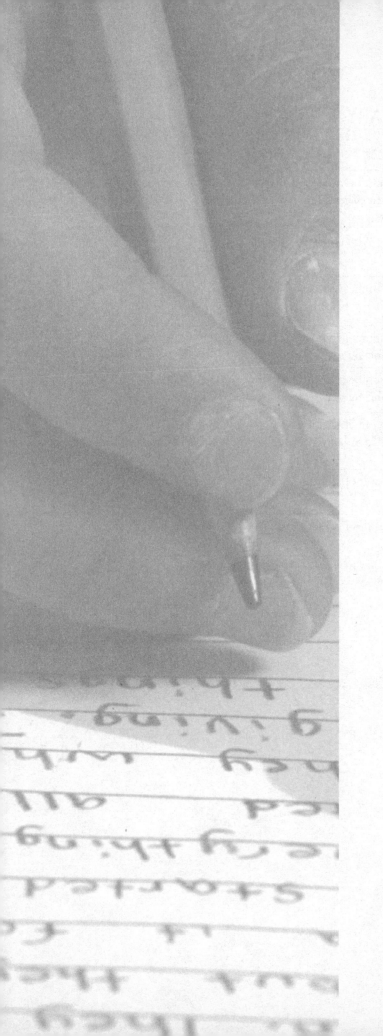

Chapter 10
Mathematics

Most of the questions in this section require you to do some amount of arithmetic. Let's take a moment to review the basics.

MATH VOCABULARY

Term	Definitions	Examples
integer	any number that does not contain either a fraction or a decimal	−4, −1, 0, 9, 15
positive number	any number greater than zero	$\frac{1}{2}$, 1, 4, 101
negative number	any number less than zero	$-\frac{1}{2}$, −1, −4, −101
even number	any number that is evenly divisible by two	−2, 0, 2, 8, 24 (*Note:* 0 is even)
odd number	any number that is not evenly divisible by two	−1, 1, 5, 35
prime number	any number that is evenly divisible only by one and itself	2, 3, 5, 7, 11, 13 (*Note:* 1 is not a prime number)
sum	the result of addition	The sum of 6 and 2 is 8.
difference	the result of subtraction	The difference between 6 and 4 is 2.
product	the result of multiplication	The product of 3 and 4 is 12.

COOP Math Vocabulary Exercise

(Answers are on page 125)

1 How many integers are there between −4 and 5?

2 How many positive integers are there between −4 and 5?

3 What is the sum of 6, 7, and 8?

4 What is the product of 2, 4, and 8?

ORDER OF OPERATIONS

How would you do the following problem?

$$4 + 5 \times 3 - (2 + 1)$$

Whenever you have a problem such as this, remember the rule.

Please Excuse My Dear Aunt Sally

Believe it or not, this sentence tells you the order in which you should solve the above problem. This stands for:

Parentheses
Exponents
Multiplication and **D**ivision (from left to right)
Addition and **S**ubtraction (from left to right)

Therefore we need to solve the parentheses first.

$$4 + 5 \times 3 - (2 + 1)$$

becomes

$$4 + 5 \times 3 - 3$$

Next, we do multiplication and division to get

$$4 + 15 - 3$$

Finally, we add and subtract to get our final answer of 16.

COOP Order of Operations Exercise

(Answers are on page 125)

1 $15 - 5 + 3 =$ _____

2 $15 - 2 \times 3 =$ _____

3 $2 \times (2 + 3) - 5 =$ _____

4 $20 + 3 \times 5 + 10 =$ _____

5 $(3 + 6) \times 3 \times 4 =$ _____

FRACTIONS

A fraction is just another way of representing division. For instance, $\frac{2}{5}$ actually means two divided by five (which is 0.4 as a decimal). Another way to think of this is to imagine a pie cut into five pieces: $\frac{2}{5}$ means two out of the five pieces. The parts of the fraction are called the numerator and the denominator. The numerator is the number on top; the denominator is the number on the bottom.

$$\frac{numerator}{denominator}$$

Reducing Fractions

Often you'll need to reduce your fractions after you have made a calculation. This means that you want to make the numbers as small as possible. To reduce a fraction, simply divide top and bottom by the same number. Don't spend too long trying to figure out the best number to divide by; use 2, 3, or 5, and keep dividing until you can't divide anymore.

For example, if you have the fraction $\frac{42}{18}$, we can divide the top and the bottom each by 3 to get $\frac{14}{6}$. Then we can divide top and bottom by 2 and get $\frac{7}{3}$. It can't be reduced any further than this, so this is your final answer.

Adding and Subtracting Fractions

To add or subtract fractions, the fractions have to have a common denominator. This means that they have to have the same number on the bottom (the denominators need to be the same). If the fractions already have a common denominator, you can add or subtract them by adding or subtracting the numbers on top.

$$\frac{4}{7} + \frac{2}{7} = \frac{6}{7}$$

If the fractions do not have a common denominator, the easiest way to add or subtract them is to use the Bowtie.

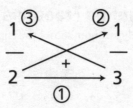

Step 1: Multiply the two bottom numbers together. Their product goes on the bottom of your two new fractions.

Step 2: Multiply diagonally from the bottom left to the top right. Write this product on the top right.

Step 3: Multiply diagonally from the bottom right to the top left. Write this product on the top left.

See—it looks like a bowtie! Now you have two fractions with a common denominator, and you can add or subtract them.

For example:

① $\dfrac{1}{2} \xrightarrow{\;\;+\;\;} \dfrac{1}{3}$　　$\dfrac{\;}{6} + \dfrac{\;}{6}$

② $\dfrac{1}{2} \;+\nearrow\; \dfrac{1}{3}$　　$\dfrac{\;}{6} + \dfrac{2}{6}$

③ $\dfrac{1}{2} \;\nwarrow+\; \dfrac{1}{3}$　　$\dfrac{3}{6} + \dfrac{2}{6} = \dfrac{5}{6}$

Multiplying and Dividing Fractions

To multiply fractions, multiply straight across the top and bottom.

$$\frac{3}{5} \times \frac{1}{3} = \frac{3 \times 1}{5 \times 3} = \frac{3}{15}$$

To divide fractions, flip the second fraction and multiply.

$$\frac{3}{5} \div \frac{1}{3} = \frac{3 \times 3}{5 \times 1} = \frac{9}{5}$$

COOP Fractions Exercise

(Answers are on page 126)

1 Reduce $\frac{12}{60}$ = _____

2 $\frac{3}{8} + \frac{2}{3}$ = _____

3 $\frac{3}{4} - \frac{2}{3}$ = _____

4 $\frac{3}{5} \times \frac{3}{2}$ = _____

5 $\frac{1}{3} \div \frac{1}{2}$ = _____

DECIMALS

Remember that decimals are just another way of writing fractions. Be sure to know the names of all the decimal places.

$$3 \ 4 \ . \ 8 \ 5 \ 7$$

tens
units
tenths
hundredths
thousandths

Adding Decimals

To add decimals, just line up the decimal places and add.

$$\begin{array}{r} 24.05 \\ +12.23 \\ \hline 36.28 \end{array}$$

Subtracting Decimals

To subtract decimals, just line up the decimal places and subtract.

$$\begin{array}{r} 24.05 \\ -12.23 \\ \hline 11.82 \end{array}$$

Multiplying Decimals

To multiply decimals, count the total number of digits to the right of the decimal point in the numbers you are multiplying. Then multiply the numbers without the decimal points. Once you have your answer, add back into the new number all of the decimal places you removed from the first two numbers.

To solve 0.2×3.4, remove two decimal places and multiply.

$$\begin{array}{r} 34 \\ \times \ 2 \\ \hline 68 \end{array}$$

Now put back the two decimal places we removed to get 0.68.

Dividing Decimals

To divide decimals, move the decimal places in both numbers the same number of places to the right until you are working with only integers. But unlike when you're multiplying decimals, you don't have to put the decimals back in when you're dividing.

$$3.4 \div 0.2 = 34 \div 2 = 17$$

Converting Decimals to Fractions

Remember that multiplying by 10 means the same thing as moving the decimal point one place to the right, and dividing by 10 means the same thing as moving the decimal points one place to the left.

$$9 \div 10 = \frac{9}{10} = 0.9$$

$$5 \div 100 = \frac{5}{100} = 0.05$$

This is why the first place to the right of the decimal is called "tenths" and the second place to the right is called "hundredths." Nine-tenths = 0.9 = $\frac{9}{10}$. Five-hundredths = 0.05 = $\frac{5}{100}$. So to convert a decimal to a fraction, all you need to do is change the numbers after the decimal to their fraction form.

$$5.24 = 5 + \frac{2}{10} + \frac{4}{100}$$

COOP Decimals Exercise

(Answers are on page 126)

1   2.43 + 5.25 =   _____

2   5.75 − 3.12 =   _____

3   1.5 × 3 =   _____

4   2.5 × 0.5 =   _____

5   2.5 ÷ 0.5 =   _____

6   What is 6.32 in fraction form?   _____

EXPONENTS, SCIENTIFIC NOTATION, AND SQUARE ROOTS

Exponents are just a short way of writing multiplication. 3^2 means to multiply two 3s together: 3×3. Likewise, 3^4 means to multiply four 3s together: $3 \times 3 \times 3 \times 3$. On the COOP you will not see very complex exponents, so the best way to solve them is to write them out longhand and multiply.

Scientific notation is also a short way of writing big numbers. Whenever you see a number such as 3.44×10^2, this means that you should move the decimal point to the right the same number of places as the exponent to the 10. In this case, you move the decimal two places to the right (10^2), and you get 344. Likewise, 4.355×10^2 is just another way of writing 435.5.

Square root is just the opposite of raising a number to the second power. $\sqrt{4} = 2$, since $2^2 = 4$. On the COOP you will not have very big square roots. Your best bet is simply to memorize these common ones.

Since $2^2 = 4$,　　$\sqrt{4} = 2$

Since $3^2 = 9$,　　$\sqrt{9} = 3$

Since $4^2 = 16$,　　$\sqrt{16} = 4$

Since $5^2 = 25$,　　$\sqrt{25} = 5$

COOP Exponents, Scientific Notation, and Square Roots Exercise

(Answers are on page 126)

1 $4^3 =$ _____

2 $2^4 =$ _____

3 $3.4 \times 10^2 =$ _____

4 $5.23 \times 10^4 =$ _____

5 $\sqrt{4} + \sqrt{16} =$ _____

SOLVE FOR X

To solve an equation, you want to get the variable (the x) on one side of the equation and put everything else on the other side.

To get only the variable on one side, follow these two steps.

Step 1: Move elements around using addition and subtraction. Put the variables on one side of the equation and numbers on the other. As long as you do the same operation on both sides of the equal sign, you aren't changing the value of the variable.

Step 2: Divide both sides of the equation by the coefficient, which is the number in front of the variable. If that number is a fraction, multiply everything by the denominator.

For example:

$$3x + 5 = 17$$

Subtract 5 from each side.

$$
\begin{array}{rl}
3x + 5 = & 17 \\
-5 = & -5 \\
\hline
3x = & 12
\end{array}
$$

Divide 3 from each side

$$
\begin{array}{rl}
3x = & 12 \\
\div 3 = & \div 3 \\
\hline
x = & 4
\end{array}
$$

Always remember the rule of equations: *Whatever you do to one side of the equation, you must also do to the other side.*

COOP Solve for x Exercise

(Answers are on page 127)

1 If $4x = 20$ then $x =$ _____

2 If $4x + 3 = 31$ then $x =$ _____

3 If $6 = 8x + 4$ then $x =$ _____

4 If $4x - 3 = 3x$ then $x =$ _____

PERCENT TRANSLATION

Everyone knows how easy it is to make a simple mistake on a percent problem. Should you write "5% of 100" as $\frac{5}{100}$ or as $\frac{100}{5}$ or as something else? To make sure to avoid silly mistakes, here's a foolproof method for solving percent questions. Any percent problem can be translated word for word into an equation if you know the mathematical equivalent of the English words. For instance, "percent" means the same thing as "divided by 100," and "of" means the same thing as "multiply." Therefore, "5% of 100" can be written as $\frac{5}{100} \times 100$, which equals 5.

The chart below shows you the mathematical translation of the English words you will probably see. To solve any percent question, read the problem back to yourself and replace the words on the left side of the chart with the math symbols on the right. Then you can easily solve.

Percent	$\div 100$
Of	$\times$
What	x (or any variable)
Is, Are, Equals	$=$

Here are two examples:

20% of 50 is?

$$\begin{array}{ccc} 20\% & \text{of} & 50 \\ \downarrow & \downarrow & \downarrow \\ \dfrac{20}{100} & \times & 50 \end{array}$$

5 is what percent of 80?

$$\begin{array}{ccccc} 5 & \text{is} & \text{what percent} & \text{of} & 80 \\ \downarrow & \downarrow & & & \\ 5 & = & \dfrac{x}{100} & \times & 80 \end{array}$$

$$5 = \frac{x}{100} \times 80$$

COOP Percent Translation Exercise

(Answers are on page 127)

1   30% of 60 =   _____

2   40% of 200 =   _____

3   15 is what percent of 60?   _____

4   What is 25% of 10% of 200?   _____

RATIOS AND PROPORTIONS

What Is a Ratio?

A ratio is a way of stating the relationship of two numbers in a reduced form. For instance, if there are 50 boys and 25 girls in a room, we can say that the ratio of boys to girls is 50 to 25. But we can also reduce this ratio just like a fraction: $\frac{50}{25} = \frac{2}{1}$. So we can also say that the ratio of boys to girls is 2 to 1. This is sometimes written as "The ratio of boys to girls is 2:1."

Of course, if we say that the ratio of boys to girls is 2 to 1, this doesn't tell us exactly how many boys and girls there are. The actual number could be 8 boys and 4 girls, or 10 boys and 5 girls, or 200 boys and 100 girls. Each of these can be reduced to the ratio 2 to 1.

But if we know one of the actual values, we can always solve for the other one. For instance, if we know that the ratio of boys to girls is 2 to 1, and there are 200 boys, we know that there must be 100 girls. Most of you can probably do that in your heads. But how do you calculate it?

Solving Ratio and Proportion Problems

The way you solve almost all ratio and proportion questions is by setting up two fractions and cross-multiplying.

$$\frac{A}{B} = \frac{C}{D}$$

Whenever you set up two equal fractions, you know that $A \times D$ is equal to $B \times C$. The only thing you have to make sure to do is keep the same thing on top and bottom of each fraction.

In this case, if we know that the ratio of boys to girls is 2 to 1 and that there are 200 boys, we can figure out the number of girls by setting up these fractions.

$$\frac{\text{boys}}{\text{girls}} \frac{2}{1} = \frac{200}{x}$$

Now we can cross multiply: We know that $2x = 1 \times 200$. This means that $x = 100$

Take a look at the following problem.

10 John has a bowl of red and blue marbles. The ratio of red to blue marbles is 5 to 4. If there are 35 red marbles in the bowl, how many blue marbles are in the bowl?

F 16

G 20

H 28

J 39

Here's How to Crack It
Let's set up our fractions with red marbles on top and blue marbles on the bottom.

$$\frac{red}{blue}\frac{5}{4} = \frac{35}{x}$$

Now we can cross-multiply. We know that $5x = 4 \times 35$. After we multiply, $5x = 140$. We can solve for x by dividing both sides by 5 to get $x = 28$. Therefore there are 28 blue marbles in the bowl, which is (H).

AVERAGES

The formula we use to figure out the average is

$$average = \frac{sum\ total}{\#\ of\ things}$$

For instance, if you take three tests on which you score 50, 55, and 57, the sum total of your scores is $50 + 55 + 57$, or 162. Since the number of tests was 3, the average on these tests must be $\frac{162}{3} = 54$.

Try the following problem.

---○---

11 During a certain month, David counted the number of apples he ate each week. He ate 2 apples during the first week, 4 apples during the second week, and 2 apples during the third week. The fourth week he ate no apples. On average, how many apples did David eat each week of the month.

A 2

B $2\frac{1}{2}$

C $3\frac{1}{3}$

D 7

Here's How to Crack It
The total number of apples David ate was 2 + 4 + 2 + 0, or 8. This sum total, over the number of weeks, will give us the average: $\frac{8}{4} = 2$.

---○---

PLUGGING IN THE ANSWER CHOICES

Very often you may think that you need to do a lot of complicated math to set up a problem. This is especially true on those long, wordy problems that give everyone a headache.

You know, however, that one of the answer choices given has to be the correct answer. All you've got to do is figure out which one. Therefore, the easiest way to solve many problems is by simply plugging in each answer choice until you find the one that works. Plugging in just means substituting numbers to figure out the answer quickly.

Take a look at the following problem.

12 If $x(x + 4) = 12$, which of the following could be the value of x?

F   –1

G   0

H   1

J   2

Here's How to Crack It

You might think that you have to do some complicated algebra to solve this problem, but you really don't. Let's just try plugging in each answer choice for the value of x and see which one makes the equation work.

If we plug in –1 for x, does $-1(-1 + 4) = 12$? No. Cross off (F). If we plug in 0 for x, does $0(0 + 4) = 12$? No. Cross off (G). If we plug in 1 for x, does $1(1 + 4) = 12$? No. Cross off (H). If we plug in 2 for x, does $2(2 + 4) = 12$? Yes, so (J) is the answer.

13 David is five years older than his brother Jim, and Jim is twice as old as Ann. If David is 10 years older than Ann, how old is Jim?

A   20

B   15

C   10

D   8

Here's How to Crack It

The question asks how old Jim is, so this is what we'll be plugging in for. Let's start with (A). Could Jim be 20? We know that David is five years older than Jim, so if Jim is 20, then David is 25. We also know that Jim is twice as old as Ann, so Ann must be 10. But the last sentence says that David should be 10 years older than Ann, which he's not. Therefore (A) can't be the answer.

How about (B)? Could Jim be 15? We know that David is five years older than Jim, so if Jim is 15, then David must be 20. We also know that Jim is twice as old as Ann, so Ann must be $7\frac{1}{2}$. But the last sentence says that David should be 10 years older than Ann, which he's not. Therefore (B) can't be the answer.

Let's try (C). Could Jim be 10? We know that David is five years older than Jim, so if Jim is 10, then David is 15. We also know that Jim is twice as old as Ann, so Ann must be 5. Does this make David 10 years older than Ann? Yes. So (C) is the answer.

———○———

Here's a slightly harder problem. Trying to solve it using algebra is difficult, but by plugging in the answer choices, it becomes very easy.

———○———

14   If the average of 4 and *x* is equal to the average of 5, 4, and *x*, what is the value of *x*?

   F   1

   G   2

   H   6

   J   8

Here's How to Crack It
Let's start with (F), and plug 1 in for *x*. Does the average of 4 and 1 (which is 2.5) equal the average of 5, 4, and 1 (which is $\frac{10}{3}$)? No, so (F) can be eliminated. Let's try (G). Does the average of 4 and 2 (which is 3) equal the average of 5, 4, and 2 (which is $\frac{11}{3}$)? No. Choice (G) can also be eliminated. How about (H)? Does the average of 4 and 6 (which is 5) equal the average of 5, 4, and 6 (which is 5)? Yes. Choice (H) is the answer.

———○———

PLUGGING IN YOUR OWN NUMBERS

The problem with doing algebra is that it's just too easy to make a mistake. Whenever you see a problem with variables (*x*'s) in the answer choices, PLUG IN. Start by picking a number for the variable in the problem (or for more than one variable, if necessary); solve the problem using that real number; then see which answer choice gives you the correct answer.

Have a look at the following problem:

───────────────○───────────────

15 If *x* is a positive integer, then 20 percent of 5*x* equals

    A   *x*

    B   2*x*

    C   5*x*

    D   15*x*

Here's How to Crack It

Let's start by picking a number for *x*. Let's plug in the nice round number 10. When we plug in 10 for *x*, we change every *x* in the whole problem into a 10. Now the problem reads:

───────────────○───────────────
───────────────○───────────────

16 If 10 is a positive integer, then 20 percent of 5(10) equals

    F   10

    G   2(10)

    H   5(10)

    J   15(10)

Here's How to Crack It

Look how easy the problem becomes! Now we can solve: 20 percent of 50 is 10. Which answer says 10? Choice (F) does.

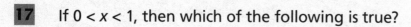

Let's try it again.

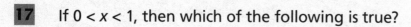

17 **If $0 < x < 1$, then which of the following is true?**

    A $x > 0$

    B $x > 1$

    C $x > 2$

    D $2x > 2$

Here's How to Crack It

This time when we pick a number for x, we have to make sure that it is between 0 and 1, because that's what the problem states. So let's try $\frac{1}{2}$. If we make every x in the problem into $\frac{1}{2}$, the answer choices now read:

    (A) $\frac{1}{2} > 0$

    (B) $\frac{1}{2} > 1$

    (C) $\frac{1}{2} > 2$

    (D) $1 > 2$

Which one of these is true? Choice (A). Plugging In is such a great technique that it makes even the hardest algebra problems easy. *Anytime you can, plug in for the variable!*

GEOMETRY

Lines and Angles

On every line, all the angles must add up to a total of 180°.

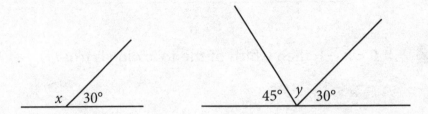

Since *x* and 30° must add up to 180°, we know that *x* must measure 180° – 30°, or 150°. Since 45°, *y*, and 30° must add up to 180°, we know that *y* must measure 180° – 45° – 30°, or 105°.

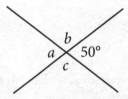

In this case, *b* and the angle measuring 50° are on a line together. This means that *b* must measure 130° (180° – 50° = 130°). Also, *c* and the angle measuring 50° are on a line together. This means that *c* must also measure 130° (180° – 50° = 130°). Finally, *a* must measure 50°, because *a* + *b* (and we already know that *b* = 130°) must measure 180° (50° + 130° = 180°).

This explains why vertical angles (the angles opposite each other when two lines cross) are always equal. Angles *b* and *c* are both 130°, and angle *a* (which is opposite the angle 50°) is 50°.

In a triangle, all the angles must add up to 180°. In a four-sided figure, all the angles must add up to 360°.

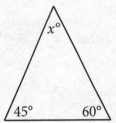 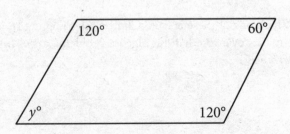

In this triangle, two of the angles are 45° and 60°. They make a total of 105°. The sum of the angles needs to equal 180°. Therefore angle x must be 180° − 105°, or 75°.

In the figure on the right, three of the angles have a total of 300°. Therefore y must be equal to 360° − 300°, or 60°.

A triangle is isosceles if it has two equal sides. This means that the two opposite angles are also equal. A triangle is *equilateral* if it has three equal sides. This means that all three angles are equal. Since these angles must equally divide 180°, they must each be 60°.

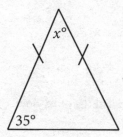

The triangle on the left is isosceles, so the two bottom angles must each be 35°. This makes a total of 70° for the two bottom angles. Since all of the angles must add up to 180°, we know that x is equal to 180° − 70°, or 110°.

Area, Perimeter, and Circumference
The area of a square or rectangle is length × width.

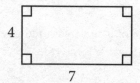

The area of this square is 4 × 4, or 16. The area of the rectangle is 4 × 7, or 28.

The area of a triangle is $\frac{1}{2}$ base × height.

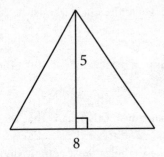 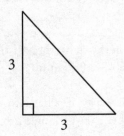

The area of the triangle on the left is $\frac{1}{2} \times 5 \times 8$, or 20.

The area of the triangle on the right is $\frac{1}{2} \times 3 \times 3$, or $4\frac{1}{2}$.

The perimeter of any object is the sum of the lengths of its sides.

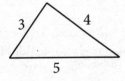 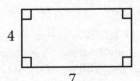

The perimeter of the triangle is 3 + 4 + 5, or 12. The perimeter of the rectangle is 4 + 7 + 4 + 7, or 22 (opposite sides are always equal to each other in a rectangle or a square).

The circumference of a circle with radius r is $2\pi r$. A circle with a radius of 5 has a circumference of 10π.

The area of a circle with radius r is πr^2. A circle with a radius of 5 has an area of 25π.

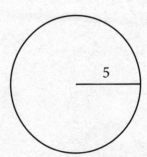

COOP Geometry Exercise

(Answers are on page 127)

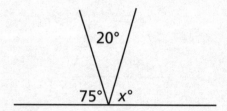

1   In the figure above, what is the value of *x*?

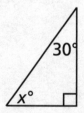

2   In the figure above, what is the value of *y* + *z*?

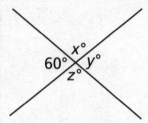

3   In the figure above, what is the value of *x*?

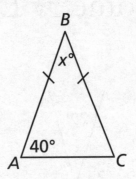

4   If triangle *ABC* is isosceles, what is the value of *x*?

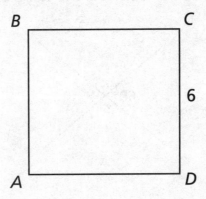

5   What is the area of square *ABCD* above?

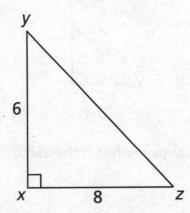

6   What is the area of triangle *XYZ* above?

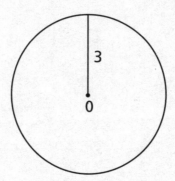

7a What is the area of the circle above with center *O*?

7b What is its circumference?

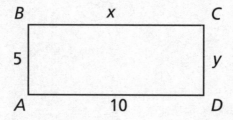

8a If *ABCD* is a rectangle, *x* = _____ and *y* = _____.

8b What is the perimeter of rectangle *ABCD*?

Now that you've reviewed all the elements of the test, time to go online and take Practice Test 2!

If you're taking the TACHS, try taking the practice test again to check out how much better you did this time!

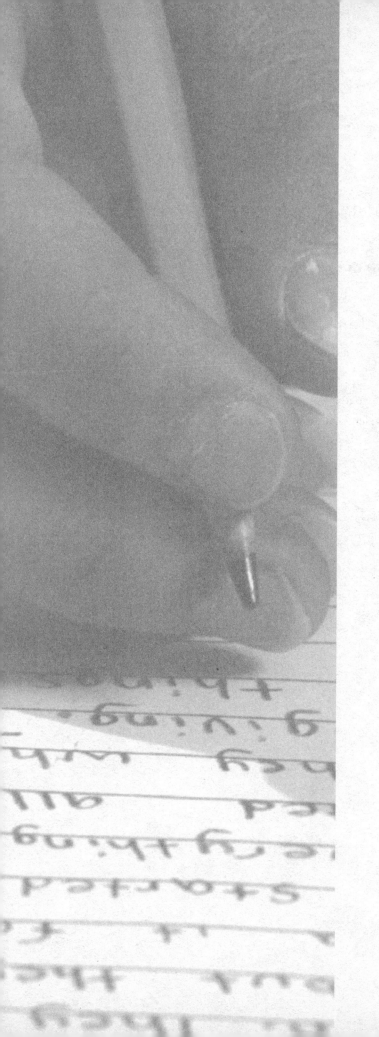

Chapter 11
Answers to
COOP Exercises

CHAPTER 4

COOP Sequence Exercise

1. **B**   The first element has 1 black dot, the second has 2, and the third has 3, so the fourth should have 4 black dots.

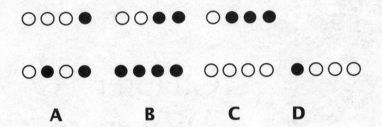

       A   **B**   **C**   **D**

2. **H**   The middle of each element should follow the pattern – + – +, so (D) can be eliminated. The first two groups have all squares, so the final two elements should have all circles.

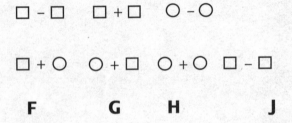

       F   **G**   **H**   **J**

3. **A**   In each element the letter "F" makes a quarter-turn. Therefore the missing element should be a quarter-turn more.

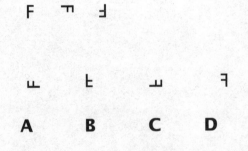

       A   **B**   **C**   **D**

4. **J**   4 (+ 4) 8 (+ 4) 12 | 11(+ 4) 19 | 21 (+ 4) 25 (+ 4) 29

       4 8 12 | 11 15 19 | 21 25 ____

      22   23   27   29

      F   **G**   **H**   **J**

5. **A** 38 (− 6) 32 (− 6) 26 | 17 (− 6) 11 (− 6) 5 | 42 (− 6) 36 (− 6) 30

38 32 26 | 17 11 5 | 42 ____ 30

36   34   32   24

A   B   C   D

6. **G** 6 (× 2) 12 (+ 4) 16 | 4 (× 2) 8 (+ 4) 12 | 5 (× 2) 10 (+ 4) 14

6 12 16 | 4 8 12 | 5 10 ____

8   14   15   20

F   G   H   J

7. **B** 10 (− 5) 5 (+ 10) 15 | 13 (− 5) 8 (+ 10) 18 | 22 (− 5) 17 (+ 10) 27

10 5 15 | 13 8 18 | 22 _____27

15   17   22   25

A   B   C   D

8. **J** 8 (× 2) 16 (+ 4) 20 | 4 (× 2) 8 (+ 4) 12 | 20 (× 2) 40 (+ 4) 44

8 16 20 | 4 8 12 | 20 ____ 44

24   28   35   40

F   G   H   J

9. **C** 20 (− 2) 18 (+ 7) 25 | 23 (− 2) 21 (+ 7) 28 | 30 (− 2) 28 (+ 7) 35

20 18 25 | 23 21 28 | 30 28 ____

25   26   35   38

A   B   C   D

10. **G** If you transform the letters into numbers, you see that they decreased by 2. For instance, HFD is the same as 8 6 4; 8 (– 2) 6 (– 2) 4. The only choice that also does this is XVT: 24 22 20; 24 (– 2) 22 (– 2) 20.

HFD | LJH | PNL | TRP | ____

RQP	XVT	VUT	YWV
F	**G**	**H**	**J**

11. **A** Since the number in each group increased by 1 from each group to the next, the missing group should contain the number 5. This will allow us to eliminate (C) and (D) because the only number in those groups is 6. If you change the letters into numbers, you see that they increase by 5. For instance, AFK is the same as 1 6 11; 1(+ 5) 6 (+ 5) 11. The only choice whose letters are each separated by 5 is MRW: 13 18 23; 13 (+ 5) 18 (+ 5) 23.

A1FK | D2IN | G3LQ | J4OT | ____

M5RW	N5QS	N5ST	U6VW
A	**B**	**C**	**D**

CHAPTER 5

COOP Analogy Exercise

1. **A** Bread is made from grain; jam is made from fruit.

2. **H** A dress hat is more formal than a baseball cap; a dress shoe is more formal than a sneaker.

3. **B** A tree grows from its trunk (or the bottom part of a tree is a trunk); a flower grows from its stem (or the bottom part of a flower is a stem).

4. **F** A fish moves with its fins; a bird moves with its wings.

5. **D** A violin is played with a bow; a piano is played with a hand.

CHAPTER 6

COOP Quantitative Reasoning Exercise

1. **C**   Subtract 3 from the number in the first column to get the number in the second column: 4 minus 3 equals 1, 7 minus 3 equals 4, and 11 minus 3 equals 8.

2. **J**   Multiply the number in the first column by 4 to get the number in the second column: 4 times 4 equals 16, 1 times 4 equals 4, and 5 times 4 equals 20.

3. **B**   Divide the number in the first column by 3 to get the number in the second column: 6 divided by 3 equals 2, 12 divided by 3 equals 4, and 9 divided by 3 equals 3.

4. **H**   There are 6 squares total. Four of the six squares are shaded. $\frac{4}{6}$ is equal to $\frac{2}{3}$.

5. **A**   The square is cut into fourths. Half of each fourth is shaded. Combine the halves together. That makes 2 full shaded squares, which means that $\frac{1}{2}$ of figure is shaded. Alternatively, the square is divided into 8 equal triangles. Four of the eight triangles are shaded. $\frac{4}{8}$ is equal to $\frac{1}{2}$.

6. **G**   The rectangle is divided into 10 squares. 2 full squares are shaded and 4 other squares are half-shaded. The 4 halves make 2 whole squares. Therefore, $\frac{4}{10}$ of the rectangle is shaded.

7. **B**   Combine the half-shaded pieces together to make two full shaded squares. The figure is divided into 8 squares, so $\frac{2}{8}$ of the figure is shaded.

8. **J**   For every one cone, there should be 2 cubes. Choice (J) has 4 cubes and 2 cones: 2 cubes for the first cone and 2 cubes for the second cone.

9. **C**   For every 3 cubes, there should be 1 cone. However, 1 cone (or 3 cubes) on the left side would balance 1 cone (or 3 cubes) on the right side. If 1 cube is added to the left side (making a total of 4 cubes) and 1 cube is added to the right side (making a total of 4 cubes), the scale is balanced.

10. **J**   If there are 3 cubes on the left side and 1 cube and 1 cone on the right side, then 1 cube on the left goes with 1 cube on the right, making the remaining 2 cubes on the left side equal to the 1 cone on the right side. Since 2 cubes are equal to 1 cone, the correct choice is (J).

11. **B**   If there is 1 cube and 1 cone on the left side and 2 cones on the right side, then the 1 cone on the left goes with 1 of the cones on the right, making the 1 cube on the left side equal to the remaining 1 cone on the right side. Therefore, 1 cube and 1 cone weigh the same, making (B) correct.

CHAPTER 7

COOP Verbal Reasoning—Words Exercise

1. **B**
2. **H**
3. **A**
4. **G**
5. **D**
6. **F**
7. **B**
8. **F**

CHAPTER 8

COOP Verbal Reasoning—Context Exercise

1. **C** If you summarized the passage well, you probably wrote something like, "People have had lights for a long time in different ways." Choice (A) is too precise, since the Egyptians are discussed in only one paragraph. Choices (B) and (D) are just details that are discussed in only one or two lines.

2. **J** In the final paragraph, the author says that "oil lamps brought with them other problems." Therefore the Romans began to use candles. Choices (G) and (H) are not stated in the paragraph, so they can be eliminated. Choice (F) is incorrect because the wording is extreme, and there is no indication the author thinks that candles are the most important discovery in human history.

3. **B** If we reread the line that mentions the word *rudimentary*, it states, "Rudimentary oil lamps, a primitive ancestor of the gaslight..." Therefore the word rudimentary must be something like primitive, or basic. This will eliminate (A), (C), and (D).

4. **J** If we skim the passage looking for Edison, we can find him mentioned in the first paragraph. There it states that "practical indoor lighting existed thousands of years before Thomas Edison invented the light bulb." Now we need to find the choice that best restates this idea. Does this sentence explain his discoveries or mention other inventors? No, so we can eliminate (F) and (G). Does the author later discuss Edison? No, so (H) can also be eliminated.

5.   **A**   The passage says that "the lamp gave off a terrible odor," and "foul-smelling" is used to describe the odor of the lamp.

6.   **H**   There is no evidence in the passage to support (F), (G), or (J). the passage does say that the "animal fat smells awful when burned," so (H) is the best answer.

7.   **C**   Nothing in the passage sounds angry, so we can eliminate (A). Choice (B) probably isn't right, since someone who was unconcerned wouldn't have written the passage. If that's as far as you get, take a guess between (C) and (D). Critical means that the author disagrees with something, but there's nothing in the passage that shows disagreement, which rules out (D).

CHAPTER 9

Errors Exercise

1.   Since "many people" is plural, it needs the plural verb form "are": "There are already many people in the auditorium."

2.   Since "my father's company" is singular, the pronoun and verb should be the singular "it is" instead of the plural "they are": "Since my father's company has so much business, it is very busy."

3.   "My uncle" is singular, so it needs the singular verb form "helps": "My uncle often helps my parents to make dinner."

4.   This is a sentence fragment. A complete sentence would read: "On his way to school, Henry ran into his friend."

5.   The first verb, "ran," is in the past tense; to maintain parallel form, the second verb, "escaping," should also be in the past tense: "The giant mouse ran through the house and escaped from the cat."

6.   The first verb, "won" is in the past tense, and the second verb, "receives," is in the present tense. You know the sentence should be in the past tense because of the clue words "last year". To maintain parallel form, the verbs should both be in the same tense: "Last year, Ines won the first prize, and received a beautiful trophy."

7.   "Most biggest" is not a valid comparative form. The sentence should simply read: "Roger finished his biggest assignment."

8.   The first verb, "cleaned," is in the past tense, but the second verb, "gives," is in the present tense. To maintain parallel form, these verbs should both be in the same tense: "Colin cleaned the bowl and gave it to his mother."

Simple Subject Exercise

1. Jonathan

2. part

3. her teacher

4. he

Simple Predicate Exercise

1. volunteered

2. drank

3. imagined

4. felt

CHAPTER 10

COOP Math Vocabulary Exercise

1. −3, −2, −1, 0, 1, 2, 3, 4 are all integers. That makes a total of 8.

2. 0, 1, 2, 3, 4, are all positive integers. That makes a total of 5.

3. $6 + 7 + 8 = 21$

4. $2 \times 4 \times 8 = 64$

COOP Order of Operations Exercise

1. 13

2. 9 (Do multiplication first!)

3. 5 (Do parentheses, then multiplication!)

4. 45 (Do multiplication first!)

5. 108 (Do parentheses first!)

COOP Fractions Exercise

1. $\dfrac{1}{5}$ (Divide the top and bottom by 12.)

2. $\dfrac{3}{8}$ ✕ $+$ $\dfrac{2}{3}$ $= \dfrac{9}{24} + \dfrac{16}{24} = \dfrac{25}{24}$

3. $\dfrac{3}{4}$ ✕ $-$ $\dfrac{2}{3}$ $= \dfrac{9}{12} - \dfrac{8}{12} = \dfrac{1}{12}$

4. $\dfrac{3}{5}$ ✕ $\times$ $\dfrac{3}{2}$ $= \dfrac{9}{10}$

5. $\dfrac{1}{3} \div \dfrac{1}{2} = \dfrac{1}{3} \times \dfrac{2}{1} = \dfrac{2}{3}$

COOP Decimals Exercise

1. 7.68

2. 2.63

3. 4.5

4. 1.25

5. 5

6. $\dfrac{632}{100}$

COOP Exponents, Scientific Notation, and Square Roots Exercise

1. $4 \times 4 \times 4 = 64$

2. $2 \times 2 \times 2 \times 2 = 16$

3. 340

4. 52,300

5. This becomes $2 + 4 = 6$

COOP Solve for *x* Exercise

1. $x = 5$

2. $x = 7$

3. $x = \dfrac{1}{4}$

4. $x = 3$

COOP Percent Translation Exercise

1. $\dfrac{30}{100} \times 60 = 18$

2. $\dfrac{40}{100} \times 200 = 80$

3. $15 = \dfrac{x}{100} \times 60 = 25$

4. $x = \dfrac{25}{100} \times \dfrac{10}{100} \times 200 = 5$

COOP Geometry Exercise

1. Since these angles must add up to 180°, $x = 85°$.

2. x and z must be 120° and y must be 60° so $y + z = 180°$.

3. The angles in a triangle must add up to 180°. Since we already have angles 90° and 30°, the remaining angle must be 60°.

4. Since this triangle is isosceles, the two bottom angles measure 40° each. To make a total of 180°, $x = 100°$.

5. The area of this square is 6×6, or 36.

6. The area of a triangle is $\dfrac{1}{2}$ base × height, or $\dfrac{1}{2} \times 8 \times 6 = 24$.

7a. The area of this circle is $3^2\pi$, or 9π.

7b. The circumference of this circle is $2(3)\pi$, or 6π.

8a. Since this figure is a rectangle, $x = 10$ and $y = 5$.

8b. The perimeter is $10 + 5 + 10 + 5 = 30$.

Part II
Cracking the HSPT

Chapter 12
What is the HSPT?

The High School Placement Test (HSPT) is a 2 1/2 hour, five-section test designed to help Catholic high schools make admissions decisions. Your score of 200 to 800 will be based on how many of the 298 questions you get right. The HSPT is fairly vocabulary-intensive, so concentrate on Chapter 2 and begin learning vocabulary as soon as possible. The test changes from year to year, so the information presented in this book is the most accurate for the year it was printed.

Along with the basic HSPT, you may be offered an optional test in Catholic religion, science, or mechanical aptitude, depending on the type of school to which you are applying. The score on these optional tests does not count toward your HSPT score, and very few schools ask for them, so we won't cover these areas in this book.

Here is the format of the HSPT.

- Verbal skills (16 minutes)
- Quantitative skills (30 minutes)
- Reading comprehension and vocabulary (25 minutes)
- Mathematics (45 minutes)
- Language (25 minutes)

Be sure to review Chapter 1 of this book ("General Test-Taking Skills") to learn the basic techniques that will help you score high on HSPT—and most any standardized test. Also review "An Introduction for Students" for basic strategy on how to approach this book. Chapters 13 to 17 will take you through each of the test sections in detail, and will review the types of problems you'll likely see. Make sure to take the practice tests in the back of the book and study the explanations to find out which areas you need to review the most to earn a high score on the HSPT. Good luck!

HSPT Study Plan
If you are taking the HSPT, follow this nine-session study plan.

Session 1
- Before you do anything else, besides reading this introduction, take the first practice HSPT in this book. Correct it and pay particularly close attention to your mistakes.
- Write down anything you notice that you had difficulty with, such as "triangle problems." This will help you remember to pay extra attention to those concepts when you study those chapters.
- If you got more than 25% incorrect in any section, tell yourself to slow down and do fewer problems. You are much better off doing only 75% of the questions and getting more of them correct than doing all of the problems and getting many of them wrong.

There are two types of HSPT exams: closed and open. The closed exam is administered by the school but scored by Scholastic Testing Service, Inc. (STS). Those scores are used in computing nationwide percentiles. The open exam is administered and scored by the school, so STS does not deal with student results.

Session 2
- Read Chapter 1: General Test-Taking Skills

Session 3
- Read Chapter 12: What is the HSPT?
- Read Chapter 2: Vocabulary

Session 4
- Read Chapter 13: Verbal Skills

Session 5
- Read Chapter 14: Quantitative Skills

Session 6
- Read Chapter 15: Reading Comprehension and Vocabulary

Session 7
- Read Chapter 16: Mathematics

Session 8
- Read Chapter 17: Language Skills

Session 9
- Take the second practice HSPT test in this book. Correct the test, "ooh" and "ahh" over how much your score improved, and then review the concepts in the book for the questions you answered incorrectly.
- Use any additional days before the test to continue to review the concepts and test-taking techniques covered in the book.

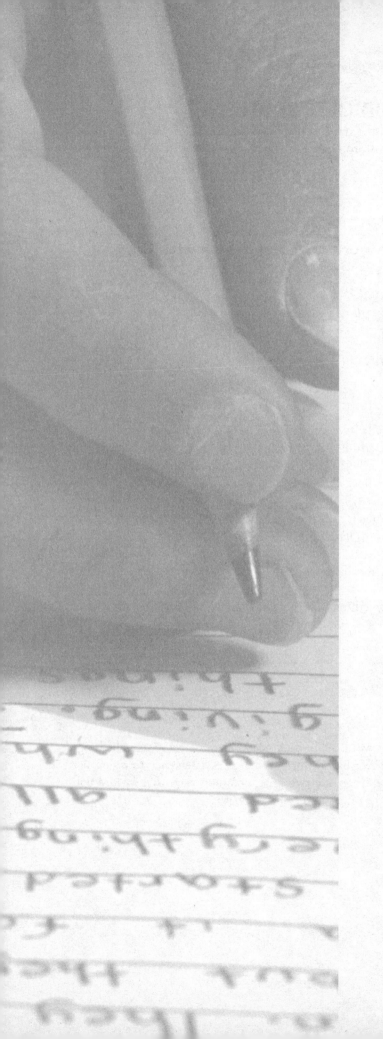

Chapter 13
Verbal Skills

WHICH ONE IS NOT LIKE THE OTHERS?

Several of the questions in the verbal skills section of the HSPT will give you four words and ask you which word does not belong with the other words. Here's a typical example:

---○---

1. **Which word does *not* belong with the others?**
   a. pencil
   b. chalk
   c. ruler
   d. pen

Here's How to Crack It

All of the choices will usually have something to do with each other—in this case, each of these objects is something that you might use at school. So we have to find something else that three of these words have in common. Then we'll know which one of them is the one that does *not* belong.

The best way to approach this is to make a sentence. Think of a sentence that will tell us what three of the words have in common.

A pencil, a pen, and chalk are all things that you can write with.

A ruler, however, is not something that you can write with. Therefore, the answer is (C).

---○---

Common Tricks

In the above example, the words all seemed related because they were all things you might find at school. We had to make a more exact sentence to figure out which one did not belong. There are two other common ways that a word will seem like it belongs with the others, even when it doesn't.

Read the following question:

---○---

2. Which word does *not* belong with the others?

   a. Shovel
   b. Hammer
   c. Tool
   d. Screwdriver

Here's How to Crack It

What kind of sentence could you make for this problem?

A shovel, a hammer, and a screwdriver are all types of tools.

In this case, tool is related to shovel, hammer, and screwdriver because these objects are all types of tools. However, it does not belong with the others because the words *shovel, hammer,* and *screwdriver* are names for tools; the word tool is the name of a category, not a name for a tool. This makes (C) the best answer.

---○---

Now try this one:

---○---

3. Which word does *not* belong with the others?

   a. trunk
   b. tree
   c. branch
   d. leaf

Here's How to Crack It

What kind of sentence could you make for this question?

A branch, a leaf, and a trunk are all parts of a tree.

All of the words in this problem seem to fit together because they are all related to trees. However, the words *branch, leaf,* and *trunk* all refer to parts of a tree; the word tree does not refer to a part of a tree. Therefore, the answer is (B).

———————————◯———————————

That's all there is to it!

ANALOGIES

What is an Analogy?

An analogy is just a fancy word that means two pairs of objects have the same relationship. For instance kittens/cat and puppies/dog are analogies. Each pair of words has the same relationship: Kittens are baby cats, just as puppies are baby dogs. On the HSPT, the way you express this analogy is by saying "Cat is to kittens as dog is to puppies."

Your job will be to complete the analogy to make a sentence like the one above. Here's an example of how an analogy question will appear on the HSPT.

———————————◯———————————

4. Apple is to fruit as beef is to
   a. restaurant
   b. vegetable
   c. meat
   d. cow

Here's How to Crack It

Make a Sentence

Just as with the last question type, the best way to figure out the relationship between words is to make a sentence. In this case, to find the relationship between the first two words, we should make a sentence with them. Then we can try to use that same sentence for each of the answer choices to see which one fits best.

Step 1: Cross out the words "is to" and "as."

Step 2: Make a sentence using the first two words in the problem. In this case, we can make the sentence "An apple is a kind of fruit."

Step 3: Try using the same sentence with each of the answer choices and see which one works best. So you'd say, "Beef is a kind of _____."

Is beef a kind of restaurant? No, so cross off A. Is beef a kind of vegetable? No, so cross off (B). Is beef a kind of meat? Yes. Is beef a kind of cow? No, so cross off (D).

The best answer is (C). It is the only choice that works with the sentence we made to define the words *apple* and *fruit*.

Making Good Sentences

Of course, some sentences you can make will be more helpful than others. If we had said, "Apple and fruit both have five letters," that wouldn't have been very useful to us in solving the problem.

When you make a sentence for the first two words, try to use one word to define the other. For example, the sentence "An apple is a kind of fruit" defines apple.

HSPT Analogy Exercise

(Answers are on page 222)

Try making sentences from the following words.

mansion / house _____

leaf / tree _____

desert / sand _____

engine / automobile _____

bread / baker _____

brush / painter _____

Synonyms and Antonyms

Other questions in the verbal skills section will ask you to identify synonyms and antonyms of words. A synonym is a word that has the same meaning as another word. Here's a trick that should help you remember: synonym = same. An antonym is a word that has the opposite (anti-) meaning of another word.

Here's an example of a synonym problem.

---○---

5. Hinder most nearly means

a. look up
b. play
c. hold back
d. protect

Here's How to Crack It

If you know the meaning of the word:

Step 1: Cover the answer choices with your hand. If you read the answer choices first, you might get confused.

Step 2: State what the word means to you in your own words.

Step 3: Uncover the answer choices and see which choice most closely matches what you said.

In this case, let's cover up the answer choices. In your own words, what does the word *hinder* mean? Maybe you came up with something like "stop" or "prevent." Now uncover the answer choices and see which best matches your word. Chances are good that you came up with something very close to hold back; therefore, the answer is (C).

---○---

If you "sort of" know what the word means:

Maybe you have a sense of what the word means but can't quite put your finger on it. Perhaps you can think of a saying that uses the word—even if you're not sure what the word means—and you should still be able to get the right answer or at least come up with a good guess. If either of these is the case, use the "side of the fence" trick. This is when you ask yourself whether the word is a positive word or a negative word. If the word is positive, you can eliminate any words that are not positive. If the word is negative, you can eliminate any words that are not negative.

Take a look at the following example.

---

6. Pretentious most nearly means
   a. intelligent
   b. arrogant
   c. inventive
   d. hidden

Here's How to Crack It

If you have a sense of the word *pretentious*—perhaps you've heard someone criticized as a really pretentious person—you may know that pretentious is a bad thing to be. It's a negative word. Since this question is asking for a synonym of the word *pretentious*, we know that the correct answer has to be another negative word.

Even if we don't know what *pretentious* means, we know that (A) and (C) are positive words, so they can be eliminated. Choice (D) really isn't positive or negative. If you know that (B) is also a negative word, you should guess (B), which is the correct answer.

If you know the meaning of the word:

Step 1: Cover the answer choices with your hand. If you read all the answer choices first, you might get confused.

Step 2: State what the word means to you in your own words.

Step 3: Uncover the answer choices and see which choice most closely matches what you said.

If you "sort of" know what the word means:

Maybe you have a sense of what the word means but can't quite put your finger on it. Perhaps you can think of a saying that uses the word—even if you're not sure what the word means—and you should still be able to get the right answer or at least come up with a good guess. If either of these is the case, use the "side of the fence" trick. This is when you ask yourself whether the word is a positive word or a negative word. If the word is positive, you can eliminate any words that are not positive. If the word is negative, you can eliminate any words that are not negative.

Try the following example:

---

7. **Courteous means the opposite of**

    a. honest
    b. unconcerned
    c. rude
    d. jealous

Here's How to Crack It

If you have a sense of the word *courteous*, you may know that it's a positive word. Since this question is asking us for an antonym, we know that the correct answer has to be a negative word.

Even if we don't know what the word *courteous* means, we know that (A) is another positive word, so eliminate it. Remember that we're looking for the opposite. Choice (B) really isn't positive or negative, so it probably isn't the answer. If you can get no further with this problem, you can take a great guess between (C) and (D). (In fact, the answer is (C).)

What if you have no idea what a word means?

Regardless of whether it's a synonym or antonym question, if you really have no idea what the word means, take your best guess and move on to the next question. Your time will be better spent on other problems in this section.

TRUE OR FALSE QUESTIONS

For a true or false question, you will be asked to read two sentences that describe people, places, or things. The third sentence will be something that we might or might not know for sure. Your job is to figure out whether the final sentence is true, false, or uncertain.

What Do "True," "False," and "Uncertain" Mean?

Look at these two statements.

- Jason scored a 92 on his math test.
- Lisa scored a 96 on her math test.

There are many things you might assume to be true, given these two statements. Here are some of them.

- Lisa is a better student than Jason.
- Lisa knows math better than Jason does.
- Lisa and Jason are in the same math class.

However, none of these choices really has to be true. Sure, they might be true, but we don't really know. These statements are all uncertain, since we can't know 100% that they are true or false. Lisa might not be a better student than Jason—maybe she just got lucky on this test, or maybe in most other subjects she scores much worse than Jason. Lisa might not be better at math—maybe she's just taking an easier math class than Jason is taking. We don't know whether they're in the same math class. We don't even know whether they're in the same grade or the same school! We can't make any assumptions on these questions.

What is something that we are certain is *true* given the information above? Lisa scored higher on her math test than Jason scored on his math test.

And what is something we are certain is *false* given the information above? Lisa scored lower on her math test than Jason scored on his math test.

How True or False Questions Appear on the HSPT

Read the following question.

8. **Mary collected more shells than Carrie and Tim. Tim collected more shells than Tracy. Mary collected more shells than Tracy. If the first two statements are true, then the third is**

   a. True
   b. False
   c. Uncertain

Here's How to Crack It

The best way to approach true or false questions is to make a diagram.

Let's make a diagram showing who has more shells, putting those with the most shells to the left.

We know that Mary collected more shells than Carrie and Tim. We can draw this:

$$M > C + Tim$$

We also know that Tim collected more than Tracy. So we can add this fact to our diagram

$$M > C + Tim$$
$$Tim > Tracy$$

Since we know that Mary has more than Tim, and that Tim has more than Tracy, we know that Mary has more than Tracy, so the third statement is true.

_____◯_____

Now try this one:

_____◯_____

9. **Mary collected more shells than Carrie and Tim. Tim collected fewer shells than Tracy. Mary collected more shells than Tracy. If the first two statements are true, then the third is**

   a. True
   b. False
   c. Uncertain

Here's How to Crack It

We can diagram the first sentence of this question the same way as before:

$$M > C + Tim$$

We now add the second sentence, which says that Tracy has more shells than Tim

$$M > C + Tim$$
$$Tracy > Tim$$

We know that Mary has more than Carrie and Tim, and that Tracy has more than Tim, but we don't know whether Mary or Tracy has more shells. We only know that they each have more than Tim does. Therefore the third statement is **uncertain**.

―――――――――――――――○―――――――――――――――

Now try some sample problems.

HSPT Verbal Skills Exercise

(Answers are on page 222)

1. **Which word does *not* belong with the others?**

   a. sad
   b. lonely
   c. feeling
   d. upset

2. **Which word does *not* belong with the others?**

   a. oregano
   b. parsley
   c. spice
   d. pepper

3. **Librarian is to library as curator is to**

   a. museum
   b. studio
   c. mall
   d. workshop

4. **Prejudice is to unbiased as worry is to**

   a. adamant
   b. active
   c. blithe
   d. unconcerned

5. **Revolve most nearly means**

   a. push against
   b. go forward
   c. leave behind
   d. turn around

6. **Fortify means the *opposite* of**

   a. load
   b. weaken
   c. sail
   d. clean

7. **Bizarre most nearly means**

   a. lonely
   b. unable
   c. odd
   d. able

8. **Opaque means the *opposite* of**

   a. dirty
   b. clear
   c. normal
   d. late

9. **Alex bought more apples than Barry and Marcia. Marcia bought more apples than Elisa and Kim. Alex bought more apples than Kim. If the first two statements are true, then the third is**

   a. True
   b. False
   c. Uncertain

10. **Alex bought more apples than Barry. Barry bought more apples than Marcia and Elisa. Elisa bought more apples than Alex. If the first two statements are true, then the third is**

    a. True
    b. False
    c. Uncertain

11. **Alex bought more apples than Barry and Marcia. Elisa bought more apples than Marcia. Alex bought more apples than Elisa. If the first two statements are true, then the third is**

    a. True
    b. False
    c. Uncertain

Chapter 14
Quantitative Skills

Most of the questions in this section require you to do some amount of arithmetic. Let's take a moment to review the basics.

MATH VOCABULARY

Term	Definitions	Examples
integer	any number that does not contain either a fraction or a decimal	−4, −1, 0, 9, 15
positive number	any number greater than zero	$\frac{1}{2}$, 1, 4, 101
negative number	any number less than zero	$-\frac{1}{2}$, −1, −4, −101
even number	any number that is evenly divisible by two	−2, 0, 2, 8, 24 (*Note:* 0 is even)
odd number	any number that is not evenly divisible by two	−1, 1, 5, 35
prime number	any number that is evenly divisible only by one and itself	2, 3, 5, 7, 11, 13 (*Note:* 1 is not a prime number)
sum	the result of addition	The sum of 6 and 2 is 8.
difference	the result of subtraction	The difference between 6 and 4 is 2.
product	the result of multiplication	The product of 3 and 4 is 12.

HSPT Math Vocabulary Exercise

(Answers are on page 223)

1. **How many integers are there between −4 and 5?**

2. **How many positive integers are there between −4 and 5?**

3. **What is the sum of 6, 7, and 8?**

4. **What is the product of 2, 4, and 8?**

ORDER OF OPERATIONS

How would you do the following problem?

$$4 + 5 \times 3 - (2 + 1)$$

Whenever you have a problem such as this, remember the rule.

Please **E**xcuse **M**y **D**ear **A**unt **S**ally

Believe it or not, this sentence tells you the order in which you should solve the above problem. This stands for:

Parentheses
Exponents
Multiplication and **D**ivision (from left to right)
Addition and **S**ubtraction (from left to right)

Therefore we need to solve the parentheses first.

$$4 + 5 \times 3 - (2 + 1)$$

becomes

$$4 + 5 \times 3 - 3$$

Next, we do multiplication and division to get

$$4 + 15 - 3$$

Finally, we add and subtract to get our final answer of 16.

HSPT Order of Operations Exercise

(Answers are on page 223)

1. $15 - 5 + 3 =$ ___

2. $15 - 2 \times 3 =$ ___

3. $2 \times (2 + 3) - 5 =$ ___

4. $20 + 3 \times 5 + 10 =$ ___

5. $(3 + 6) \times 3 \times 4 =$ ___

FRACTIONS

A fraction is just another way of representing division. For instance, $\frac{2}{5}$ actually means two divided by five (which is 0.4 as a decimal). Another way to think of this is to imagine a pie cut into five pieces: $\frac{2}{5}$ means two out of the five pieces. The parts of the fraction are called the numerator and the denominator. The numerator is the number on top; the denominator is the number on the bottom.

$$\frac{\text{numerator}}{\text{denominator}}$$

Reducing Fractions

Often you'll need to reduce your fractions after you have made a calculation. This means that you want to make the numbers as small as possible. To reduce a fraction, simply divide top and bottom by the same number. Don't spend too long trying to figure out the best number to divide by; use 2, 3, or 5, and keep dividing until you can't divide anymore.

For example, if you have the fraction $\frac{42}{18}$, you can divide the top and the bottom each by 3 to get $\frac{14}{6}$. Then you can divide top and bottom by 2 and get $\frac{7}{3}$. It can't be reduced any further than this, so this is your final answer.

Adding and Subtracting Fractions

To add or subtract fractions, the fractions have to have a common denominator. This means that they have to have the same number on the bottom (the denominators need to be the same). If the fractions already have a common denominator, you can add or subtract them by adding or subtracting the numbers on top.

$$\frac{4}{7} + \frac{2}{7} = \frac{6}{7}$$

If the fractions do not have a common denominator, the easiest way to add or subtract them is to use the Bowtie.

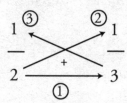

Step 1: Multiply the two bottom numbers together. Their product goes on the bottom of your two new fractions.

Step 2: Multiply diagonally from the bottom left to the top right. Write this product on the top right.

Step 3: Multiply diagonally from the bottom right to the top left. Write this product on the top left.

See—it looks like a bowtie! Now you have two fractions with a common denominator, and you can add or subtract them.

For example:

① $\dfrac{1}{2} + \dfrac{1}{3}$ $\dfrac{}{6} + \dfrac{}{6}$

② $\dfrac{1}{2} + \dfrac{1}{3}$ $\dfrac{}{6} + \dfrac{2}{6}$

③ $\dfrac{1}{2} + \dfrac{1}{3}$ $\dfrac{3}{6} + \dfrac{2}{6} = \dfrac{5}{6}$

Multiplying and Dividing Fractions

To multiply fractions, multiply straight across the top and bottom.

$$\frac{3}{5} \times \frac{1}{3} = \frac{3 \times 1}{5 \times 3} = \frac{3}{15}$$

To divide fractions, flip the second fraction and multiply.

$$\frac{3}{5} \div \frac{1}{3} = \frac{3 \times 3}{5 \times 1} = \frac{9}{5}$$

HSPT Fractions Exercise

(Answers are on page 223)

1. **Reduce** $\dfrac{12}{60}$ = _____

2. $\dfrac{3}{8} + \dfrac{2}{3}$ = _____

3. $\dfrac{3}{4} - \dfrac{2}{3}$ = _____

4. $\dfrac{3}{4} \times \dfrac{3}{2}$ = _____

5. $\dfrac{1}{3} \div \dfrac{1}{2}$ = _____

DECIMALS

Remember that decimals are just another way of writing fractions. Be sure to know the names of all the decimal places.

$$3\ 4\ .\ 8\ 5\ 7$$

tens
units
tenths
hundredths
thousandths

Adding Decimals

To add decimals, just line up the decimal places and add.

$$
\begin{array}{r}
24.05 \\
+12.23 \\
\hline
36.28
\end{array}
$$

Subtracting Decimals

To subtract decimals, just line up the decimal places and subtract.

$$
\begin{array}{r}
24.05 \\
-12.23 \\
\hline
11.82
\end{array}
$$

Multiplying Decimals

To multiply decimals, count the total number of digits to the right of the decimal point in the numbers you are multiplying. Then multiply the numbers without the decimal points. Once you have your answer, add all of the decimal places you removed from the first two numbers back into the new number.

To solve 0.2×3.4, remove two decimal places and multiply.

$$
\begin{array}{r}
34 \\
\times\ 2 \\
\hline
68
\end{array}
$$

Now put back the two decimal places we removed to get 0.68.

Dividing Decimals

To divide decimals, move the decimal places in both numbers the same number of places to the right until you are working with only integers. But unlike when you're multiplying decimals, you don't have to put the decimals back in when you're dividing.

$$3.4 \div 0.2 = 34 \div 2 = 17$$

Converting Decimals to Fractions

Remember that multiplying by 10 means the same thing as moving the decimal point one place to the right, and dividing by 10 means the same thing as moving the decimal points one place to the left.

$$9 \div 10 = \frac{9}{10} = 0.9$$

$$5 \div 100 = \frac{5}{100} = 0.05$$

This is why the first place to the right of the decimal is called "tenths" and the second place to the right is called "hundredths." Nine-tenths = $0.9 = \frac{9}{10}$. Five-hundredths = $0.05 = \frac{5}{100}$. So to convert a decimal to a fraction, all you need to do is change the numbers after the decimal to their fraction form.

$$5.24 = 5 + \frac{2}{10} + \frac{4}{100}$$

HSPT Decimals Exercise

(Answers are on page 224)

1. 2.43 + 5.25 =   _____

2. 5.75 − 3.12 =   _____

3. 1.5 × 3 =   _____

4. 2.5 × 0.5 =   _____

5. 2.5 ÷ 0.5 =   _____

6. What is 6.32 in
   fraction form?   _____

EXPONENTS, SCIENTIFIC NOTATION, AND SQUARE ROOTS

Exponents are just a short way of writing multiplication. 3^2 means to multiply two 3s together: 3×3. Likewise, 3^4 means to multiply four 3s together: $3 \times 3 \times 3 \times 3$. On the HSPT you will not see very complex exponents, so the best way to solve them is to write them out longhand and multiply.

Scientific notation is also a short way of writing big numbers. Whenever you see a number such as 3.44×10^2, this means that you should move the decimal point to the right the same number of places as the exponent to the right of the 10. In this case, you move the decimal two places to the right (10^2), and you get 344. Likewise, 4.355×10^2 is just another way of writing 435.5.

Square root is just the opposite of raising a number to the second power. $\sqrt{4} = 2$, since $2^2 = 4$. On the HSPT you will not have very big square roots. Your best bet is simply to memorize these common ones.

Since $2^2 = 4$, $\sqrt{4} = 2$

Since $3^2 = 9$, $\sqrt{9} = 3$

Since $4^2 = 16$, $\sqrt{16} = 4$

Since $5^2 = 25$, $\sqrt{25} = 5$

HSPT Exponents, Scientific Notation, and Square Roots Exercise

(Answers are on page 224)

1. $4^3 =$ ____

2. $2^4 =$ ____

3. $3.4 \times 10^2 =$ ____

4. $5.23 \times 10^4 =$ ____

5. $\sqrt{4} + \sqrt{16} =$ ____

SOLVE FOR *X*

To solve an equation, you want to get the variable (the *x*) on one side of the equation and put everything else on the other side.

To get only the variable on one side, follow these two steps.

Step 1: Move elements around using addition and subtraction. Put the variables on one side of the equation and numbers on the other. As long as you do the same operation on both sides of the equal sign, you aren't changing the value of the variable.

Step 2: Divide both sides of the equation by the coefficient, which is the number in front of the variable. If that number is a fraction, multiply everything by the denominator.

For example:

$$3x + 5 = 17$$

Subtract 5 from each side.

$$\begin{aligned} 3x + 5 &= 17 \\ -5 &= -5 \\ \hline 3x &= 12 \end{aligned}$$

Divide 3 from each side

$$\begin{aligned} 3x &= 12 \\ \div 3 &= \div 3 \\ \hline x &= 4 \end{aligned}$$

Always remember the rule of equations: *Whatever you do to one side of the equation, you must also do to the other side.*

HSPT Solve for x Exercise

(Answers are on page 224)

1. If $4x = 20$ then $x =$ ____

2. If $4x + 3 = 31$ then $x =$ ____

3. If $6 = 8x + 4$ then $x =$ ____

4. If $4x - 3 = 3x$ then $x =$ ____

PERCENT TRANSLATION

Everyone knows how easy it is to make a simple mistake on a percent problem. Should you write "5% of 100" as $\frac{5}{100}$ or as $\frac{100}{5}$ or as something else? To make sure to avoid silly mistakes, here's a foolproof method for solving percent questions. Any percent problem can be translated word for word into an equation if you know the mathematical equivalent of the English words. For instance, "percent" means the same thing as "divided by 100," and "of" means the same thing as "multiply." Therefore, "5% of 100" can be written as $\frac{5}{100} \times 100$, which equals 5.

The chart below shows you the mathematical translation of the English words you will probably see. To solve any percent question, read the problem back to yourself and replace the words on the left side of the chart with the math symbols on the right. Then you can easily solve.

Percent	$\div 100$
Of	$\times$
What	x (or any variable)
Is, Are, Equals	$=$

Here are two examples:

20% of 50 is?

$$\begin{array}{ccc} 20\% & \text{of} & 50 \\ \downarrow & \downarrow & \downarrow \\ \dfrac{20}{100} & \times & 50 \end{array}$$

5 is what percent of 80?

$$\begin{array}{cccc} 5 & \text{is} & \text{what percent} & \text{of } 80 \\ \downarrow & \downarrow & & \\ 5 & = & \dfrac{x}{100} & \times \ 80 \end{array}$$

$$5 = \frac{x}{100} \times 80$$

HSPT Percent Translation Exercise

(Answers are on page 224)

1. **30% of 60 =** ____

2. **40% of 200 =** ____

3. **15 is what percent of 60?** ____

4. **What is 25% of 10% of 200?** ____

COMPUTATION QUESTIONS

Several of the questions on the HSPT will ask you to perform basic arithmetic computations. Don't worry about variables here; you won't see any—just addition, subtraction, multiplication, and division. The trick here is to work carefully and in bite-size pieces to make sure that you don't make any careless errors.

Here's an example of a computation question.

───────────◯───────────

10. **What number is 4 more than $\frac{1}{4}$ of 32?**

    a. 6

    b. 8

    c. 10

    d. 12

Here's How to Crack It

The most common mistakes in computation problems stem from trying to do the whole problem at once. Let's just take it one step at a time—in bite-size pieces—and get the right answer. First, let's solve $\frac{1}{4}$ of 32. $\frac{1}{4}$ of 32 is 8. So now the question reads: What number is 4 more than 8? 4 + 8 = 12. The answer is (D)

───────────◯───────────

If you are careful and have mastered basic arithmetic, these questions shouldn't give you too much trouble.

HSPT Computation Exercise

(Answers are on page 225)

1. **What is three times the difference of 75 and 30?** ____

2. **What is $\frac{1}{8}$ of the sum of 50 and 14?** ____

3. **What is 16 more than half of 30?** ____

4. **What number is 160% of 40?** ____

5. **What number is 2 more than the difference of 6^2 and 5^2?** ____

SERIES QUESTIONS

A series is a list of numbers that follow a pattern. For instance, the numbers 2, 4, 6, 8 make a series because each number is 2 more than the number before it. On the HSPT, several questions will show you a series with a blank in it and ask you to figure out what number should fill the blank. What you need to do is figure out the pattern.

To see how to solve one, let's look at the following example.

---○---

11. What number should come next in this series: 1, 5, 9, ___?

Here's How to Crack It

Between the numbers, write the number that—by performing an operation like adding, subtracting, multiplying, or dividing—takes you from the first number to the next and so on.

$$1 \ (+4) \ 5 \ (+4) \ 9 \ \_\_\_$$

Since each number is 4 more than the previous number, the next number in the series must be 13.

Sometimes you will need to try more than one kind of operation between each pair of numbers. On more complicated problems, you may need to try subtraction, multiplication, and division.

---○---

Here's another example.

---○---

12. What number should come next in this series: 7, 5, 12, 10, 17, ___?

Here's How to Crack It

$$
\begin{array}{ccc|ccc|cc}
 & -2 & +7 & & -2 & +7 & -2 & \\
7 & 5 & 12 & 12 & 10 & 17 & 17 & \_\_\_
\end{array}
$$

Since the series goes (– 2) then (+ 7), then next element should be 2 less than 17, or 15.

———————○———————

Try this one.

———————○———————

13. What number should come next in the series: 2, 4, 5, 10, 11, 22, ___?

Here's How to Crack It

$$
\begin{array}{ccc|ccc|ccc}
\times 2 & +1 & & \times 2 & +1 & & \times 2 & +1 & \\
2 & 4 & 5 & 5 & 10 & 11 & 11 & 22 & \rule{1em}{0.4pt}
\end{array}
$$

This series goes (× 2) then (+ 1), so the next element should be 1 more than 22, or 23.

———————○———————

Sometimes the blank will be in the middle of the series rather than at the end. Follow the same technique, and double-check your answer by making sure that the number you put in the blank works with the number(s) that follow.

———————○———————

14. What number should fill the blank in the series: 3, 5, 10, 12, 24, ___, 52?

Here's How to Crack It

$$
\begin{array}{ccc|ccc|ccc}
+2 & \times 2 & & +2 & \times 2 & & +2 & \times 2 & \\
3 & 5 & 10 & 10 & 12 & 24 & 24 & \rule{1em}{0.4pt} & 52
\end{array}
$$

This series goes (+2) then (× 2), so the missing number should be 2 more than 24, or 26. We can double-check this by making sure that $26 \times 2 = 52$, which it does.

———————○———————

That's all there is to series questions! Now give it a try.

HSPT Series Exercise

(Answers are on page 225)

1. 4, 8, 12, 16, 20, ___?

2. 38, 32, 26, 20, ___?

3. 6, 12, 16, 32, 36, 72, ___?

4. 10, 5, 15, 10, 20, 15, ___?

5. 7, 14, 12, 24, 22, 44, ___?

6. 8, 16, 20, 40, ___, 88?

7. 20, 18, 25, 23, ___, 28?

COMPARISON PROBLEMS

The rest of the problems in this section of the HSPT will ask you to compare three values or three quantities. You may be asked to perform some simple arithmetic operations or do simple geometry. (For the geometry review, see Chapter 16.)

Here's an example of a question that asks you to compare three values.

———————○———————

15. **Examine the following and find the best answer.**

    1. $\dfrac{6}{10}$

    2. $\dfrac{40}{100}$

    3. $\dfrac{9}{100}$

    a. 1 > 2 > 3
    b. 1 = 2 = 3
    c. 2 > 1 = 3
    d. 2 > 1 > 3

Here's How to Crack It
Solve for the values of (1), (2), and (3).

In this case, (1) = 0.6, (2) = 0.44, and (3) = 0.9

Once you have the values for (1), (2), and (3), carefully look at the answer choices to see which accurately represents their relationships. Use the Process of Elimination to cross off any choices that you know are wrong, and be sure to read carefully!

Since (1) is the largest, we can eliminate answers (B), (C), and (D). Therefore, (A) is the answer.

———————○———————

Here's another example of a question that asks you to compare three quantities.

16. Examine (A), (B), and (C) and find the best answer.

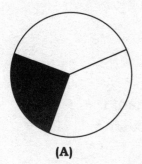 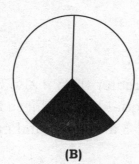 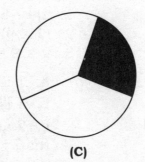

(A)　　　　　　　(B)　　　　　　　(C)

a. (A) is more shaded than (B)

b. (A) is less shaded than (B) and more shaded than (C)

c. (C) is more shaded than both (A) and (B)

d. (A), (B), and (C) are equally shaded

Here's How to Crack It

In this case, you should inspect circles A, B, and C. Figure out what the relationship is among them and use Process of Elimination to find the best choice. Since A and B are equally shaded, choices (A) and (B) can be eliminated. Since B and C are equally shaded, choice (C) can also be eliminated. Therefore, choice (D) must be the answer.

HSPT Comparison Exercise

(Answers are on page 225)

1. **Examine the following and find the best answer.**

   1. $2(9 - 5)$
   2. $(2 \times 9) - 5$
   3. $2 \times 9 - 5$

      a. 1 is greater than 2 and 3
      b. 1 is equal to 2 and less than 3
      c. 2 and 3 are equal and greater than 1
      d. 1, 2, and 3 are equal

2. **Examine the following and find the best answer.**

   1. 40% of 60
   2. 60% of 40
   3. 50% of 90

      a. 1 is greater than 2 and 3
      b. 1 is equal to 2 and less than 3
      c. 2 and 3 are equal and greater than 1
      d. 1, 2, and 3 are equal

3. **Examine the following and find the best answer.**

   1. 2.3×10^2
   2. 2,300
   3. 2.3×10^3

      a. 1 is greater than 2 and 3
      b. 1 is equal to 2 and less than 3
      c. 2 and 3 are equal and greater than 1
      d. 1, 2, and 3 are equal

4. Examine the following and find the best answer.

1. the area of a square with side 6
2. the perimeter of a square with side 6
3. half the area of a square with side 8

   a. 1 is greater than 2, which is less than 3

   b. 1 is equal to 2 and less than 3

   c. 2 and 3 are equal and greater than 1

   d. 1, 2, and 3 are equal

5. Triangle *ABC* is isosceles. Angle *a* measures 40°. Find the best answer.

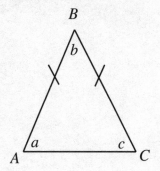

   a. *a* is greater than *b* + *c*

   b. *a* is less than *b* + *c*

   c. *a* is equal to *b* + *c*

   d. *a*, *b*, and *c* are all equal

Chapter 15
Reading Comprehension and Vocabulary

A WORD ABOUT TIMING

This section of the HSPT combines two very different question types: reading comprehension and reading vocabulary. How should you spend your time?

The reading vocabulary questions are very much like the synonym questions we discussed in Chapter 13. You should go through them very quickly, since you probably either know the word or you don't. This means you should spend the majority of your time on the reading comprehension. Slow down, take your time, and get your points on reading comprehension, because taking extra time on vocabulary probably won't help. Of your 25 minutes, the first five should be spent on the vocab, and the rest of time can be used on reading comprehension.

HOW TO THINK ABOUT READING COMPREHENSION

Reading the passages on the HSPT is different from most other kinds of reading that you will do in school. You might think that you have to read slowly enough to learn all the information in the passage. But there is much more information in the passage than you can learn in a short time, and you will be asked about only a few facts from the passage. So trying to understand all of the facts in the passage is not the best use of your time.

Most importantly, you don't get points for understanding everything in the passage. You only get points for answering questions correctly. Therefore, we're going to teach you the best strategy to get the most correct answers.

There is one more important thing to know, which works to your advantage: *The answer to every question can be found somewhere in the passage.* All you've got to do is find it. This means that you should think of reading comprehension like a treasure hunt: You need to use clues in the questions to find the answers in the passage and earn your points.

STRATEGY FOR ATTACKING READING COMPREHENSION

Step 1: Read the passage and label each paragraph. Don't try to learn every single fact in the passage; you can always go back later. It is important to only get a general idea of what the paragraph talks about.

Step 2: Answer the general questions based on your paragraph labels.

Step 3: Answer the specific questions by looking back at the passage and finding the answer.

Important! In steps 2 and 3, answer your questions by using Process of Elimination. The test-writers will often try to disguise the correct answer by using different words that mean basically the same thing as the words used in the passage. You might not recognize these words right away as the ones used in the passage. Why do the test-writers do this? If they gave you the exact words straight out of the passage, that would be too easy. So your best bet is the cross off the choices that you know are wrong and pick from the choices that are left.

Now let's look at each step in more detail.

Step 1: Label Your Paragraphs

Every good treasure hunt needs a map, which will help you locate the answers in the passage. The best way to make a map is to label your paragraphs as you read. This will help you understand the main idea of the passage and at the same time make it easier to locate facts in the passage while you're reading.

After you finish each paragraph, stop for a moment and ask yourself, "What is this paragraph about?" Try to summarize the idea of this paragraph in seven or eight words, and quickly write this summary in the margin. This way, you'll have a guide to important parts of the passage when you have to answer a question.

After you have read the entire passage, take a moment and ask yourself, "What is this whole passage about?" Write a one sentence summary at the bottom of the page. This will help you answer any main idea questions you may see.

Try doing Step 1 for the following passage

Contrary to popular belief, the first European known to lay eyes on America was not Christopher Columbus or Amerigo Vespucci, but a little-known Viking named Bjarni Herjolfsson. In the summer of 966, Bjarni sailed from Norway to Iceland, heading for the Viking settlement where his father Heriulf resided.

When he arrived in Iceland, Bjarni discovered that his father had already sold his land and estates and set out for the latest Viking settlement on the subartic island called Greenland. Discovered by an infamous murderer and criminal named

Erik the Red, Greenland lay at the limit of the known world. Dismayed, Bjarni set out for this new colony.

Since the Vikings traveled without a chart or compass, it was not uncommon for them to lose their way in the unpredictable northern seas. Beset by fog, the crew lost their bearings. When the fog finally cleared, they found themselves before a land that was level and covered with woods. They traveled farther up the coast, finding more flat, wooded country. Farther north, the landscape revealed glaciers and rocky mountains. Without knowing it, Bjarni had arrived in North America.

Though Bjarni realized this was an unknown land, he was no intrepid explorer. Rather, he was a practical man who had simply set out to find his father. Refusing his crew's request to go ashore, he promptly turned his bow back to sea. After four days' sailing, Bjarni landed at Herjolfsnes on the southwestern tip of Greenland, the exact place he had been seeking all along.

_____

_____

_____

_____

What is this whole passage about?

Your labels and passage summary should look something like this.

Paragraph 1: America was first visited by Bjarni Herjolfsson.

Paragraph 2: Herjolfsson wanted to follow his father to Greenland.

Paragraph 3: He got lost and ended up at America.

Paragraph 4: He turned around and finally reached Greenland.

Summary: How Bjarni Herjolfsson got lost and saw America before anyone else.

Now we have a good picture of the overall point of the passage, and we should be able to look back and find any details we need. So let's turn to the questions.

Step 2: Answer the General Questions

It's usually best to answer the general questions first. These questions ask you about the passage as a whole. There are several types of general questions, and they look like this.

Main Idea/Purpose
- The passage is mostly about
- The main idea of this passage is
- The best title for this passage would be
- The purpose of this passage is to
- The author wrote this passage in order to

Tone/Attitude
- The author's tone is best described as
- The attitude of the author is one of

General Interpretation
- The author would most likely agree that
- It can be inferred from the passage that
- The passage implies that
- You would probably find this passage in a
- This passage is best described as

To answer a main idea/purpose question, ask yourself, "What did the passage talk about most?" Look at the choices and cross off anything that was not discussed or that was only a detail of the passage.

To answer a tone/attitude question, ask yourself, "How does the author feel about the subject?" Cross off anything that was not discussed in the paragraph or that does not agree with the author's view.

Let's take a look at some general questions for this passage.

---

1. **The passage is mostly about**

   a. the Vikings and their civilization

   b. the waves of Viking immigration

   c. sailing techniques of Bjarni Herjolfsson

   d. one Viking's glimpse of America

Here's How to Crack It

To answer this question, let's look back at our labels and our summary of the passage. We said that the main idea of the passage was how Bjarni Herjolfsson got lost and saw America before anyone else. Choices (A) and (D) are about the Vikings in general and not about Herjolfsson, so they can be eliminated. Choice (C) is about Herjolfsson, but his sailing techniques are not really discussed. This makes (D) the best choice.

---

2. **Which of the following can be inferred from the passage?**

   a. The word *America* was first used by Herjolfsson.

   b. Herjolfsson's discovery of America was an accident.

   c. Herjolfsson was helped by Native Americans.

   d. Greenland and Iceland were the Vikings' most important discoveries.

Here's How to Crack It

You should make quick work of this problem using Process of Elimination. The passage never says anything about Native Americans, so (C) can be eliminated.

Also, it doesn't say that Herjolfsson ever used the word *America*, so you can cross off (A). (If you're not positive whether this is true or not, quickly skim back and double-check this in the passage.) We're already down to two choices. Choice (D) is an extreme choice—meaning it uses strong language that makes something absolutely true or false—due to the word *most*, so it probably is not the answer. If you check the passage, you can see that (D) is never stated. Therefore (B) is the best choice.

Step 3: Answer the Specific Questions

Specific questions ask you about a fact or detail mentioned in the passage. For these questions, look back at the passage to find your answer. These are different kinds of specific questions.

Fact
- According to the passage
- According to the author
- Which of these questions is answered by the passage?

Vocabulary in Context
- The word <u>pilfer</u> probably means
- What does the passage mean by <u>pilfer</u>?

Specific Interpretation/ Purpose
- The author mentions Mother Goose in order to
- From the information in the passage, Mother Goose would probably

To answer a **fact** question, look back at the passage and find the lines that mention the thing you are asked about. Use your passage labels to find the information quickly, or simply skim until you find it. Reread those lines to see exactly what the passage says. Then look for a choice that best restates what the passage says. Cross off anything that is never stated or that says the opposite of the information in the passage.

To answer a **Vocabulary in Context** question, look back at the passage and find the underlined word. It will probably be a prod that you don't know. Cover the word with your finger. Reread the lines around that word, and think of the word that you should put there. If you can't think of the exact word, it's okay to simply note that the word should be a "positive word" or a "negative word."

To answer a **Specific Interpretation/Purpose** question, look back at the passage and find the lines that discuss the thing you are asked about. Use your passage labels or skim the passage. Reread those lines to see exactly what the passage says.

The correct answer will always be very closely based on the information in the passage. For instance, if a passage tells us that John likes to play tennis, we can infer that he will probably play tennis if he is given the chance. Cross off any choices that are not stated in the passage or sound very far off from what the passage says.

---

3. According to the passage, Greenland was discovered by

   a. Amerigo Vespucci
   b. Bjarni Herjolfsson's father
   c. Bjarni Herjolfsson
   d. Erik the Red

Here's How to Crack It

To answer this question, we should look back at the passage and find the line that talks about the discovery of Greenland. If you skim for the word Greenland, you'll find it in the second paragraph: "Discovered by an infamous murderer and criminal named Erik the Red, Greenland lay at the limit of the known world." Therefore the answer is (D).

---

4. The word infamous probably means

   a. lazy
   b. strong
   c. wicked
   d. intelligent

Here's How to Crack It

Let's reread the line that mentions the word *infamous*: "Discovered by an infamous murderer and criminal named Erik the Red..." Since the word *infamous* describes a *murderer and criminal*, it must be a word that describes someone who is bad. Choices (B) and (D) are positive words, so you can eliminate them. Choice (C) sounds much more like a description of a bad person than (A), so the best choice is (C).

---

5. According to the passage, Bjarni Herjolfsson left Norway to

a. start a new colony

b. open a trade route to America

c. visit his relatives

d. map the North Sea

Here's How to Crack It

The end of the first paragraph discusses Herjolfsson's departure. There it states, "Bjarni sailed from Norway to Iceland, heading for the Viking settlement where his father resided." The correct answer will use different words, but it should restate the same idea. Can we find anything here about starting a colony? No, so (A) can be eliminated. Does it mention opening a trade route to America? No, so (B) can also be eliminated. (It's true that he does eventually reach America, but that isn't the reason why he left.) Does it mention visiting his relatives? Well, it does say that he wanted to find his father. So let's leave (C). Does this sentence mention mapping the North Sea? No. Choice (D) is incorrect, too, so (C) is the answer.

6. Bjarni's reaction upon landing in Iceland can best be described as

a. disappointed

b. satisfied

c. amused

d. fascinated

Here's How to Crack It

Where can we find a description of Bjarni Herjolfsson's arrival in Iceland? At the beginning paragraph. There it states, "When he arrived in Iceland, Bjarni discovered that his father had already sold his land and estates and set out for the latest Viking settlement on the subarctic island called Greenland." Feeling "dismayed," Bjarni left to look for the new colony. Since he had missed his father, he was unhappy. Which word best states this idea? Choice (A).

7. When the author says, "The crew lost their bearings," this probably means that

a. the ship was damaged beyond repair

b. the sailors did not know which way they were going

c. the sailors were very angry

d. the sailors misplaced their clothes

Here's How to Crack It

Let's reread the lines around "the crew lost their bearings": "Since the Vikings traveled without chart or compass, it was not uncommon for them to lose their way in the unpredictable northern sea. Beset by fog, the crew lost their bearings." Since the story says that the crew would often "lose their way" the best answer is (B).

PROCESS OF ELIMINATION

If you're stuck on which answer is correct, remember to use the Process of Elimination to cross off answers you know are wrong.

On general questions, you'll usually want to cross off answers that

- are not mentioned in the passage
- are too detailed—if the passage mentions something in only one line, it is a detail, not a main idea
- go against, or say the opposite of, information in the passage
- are too big—you can't say much in four or five paragraphs, so any answer that says something like, "The passage proves that the theory Einstein spent his entire life creating was right" is probably a wrong answer
- are too extreme—if a choice uses absolute terms such as "all," "every," "never," or "always," it's probably a wrong answer
- go against common sense

On specific questions, you should probably cross off answers that

- are extreme
- go against information in the passage
- are not mentioned in the passage
- go against common sense

If you look back at the questions in the sample reading comp passage above, you'll see that following guidelines eliminates many of the wrong answer choices. Use these guidelines when you take the HSPT.

What Kind of Answers Do I Keep?

Correct answers tend to be

- restatements or paraphrases of what is said in the passage
- traditional and conservative
- moderate, using words such as "may," "can," and "often"

HSPT Reading Comprehension Exercise

(Answers are on page 226)

Try the following reading comprehension passage. Don't forget to label your paragraphs!

Although many people associate indoor lighting with modern electrical wiring, practical indoor lighting existed thousands of years before Thomas Edison invented the light bulb. <u>Rudimentary</u> oil lamps, a primitive ancestor of the gaslight, were used in the caves in which prehistoric humans lived.

_____

Approximately 50,000 years ago, cave-dwelling humans fashioned a basic oil-based lamp out of animal fat that was kept inside a stone base as well as a wick made out of a clothlike material. Due to the fact that animal fat smells awful when burned, the lamp gave off a terrible odor.

_____

Thousands of years later, during the Egyptian era (around 1300 B.C.E.) the structure and design of the lamp changed. Instead of using only stone, the Egyptians used a form of decorated pottery with a papyrus-based wick and vegetable oil instead of the <u>foul</u>-smelling animal fat.

_____

In times of need people burned whatever oil was plentiful. Because vegetable oil and animal fat are both edible, in times of hunger people did not burn lamps; they used the oil for food. But oil lamps brought with them other problems. Wicks for the lamps did not always burn away and had to be changed periodically. Soon the oil lamp gave way to the first candle, which became a popular source of light in Rome during the first century B.C.E.

_____

1. **What is this passage mostly about?**

   a. how Egyptians lit their homes
   b. why the candle is better than the oil lamp
   c. the history of indoor lighting
   d. why vegetable oil replaced animal fat in oil lamps

2. **It can be inferred that the author views the change from oil lamps to candles as**

   a. the most important discovery of human history
   b. a mistake made by the Romans
   c. important to the discovery of electricity
   d. a step in the development of indoor lighting

3. **The word <u>rudimentary</u> most likely means**

   a. expensive
   b. basic
   c. colorful
   d. handy

4. **The author mentions Thomas Edison in the passage in order to**

   a. explain his discoveries
   b. compare him with other modern inventors
   c. introduce someone that the author will discuss later
   d. show that Edison was not the first to discover indoor lighting

5. **The word <u>foul</u> probably means**

   a. awful
   b. sweet
   c. fruity
   d. clean

6. **People probably stopped burning animal fat in lamps because**

   a. vegetable oil was more plentiful
   b. they needed the animal fat for cooking
   c. animal fat smelled bad
   d. burning animal fat was against the law

7. **The author's tone can best be described as**

   a. angry
   b. unconcerned
   c. instructive
   d. critical

READING VOCABULARY

The vocab section of this test should only take you about five minutes. As mentioned earlier, these questions are very much like the synonym questions in Chapter 13, and can be solved using the same techniques.

----------○----------

1. **To <u>recall</u> an event**
   a. plan
   b. leave
   c. remember
   d. attend

Here's How to Crack It
If you know the meaning of the word:

Step 1: Cover the answer choices with your hand. If you read the answer choices first, you might get confused.

Step 2: State what the word means to you in your own words.

Step 3: Uncover the answer choices and see which choice most closely matches what you said.

In this case, let's cover up the answers choices. In your own words, what does the word *recall* mean? Maybe you came up with something like "remember" or "think about." Now uncover the answer choices and see which best matches your word. Chances are good that you came up with something very close to (C).

----------○----------

If you "sort of" know what the word means:

Maybe you have a sense of what the word means but can't quite put your finger on it. Perhaps you can think of a saying that uses the word—even if you're not sure what the word means—and you should still be able to get the right answer or at least come up with a good guess. If either of these is the case, use the "side of the fence" trick. This is when you ask yourself whether the word is a positive word or negative word. If the word is positive, you can eliminate any words that are not positive. If the word is negative, you can eliminate any words that are not negative.

Take a look at the following example.

---○---

2. A <u>surplus</u> of food

   a. basket

   b. excess

   c. lack

   d. field

Here's How to Crack It

You might have a sense that the word *surplus* is positive, especially because the word *plus*, which you can see inside it. Then you may guess that the word *surplus* means something like "a lot." If so, you can eliminate (A) and (C), and take your best guess from the remaining choices. (The answer is (B).)

---○---

What if you have no idea what the word means?

If you have no idea what the word means, take your best guess and move on to the next problem. This is the perfect time to use the Process of Elimination or your LOTD.

You're on a learning roll! Now it's time to take a stroll!

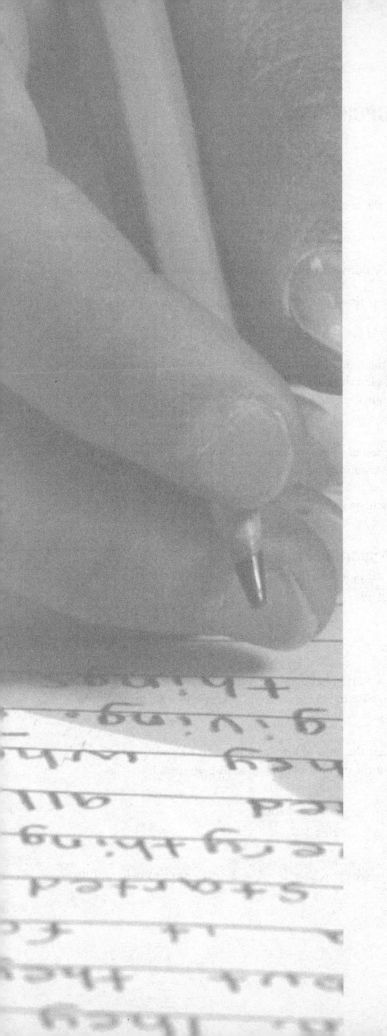

Chapter 16
Mathematics

RATIOS AND PROPORTIONS

What Is a Ratio?

A ratio is a way of stating the relationship of two numbers in a reduced form. For instance, if there are 50 boys and 25 girls in a room, we can say that the ratio of boys to girls is 50 to 25. But we can also reduce this ratio just like a fraction: $\frac{50}{25} = \frac{2}{1}$. So we can also say that the ratio of boys to girls is 2 to 1. This is sometimes written as "The ratio of boys to girls is 2:1."

Of course, if we say that the ratio of boys to girls is 2 to 1, this doesn't tell us exactly how many boys and girls there are. The actual number could be 8 boys and 4 girls, or 10 boys and 5 girls, or 200 boys and 100 girls. Each of these can be reduced to the ratio 2 to 1.

But if we know one of the actual values, we can always solve for the other one. For instance, if we know that the ratio of boys to girls is 2 to 1, and there are 200 boys, we know that there must be 100 girls. Most of you can probably do that in your heads. But how do you calculate it?

Solving Ratio and Proportion Problems

The way you solve almost all ratio and proportion questions is by setting up two fractions and cross multiplying.

$$\frac{A}{B} = \frac{C}{D}$$

Whenever you set up two equal fractions, you know that $A \times D$ is equal to $B \times C$. The only thing you have to make sure to do is keep the same thing on top and bottom of each fraction.

In this case, if we know that the ratio of boys to girls is 2 to 1 and that there are 200 boys, we can figure out the number of girls by setting up these fractions.

$$\frac{\text{boys}}{\text{girls}} \frac{2}{1} = \frac{200}{x}$$

Now we can cross-multiply: We know that $2x = 1 \times 200$. This means that $x = 100$.

Take a look at the following problem.

---⌒---

1. **John has a bowl of red and blue marbles. The ratio of red to blue marbles is 5 to 4. If there are 35 red marbles in the bowl, how many blue marbles are in the bowl?**

   a. 16
   b. 20
   c. 28
   d. 39

Here's How to Crack It
Let's set up our fractions with red marbles on top and blue marbles on the bottom. It will look like this:

$$\frac{\text{red}}{\text{blue}} \frac{5}{4} = \frac{35}{x}$$

Now we can cross-multiply. We know that $5x = 4 \times 35$. After we multiply, $5x = 140$. We can solve for x by dividing both sides by 5 to get $x = 28$. Therefore, there are 28 blue marbles in the bowl, which is (C).

---⌒---

AVERAGES

The formula we use to figure out the average is:

$$\text{average} = \frac{\text{sum total}}{\text{\# of things}}$$

For instance, if you take 3 tests on which you score 50, 55, and 57, the sum total of your scores is $50 + 55 + 57$, or 162. Since there were 3 tests, the average must be $\frac{162}{3} = 54$.

Try the following problem.

---

2. **During a certain month, David counted the number of apples he ate each week. He ate 2 apples during the first week, 4 apples during the second week, and 2 apples during the third week. The fourth week he ate no apples. On average, how many apples did David eat each week of the month.**

   a. 2

   b. $2\frac{1}{2}$

   c. $3\frac{1}{3}$

   d. 7

Here's How to Crack It

The total number of apples David ate was 2 + 4 + 2 + 0, or 8. This sum total, over the number of weeks, will give us the average: $\frac{8}{4} = 2$.

PLUGGING IN THE ANSWER CHOICES

Very often you may think that you need to do a lot of complicated math to set up a problem. This is especially true on those long, wordy problems that give everyone a headache.

You know, however, that one of the answer choices given has to be the correct answer. All you've got to do is figure out which one. Therefore, the easiest way to solve many problems is by simply plugging in each answer choice until you find the one that works. Plugging in just means substituting numbers to figure out the answer quickly.

Take a look at the following problem.

───────○───────

3. If $x(x + 4) = 12$, which of the following could be the value of x?

    a. −1
    b. 0
    c. 1
    d. 2

Here's How to Crack It

You might think that you have to do some complicated algebra to solve this problem, but you really don't. Let's just try plugging in each answer choice for the value of x and see which one makes the equation work.

If we plug in −1 for x, does $-1(-1 + 4) = 12$? No. Cross off (A). If we plug in 0 for x, does $0(0 + 4) = 12$? No. Cross off (B). If we plug in 1 for x, does $1(1 + 4) = 12$? No. Cross off (C). If we plug in 2 for x, does $2(2 + 4) = 12$? Yes, so (D) is the answer.

───────○───────

───────○───────

4. David is five years older than his brother Jim, and Jim is twice as old as Ann. If David is 10 years older than Ann, how old is Jim?

    a. 20
    b. 15
    c. 10
    d. 8

Here's How to Crack It

The question asks how old Jim is, so this is what we'll be plugging in for. Let's start with (A). Could Jim be 20? We know that David is five years older than Jim, so if Jim is 20, then David is 25. We also know that Jim is twice as old as Ann, so Ann must be 10. But the last sentence says that David should be 10 years older than Ann, which he's not. Therefore (A) can't be the answer.

How about (B)? Could Jim be 15? We know that David is five years older than Jim, so if Jim is 15, then David must be 20. We also know that Jim is twice as old as Ann, so Ann must be $7\frac{1}{2}$. But the last sentence says that David should be 10 years older than Ann, which he's not. Therefore (B) can't be the answer.

Let's try (C). Could Jim be 10? We know that David is five years older than Jim, so if Jim is 10, then David is 15. We also know that Jim is twice as old as Ann, so Ann must be 5. Does this make David 10 years older than Ann? Yes. So (C) is the answer.

———————◯———————

Here's a slightly harder problem. Trying to solve it using algebra is difficult, but by plugging in the answer choices, it becomes very easy.

———————◯———————

5. **If the average of 4 and *x* is equal to the average of 5, 4, and *x*, what is the value of *x*?**

    a. 1
    b. 2
    c. 6
    d. 8

Here's How to Crack It
Let's start with (A), and plug 1 in for *x*. Does the average of 4 and 1 (which is 2.5) equal the average of 5, 4, and 1 (which is $\frac{10}{3}$)? No, so (A) can be eliminated. Let's try (B). Does the average of 4 and 2 (which is 3) equal the average of 5, 4, and 2 (which is $\frac{11}{3}$)? No. Choice (B) can also be eliminated. How about (C)? Does the average of 4 and 6 (which is 5) equal the average of 5, 4, and 6 (which is 5)? Yes. Choice (C) is the answer.

———————◯———————

PLUGGING IN YOUR OWN NUMBERS

The problem with doing algebra is that it's just too easy to make a mistake. Whenever you see a problem with variables (x's) in the answer choices, PLUG IN. Start by picking a number for the variable in the problem (or for more than one variable, if necessary); solve the problem using that real number; then see which answer choice gives you the correct answer.

Have a look at the following problem:

———————————○———————————

6. If x is a positive integer, then 20 percent of $5x$ equals

    a. x

    b. $2x$

    c. $5x$

    d. $15x$

Here's How to Crack It

Let's start by picking a number for x. Let's plug in the nice round number 10. When we plug in 10 for x, we change every x in the whole problem into a 10. Now the problem reads:

———————————○———————————

———————————○———————————

7. If 10 is a positive integer, then 20 percent of 5(10) equals

    a. 10

    b. 2(10)

    c. 5(10)

    d. 15(10)

Here's How to Crack It

Look how easy the problem becomes! Now we can solve: 20 percent of 50 is 10. Which answer says 10? Choice (A) does.

———————————○———————————

Let's try it again.

⎯⎯⎯⎯⎯⎯⎯⎯⎯⎯◯⎯⎯⎯⎯⎯⎯⎯⎯⎯⎯

8. If $0 < x < 1$, then which of the following is true?

   a. $x > 0$

   b. $x > 1$

   c. $x > 2$

   d. $2x > 2$

Here's How to Crack It

This time when we pick a number for x, we have to make sure that it is between 0 and 1, because that's what the problem states. So let's try $\frac{1}{2}$. If we make every x in the problem into $\frac{1}{2}$, the answer choices now read:

(a) $\frac{1}{2} > 0$

(b) $\frac{1}{2} > 1$

(c) $\frac{1}{2} > 2$

(d) $1 > 2$

Which one of these is true? Choice (A). Plugging In is such a great technique that it makes even the hardest algebra problems easy. *Anytime you can, plug in!*

⎯⎯⎯⎯⎯⎯⎯⎯⎯⎯◯⎯⎯⎯⎯⎯⎯⎯⎯⎯⎯

GEOMETRY

Lines and Angles

On every line, all the angles must add up to a total of 180°.

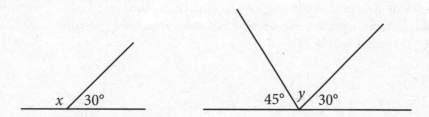

Since x and 30° must add up to 180°, we know that x must measure 180° – 30°, or 150°. Since 45°, y, and 30° must add up to 180°, we know that y must measure 180° – 45° – 30°, or 105°.

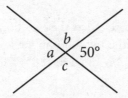

In this case, b and the angle measuring 50° are on a line together. This means that b must measure 130° (180° – 50° = 130°). Also, c and the angle measuring 50° are on a line together. This means that c must also measure 130° (180° – 50° = 130°). Finally, a must measure 50°, because a + b (and we already know that b = 130°) must measure 180° (50° + 130° = 180°).

This explains why vertical angles (the angles opposite each other when two lines cross) are always equal. Angles b and c are both 130°, and angle a (which is opposite the angle 50°) is 50°.

In a triangle, all the angles must add up to 180°. In a four-sided figure, all the angles must add up to 360°.

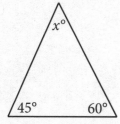
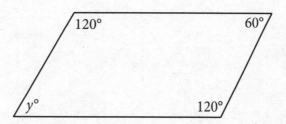

In this triangle, two of the angles are 45° and 60°. They make a total of 105°. The sum of the angles needs to equal 180°. Therefore angle *x* must be 180° – 105°, or 75°.

In the figure on the right, three of the angles have a total of 300°. Therefore *y* must be equal to 360° – 300°, or 60°.

A triangle is *isosceles* if it has two equal sides. This means that the two opposite angles are also equal. A triangle is *equilateral* if it has three equal sides. This means that all three angles are also equal. Since these angles must equally divide from 180°, they must each be 60°.

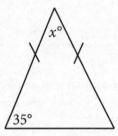

The triangle on the left is isosceles, so the two bottom angles must each be 35°. This makes a total of 70° for the two bottom angles. Since all of the angles must add up to 180°, we know that *x* is equal to 180° – 70°, or 110°.

Area, Perimeter, and Circumference

The area of a square or rectangle is length × width.

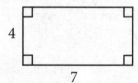

The area of this square is 4 × 4, or 16. The area of the rectangle is 4 × 7, or 28.

The area of a triangle is $\frac{1}{2}$ base × height.

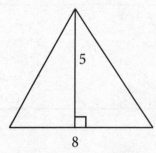

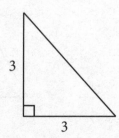

The area of the triangle on the left is $\frac{1}{2} \times 5 \times 8$, or 20.

The area of the triangle on the right is $\frac{1}{2} \times 3 \times 3$, or $4\frac{1}{2}$.

The perimeter of any object is the sum of the lengths of its sides.

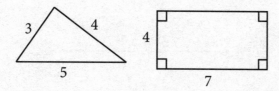

The perimeter of the triangle is 3 + 4 + 5, or 12. The perimeter of the rectangle is 4 + 7 + 4 + 7, or 22 (opposite sides are always equal to each other in a rectangle or a square).

The circumference of a circle with radius r is $2\pi r$. A circle with a radius of 5 has a circumference of 10π.

The area of a circle with radius r is πr^2. A circle with a radius of 5 has an area of 25π.

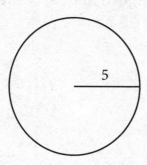

HSPT Geometry Exercise

(Answers are on page 227)

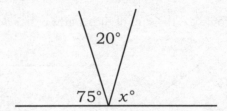

1. In the figure above, what is the value of *x*?

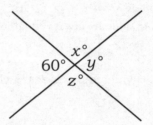

2. In the figure above, what is the value of *y* + *z*?

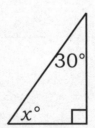

3. In the figure above, what is the value of *x*?

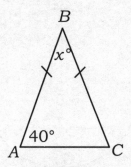

4. If triangle *ABC* is isosceles, what is the value of *x*?

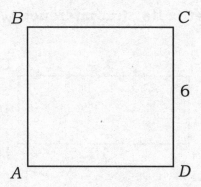

5. What is the area of square *ABCD* above?

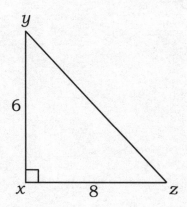

6. What is the area of triangle *XYZ* above?

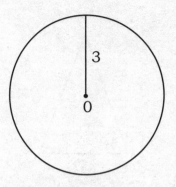

7a. What is the area of the circle above with center _O_?

7b. What is its circumference?

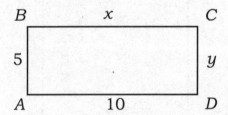

8a. If _ABCD_ is a rectangle, _x_ = ____ and _y_ = ___.

8b. What is the perimeter of rectangle _ABCD_?

Chapter 17
Language Skills

USAGE QUESTIONS

Most of the questions in the language expressions section of the HSPT will ask you to look at four sentences and figure out which one, if any, contains an error. If the sentence contains no error, pick (D), "No mistake."

ERRORS

What kind of errors should you look for? The HSPT tests only a few kinds of errors. Learn them, and you'll know what to look for to greatly increase your score.

Subject/ Verb Agreement

What is wrong with the following sentences?

1. **The cats in the house watches the bird.**

2. **A wild dingo from Sydney were caught last year.**

To spot subject/verb agreement errors, always find the subject and the verb in the given sentence. To find the subject, ask yourself, "Who or what is acting or being described?" To find the verb, find the action word by asking yourself, "What is the subject doing?" Then make sure that the subject and the verb agree. Subjects and verbs have to agree in both number (singular or plural) and person (I, she, we, you). You may have to read around other parts of the sentence to make it clear to yourself.

What is the subject in sentence 1? It's the cats who are watching the bird. Can you say, "The cats **watches** the bird?" No. *Cats*, in this case, is plural—more than one cat—so the verb has to agree. It should be "The cats **watch** the bird."

What is the subject in sentence 2? A *wild dingo* is the thing being described. Can you say, "A wild dingo **were** caught last year"? No; in this case *dingo* is singular, and the verb has to agree with a singular subject. It should be "A wild dingo **was** caught last year."

Verb Form and Tense

What is wrong with the following sentences?

> **3. Yesterday, John is going to the playground.**

> **4. Patricia has took her hamster to the vet.**

Verb Tense

The word *yesterday* in sentence 3 tells us that the verb should be in the past tense. You can see that this sentence has an error because it clearly says that the action happened yesterday, but the verb "is going" is in the present tense. The sentence should read "Yesterday, John **went** to the playground." *Went* is the past tense of the infinitive verb *to go*. To spot tense problems, look for words and phrases that indicate present or past, such as

- today (present)
- now (present)
- yesterday (past)
- last week (past)
- in 1956 (past)
- once (past)
- a long time ago (past)
- during the Second World War (past)

Verb Form

Sometimes the error will be in the verb form, such as in sentence 4. Recognizing correct verb form is as simple as knowing the proper present, past, and future forms of verbs. The HSPT will ask you not to identify and name verb forms, just to choose the correct version of the sentence. Usually, it should be obvious to you when a verb form is wrong because the sentence just won't make sense. The past tense form of the verb *to take* would be either *took* or *has taken*. You could say, "Patricia **took** her hamster to the vet" or "Patricia **has taken** her hamster to the vet." But *has took* is not a possible form. Make sure that you review proper verb forms as part of your preparation for the HSPT.

Adjective/ Adverbs

What is wrong with the following sentence?

5. Kim ran quick around the track.

What is the word *quick* describing? The way that Kim ran around the track. If a word describes a person or a thing, it should be an adjective like *quick*. But if a word describes an action (verb), it should be an adverb like *quickly*. Don't forget: Most adverbs end in *-ly*.

Remember this rule: Adjectives modify nouns; adverbs modify everything else.

Comparison Words

What is wrong with the following sentences?

6. He was one of the most greatest authors of his time.

7. She is intelligenter than he is.

Some questions on the HSPT will ask you to determine the right form of a comparison word. In the sentences above, *greatest* and *more intelligent* are the correct forms of the comparison words. For most adjectives that have only one syllable, we make them into comparison words by adding *–er* and *–est* to the end of the word, such as big, bigger, biggest and great, greater, greatest.

For most adjectives with more than one syllable, we make the comparison using the words more and most, as with intelligent, more intelligent, most intelligent and interesting, more interesting, most interesting.

Pronoun Agreement and Case

8. The dog ran away, but they came back soon.

9. Murray is a man which loves to play the piano.

10. Olivia gave the assignment to Peter and I.

Pronouns are words, such as *I, it, they, me,* and *she,* that take the place of nouns. Whenever you see pronouns in a sentence, check to make sure that they agree with the nouns they stand for and that they are in the proper case. Pronoun *agreement* means that singular pronouns stand in for singular nouns, and plural pronouns stand in for plural nouns. In sentence 8, the subject is "the dog," which is singular, but the pronoun "they" is plural. The sentence should read "The dog ran away, but it came back soon."

Another important rule to remember is to use the pronoun *who* for people and *which* or *that* for things. Therefore sentence 9 should read "Murray is a man **who** loves to play the piano."

Pronoun *case* means that the subject of the sentence (the thing doing the acting) needs a subject pronoun, and the object of a sentence (the thing receiving the action) needs an object pronoun. In the sentence "Mary threw the ball to John," Mary is the subject and John is the object. Below is a chart that tells you how to use a pronoun whether it is the subject or the object.

Subject	Example
I	I left the office.
You	You should get some rest.
He/she/it	He knew the best route to take.
We	We love to visit our grandparents.
They	They live in California.
Object	Example
Me	My boss told me to go home.
You	A good night's sleep would do you some good.
Him/her/it	Jenny refused to tell him the best route to take.
Us	Our grandparents love us.
Them	We visited them in California.

In sentence 10, does the word *I* describe someone who is giving the book (a subject) or someone to whom the book was given (an object)? Think about it this way: We say *I* gave it to *him,* but *he* gave it to *me.* In the example sentence, the word *I* describes someone who received the action, not someone who was doing the action. So the pronoun used should be the object pronoun, and the sentence should read "Olivia gave the assignment to Peter and *me.*" If you are confused about the correct answer, try this trick: Take away the word *Peter* and see what is left. You wouldn't say, "Olivia gave the assignment to I," but you would say, "Olivia gave the assignment to me."

Important note: Whenever a pronoun follows a preposition (such as *to, of, in, at, around, between,* and *from*) the pronouns are *always* in the object case.

Here are some common pronoun mix-ups. Don't forget them because recognizing them is a simple way to rack up points on the HSPT.

It's = it is	It's raining outside.
Its = belongs to it	The dog eats its bone.
You're = you are	You're a great friend.
Your = belongs to you	I love your shoes.
Who's = who is	Who's at the door?
Whose = belongs to who	Whose car is this?

Sentence Fragments

What is wrong with the following sentences?

11. Told me that I would have to see the dentist.

12. The elephant, after eating dinner, walking around the zoo.

Every sentence has to express a complete thought and have both a subject and a verb. What is the subject in sentence 11? Who or what told me to go to the dentist? There is no subject in this sentence, and therefore it is only a sentence fragment. Sentence fragments are not complete sentences and are never the correct answer on the HSPT.

Sentence 12 has a subject—the elephant—but it has no true verb. It is also a fragment so we know it's an error!

Parallelism

What is wrong with the following sentences?

13. Lawrence left the house and going to school.

14. Erica wanted to eat lunch, visit her friend, and to play soccer.

Whenever you read a sentence that contains a list of actions or objects, check to make sure that the items in the list are all in the same form. For instance, in sentence 13 there are two actions. The first action is that Lawrence left the house. So the second action must be in the same form; however, *left* and *going* aren't in the same form. The second part of the sentence should read "Lawrence went to school" to make this a parallel sentence.

In sentence 14, there are three things that Erica wanted to do: to *eat* lunch, *visit* her friend, and to *play* soccer. Are these three things in the same form? No. the first and the third things on the list use the infinitive verb forms—*to eat* and *to play*—but the second does not. To be parallel and correct, the sentence should read "Erica wanted to eat lunch, to visit her friend, and to play soccer." You could also say "Erica wanted to eat lunch, visit her friend, and play soccer." Make sure you check to see what your answer choices are.

Double Negative

What is wrong with the following sentence?

15. Paul has hardly seen no birds today.

In English, you should have only one negative word in the same phrase. When a sentence has two, it is called a double negative. All of the following are double negatives, and are always considered incorrect.

- can't hardly
- can't never
- barely none
- barely never
- won't never
- won't hardly
- hardly never
- hardly none
- hasn't got none

Capitalization and Punctuation

Always capitalize proper names, including names of the following:

- people (Jim)
- places (Alaska)
- holidays (Independence Day)
- months of the year (March)
- geographical features (Rocky Mountains)
- important words in the titles of books or movies (*All Quiet on the Western Front*)
- official titles when they are followed by a proper name (Chief Smith, Aunt Maggie)
- names of languages and peoples (French, Cuban)
- closings of letters (Sincerely, *but* Sincerely yours,)

Punctuation

Some of the questions will involve punctuation errors. Most of the punctuation problems on the HSPT involve problems with commas.

Remember to always use a comma in the following cases:

- between the name of a city and a state (Seattle, Washington)
- between the date and the year (April 19, 1999)
- between elements in a list (John, Amelia, Robert, and I)
- when addressing a person (Penelope, can you come here?)
- openings and closings of letters (Dear Bob,; Sincerely yours,)

A comma should NOT be used between a subject and its verb or between a verb and its object.

- INCORRECT: Alexandra, discovered a bone in her backyard.
- INCORRECT: David hit, the ball so hard that it broke a window.

HSPT Language Exercise

(Answers are on page 227)

1. There is already many people in the auditorium.

2. Since my father's company has so much business, they are very busy.

3. My uncle often help my parents to make dinner.

4. Henry going to school, runs into his friend.

5. The giant mouse ran through the house and escaping from the cat.

6. I met her on March 1 2010.

7. Last year, Ines won the first prize and receives a beautiful trophy.

8. Roger finished his most biggest assignment.

9. Colin cleaned the bowl and gives it to his mother.

10. Rachel read the letter to my brother and I.

SPELLING QUESTIONS

A few questions on the HSPT will ask you to identify which sentence, if any, contains a misspelled word. If none of the words is misspelled, choose (D), "No mistake." To approach these questions, read carefully through (A), (B), and (C). Pay close attention to the long or unusual words. If you find an error, pick it. If you can't find an error, pick (D).

COMPOSITION QUESTIONS

Other questions in the language section will ask you to find the sentence that is correctly written. For these questions, three of the choices will contain grammatical errors or awkward constructions.

Here's the procedure for attacking composition questions.

Step 1: Read all five sentences and eliminate any choice that breaks a rule of grammar.

Step 2: Reread the choices that are left, and cross off any choices that are awkward or don't make sense.

Step 3: Make your choice. The sentence you are left with may not sound great, but you should always pick the one that is the best of the bunch—the one that makes the most sense. If you can't get it down to only one sentence, that's okay. Cross off what you can, and guess from among the remaining choices.

SENTENCE COMPLETIONS

A few questions in the language section will ask you to complete a sentence by filling in a blank. Some of the questions in this section of the HSPT will test how well you can pick the correct word based on the "direction" of the sentence.

How would you fill in the blanks in the following sentences?

1. **I really like you _____ you are very friendly.**

2. **I really like you _____ you are a very nasty person.**

In sentence 1, you probably picked a word like "because." How did you know that this word was the right one to choose? Because the idea after the blank ("are very friendly") kept going in the *same direction* as the idea before the blank ("I really like you"). The sentence started out with a positive idea and continued with a positive idea.

In sentence 2, you probably picked something like "but," "although," or "even though." Why? Because the idea after the blank ("you are a very nasty person") went in the *opposite direction* from the idea before the blank ("I really like you"). The sentence started out with a positive idea and then changed to a negative idea.

Here are lists of same-direction and opposite-direction words.

Same-Direction
- and
- moreover
- in fact
- for instance
- for example
- so
- therefore
- because
- since

Opposite-Direction
- however
- but
- yet
- although
- though
- nevertheless
- nonetheless
- despite
- rather
- instead
- in contrast

Try the following example:

_____

3. Fill in the blank.

Susie's mother wanted her to be a dancer; _____ Susie felt like becoming a doctor.

  a. because,

  b. however,

  c. in fact,

  d. rather,

Here's How to Crack It

In this case, the idea after the blank ("becoming a doctor") goes in the opposite direction from the idea before the blank ("be a dancer"). Therefore we can eliminate (A) and (C). If you get no further, you have a great guess. The best choice is (B).

_____

STRUCTURE QUESTIONS

A few questions in this section will ask you to choose which sentences fit best with our other sentences in a paragraph. You may be asked to find the following:

- Where does the sentence belong in the paragraph?
- Which sentence does not belong in the paragraph?

To answer these questions, make sure that the ideas are in a logical order from one sentence to the next.

To answer a question that asks you where a sentence belongs in the paragraph, read the sentence and ask yourself what the sentence is about. Then read the paragraph and ask yourself, "Where in the paragraph is this same idea discussed?"

To answer a question that asks you which sentence does not belong, read the paragraph and ask yourself what the paragraph is about. Then reread it, and find the sentence that does not discuss this same idea or suddenly changes the topic.

Take a look at the following examples.

4. **Where should the sentence "At first it was rough" be placed in the paragraph?**

   1) Paper has a long and interesting history. 2) It was first made in China around 100 B.C.E. from bits of plants and tree bark. 3) This made it difficult to use for writing. 4) Soon, however, people found ways to make it flat and even. 5) Over the next few hundred years, paper was introduced to the rest of Asia, where it was used to keep government documents and religious inscriptions.

   a. After sentence 1
   b. After sentence 2
   c. After sentence 3
   d. After sentence 4

Here's How to Crack It

If we read the paragraph, we see that it discusses the history of paper, from early years to later years. The sentence "At first it was rough" belongs in the discussion of the early years of paper. Sentence 3 discusses the properties of early paper, so the new sentence should come right after sentence 2.

5. **Which of the following sentences does not belong in the paragraph?**

1) One of the most loved musical styles today is blues. 2) Blues originated in the early 1900s in America. 3) It was born from a combination of African-American work chants and gospel songs. 4) The blues got its name from the introduction of special "blue notes," which are created by "bending" normal notes up or down. 5) These blue notes give the song a certain sad sound that people recognize as part of the blues. 6) While some people like sad music, other people prefer happier songs. 7) In the 1920s, blues began to incorporate elements from jazz, dance music, and show tunes. 8) Today, blues has spread to many different countries and is one of the most popular types of music in the world.

a. Sentence 3
b. Sentence 4
c. Sentence 5
d. Sentence 6

Take a break from studying with a quick solo dance party!

Here's How to Crack It

If we read the paragraph, we see that it is about the musical style called blues. Each sentence talks about this idea except for sentence 6, which talks about whether people like happy or sad music. This makes (D) the best choice.

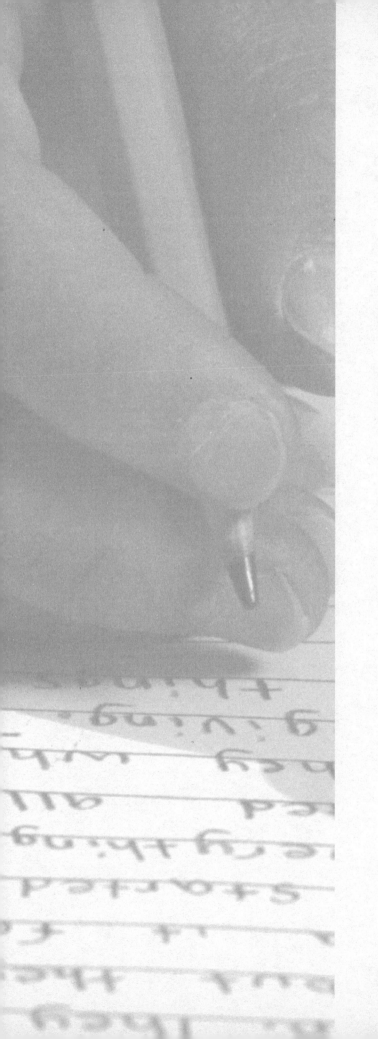

Chapter 18
Answers to
HSPT Exercises

CHAPTER 13

HSPT Analogy Exercise

A mansion is a very large house.

A leaf is part of a tree.

A desert is full of sand.

An engine allows an automobile to run.

Bread is made by a baker.

A brush is used by a painter.

HSPT Verbal Skills Exercise

1. **C**

2. **C**

3. **A**

4. **D**

5. **D**

6. **B**

7. **C**

8. **B**

9. **A**

10. **B**

11. **C**

CHAPTER 14

HSPT Math Vocabulary Exercise

1. −3, −2, −1, 0, 1, 2, 3, 4 are all integers. That makes a total of 8.

2. 0, 1, 2, 3, 4, are all positive integers. That makes a total of 5.

3. 6 + 7 + 8 = 21

4. 2 × 4 × 8 = 64

HSPT Order of Operations Exercise

1. 13

2. 9 (Do multiplication first!)

3. 5 (Do parentheses, then multiplication!)

4. 45 (Do multiplication first!)

5. 108 (Do parentheses first!)

HSPT Fractions Exercise

1. $\frac{1}{5}$ (Divide the top and bottom by 12.)

2. $\frac{3}{8} \; + \; \frac{2}{3} = \frac{9}{24} + \frac{16}{24} = \frac{25}{24}$

3. $\frac{3}{4} \; - \; \frac{2}{3} = \frac{9}{12} - \frac{8}{12} = \frac{1}{12}$

4. $\frac{3}{5} \; \times \; \frac{3}{2} = \frac{9}{10}$

5. $\frac{1}{3} \div \frac{1}{2} = \frac{1}{3} \times \frac{2}{1} = \frac{2}{3}$

HSPT Decimals Exercise

1. 7.68

2. 2.63

3. 4.5

4. 1.25

5. 5

6. $\dfrac{632}{100}$

HSPT Exponents, Scientific Notation, and Square Roots Exercise

1. $4 \times 4 \times 4 = 64$

2. $2 \times 2 \times 2 \times 2 = 16$

3. 340

4. 52,300

5. This becomes $2 + 4 = 6$.

HSPT Solve for *X* Exercise

1. $x = 5$

2. $x = 7$

3. $x = \dfrac{1}{4}$

4. $x = 3$

HSPT Percent Translation Exercise

1. $\dfrac{30}{100} \times 60 = 18$

2. $\dfrac{40}{100} \times 200 = 80$

3. $15 = \dfrac{x}{100} \times 60 = 25\%$

4. $x = \dfrac{25}{100} \times \dfrac{10}{100} \times 200 = 5$

HSPT Computation Exercise

1.   The difference of 75 and 30 is 45; $3 \times 45 = 135$.

2.   The sum of 50 and 14 is 64; $\frac{1}{8} \times 64 = 8$.

3.   Half of 30 is 15; $16 + 15 = 31$

4. $\frac{160}{100} \times 40 = 64$

5. $6^2 = 36$ and $5^2 = 25$; the difference of 36 and 25 is 11; $11 + 2 = 13$

HSPT Series Exercise

1.   4 (+ 4) 8 (+ 4) 12 (+ 4) 16 (+ 4) 20 (+ 4) 24

2.   38 (− 6) 32 (− 6) 26 (− 6) 20 (− 6) 14

3.   6 (× 2) 12 (+ 4) 16 (× 2) 32 (+ 4) 36 (× 2) 72 (+ 4) 76

4.   10 (− 5) 5 (+ 10) 15 (− 5) 10 (+ 10) 20 (− 5) 15 (+ 10) 25

5.   7 (× 2) 14 (− 2) 12 (× 2) 24 (− 2) 22 (× 2) 44 (− 2) 42

6.   8 (× 2) 16 (+ 4) 20 (× 2) 40 (+ 4) 44 (× 2) 88

7.   20 (− 2) 18 (+ 7) 25 (− 2) 23 (+ 7) 30 (− 2) 28

HSPT Comparison Exercise

1.   **C**   (1) is $2 \times 4 = 8$. (2) is $18 − 5 = 13$. (3) is $18 − 5 = 13$. Therefore, (2) and (3) are equal and greater than (1).

2.   **B**   (1) is $\frac{40}{100} \times 60 = 24$. (2) is $\frac{60}{100} \times 40 = 24$. (3) is $\frac{50}{100} \times 90 = 45$. So (1) is equal to (2) and less than (3).

3.   **C**   (1) is 230. (2) is 2,300. (3) is 2,300. So (2) and (3) are equal and greater than (1).

4.   **A**   The area of a square is one side squared, so (1) is $6 \times 6 = 36$. The perimeter of a square is the sum of all sides, which are equal, so (2) is $6 + 6 + 6 + 6 = 24$. (3) is $\frac{1}{2} \times 8 \times 8$ (one-half times one side squared) = 32. Therefore, (1) is greater than (2), which is less than (3).

5.   **B**   Since angle a measures 40° and the triangle is isosceles, we know that angle c is also 40°, and therefore angle b must be 100°. So angle a is less than angles $b + c$.

CHAPTER 15

HSPT Reading Comprehension Exercise

1. **C**   If you summarized the passage well, you probably wrote something like "People have had indoor lighting way before Thomas Edison invented the electric light." Choice (A) is too precise, since the Egyptians are discussed in only one paragraph. Choices (B) and (D) are just details that are discussed in only one or two lines.

2. **D**   In the final paragraph, the author says that "oil lamps brought with them other problems." Therefore the Romans began to use candles. Choices (B) and (C) are not stated in the paragraph, so they can be eliminated. Choice (A) is extreme because of the term *most important*.

3. **B**   If we reread the line that mentions the word *rudimentary*, it states, "Rudimentary oil lamps, a primitive ancestor of the gaslight..." Therefore, the word *rudimentary* must be something like *primitive*. This will eliminate (A), (C), and (D).

4. **D**   If we skim the passage looking for Edison, we can find him mentioned in the first paragraph. It states that "practical indoor lighting existed thousands of years before Thomas Edison invented the light bulb." Does this sentence explain his discoveries or mention other inventors? No, so we can eliminate (A) and (B). Does the author later discuss Edison? No, so (C) can also be eliminated.

5. **A**   The passage says that "the lamp gave off a terrible odor," and "foul-smelling" is used to describe the odor of the lamp.

6. **C**   There is no evidence in the passage to support (A), (B), or (D). The passage does say that the "animal fat smells awful when burned," so (C) is the best answer.

7. **C**   Nothing in the passage sounds angry, so we can eliminate (A). Choice (B) probably isn't right since someone who was unconcerned wouldn't have written the passage. If that's as far as you got, take a guess between (C) and (D). Critical means that the author disagrees with something, but there's nothing in the passage that shows disagreement, which rules out (D). Choice (C) is the best answer.

CHAPTER 16

HSPT Geometry Exercise

1. Since these angles must add up to 180°, $x = 85°$.

2. x and z must be 120° each, and y must be 60°, so $y + z = 180°$.

3. The angles in a triangle must add up to 180°. Since we already have angles 90° and 30°, the remaining angle must be 60°.

4. Since this triangle is isosceles, the two bottom angles measure 40° each. To make a total of 180°, $x = 100°$.

5. The area of this square is 6×6, or 36.

6. The area of a triangle is $\frac{1}{2}$ base × height, or $\frac{1}{2} \times 8 \times 6 = 24$.

7a. The area of this circle is $3^2\pi$, or 9π.

7b. The circumference of this circle is $2(3)\pi$, or 6π.

8a. Since this figure is a rectangle, $x = 10$ and $y = 5$.

8b. The perimeter is $10 + 5 + 10 + 5 = 30$.

CHAPTER 17

HSPT Language Exercise

1. Since "many people" is plural, it needs the plural verb form *are*: "There **are** already many people in the auditorium."

2. Since "my father's company" is singular, the pronoun and verb should be singular *it is* instead of the plural *they are*: "Since my father's company has so much business, it is very busy."

3. "My uncle" is singular, so it needs the singular verb form *helps*: "My uncle often **helps** my parents to make dinner."

4. This is a sentence fragment. A complete sentence would read: "On his way to school, Henry ran into his friend."

5.	The first verb, "ran," is in the past tense; to maintain parallel form, the second verb, "escaping," should also be in the past tense: "The giant mouse ran through the house and **escaped** from the cat."

6.	There should be a comma after the date and before the year: "I met her on March 1, 2010."

7.	The first verb, "won" is in the past tense, and the second verb, "receives," is in the present tense. You know the sentence should be in the past tense because of the clue words "last year." To maintain parallel form, the verbs should both be in the same tense: "Last year, Ines won the first prize and **received** a beautiful trophy."

8.	"Most biggest" is not a valid comparative form. The sentence should simply read "Roger finished his **biggest** assignment."

9.	The first verb, "cleaned," is in the past tense, but the second verb, "gives," is in the present tense. To maintain parallel form, these verbs should both be in the same tense: "Colin cleaned the bowl and **gave** it to his mother."

10.	Since "my brother and I" are the people being read to, not doing the reading, the pronoun should be objective: "Rachel read the letter to my brother and **me**."

Part IV
HSPT
Practice Tests

Chapter 19
HSPT
Practice Test 1

Verbal Skills

Questions 1-60, 15 Minutes

1. **Conquer most nearly means**
   a. defeat
   b. fear
   c. dislike
   d. calm

2. **Company is to president as army is to**
   a. battle
   b. general
   c. soldier
   d. weapon

3. **Fortify means the *opposite* of**
   a. load
   b. weaken
   c. sail
   d. clean

4. **Which word does *not* belong with the others?**
   a. sad
   b. lonely
   c. feeling
   d. upset

5. **Compelling most nearly means**
   a. serious
   b. interesting
   c. insulting
   d. funny

6. **Gigantic is to large as hilarious is to**
   a. serious
   b. interesting
   c. insulting
   d. funny

7. **Opaque means the *opposite* of**
   a. dirty
   b. clear
   c. normal
   d. late

8. **Which word does *not* belong with the others?**
   a. oregano
   b. parsley
   c. spice
   d. pepper

9. **Fragile most nearly means**
   a. important
   b. dangerous
   c. clean
   d. delicate

10. **John has more marbles than Alice. Alice has fewer marbles than Kenny. John has more marbles than Kenny. If the first two statements are true, the third is**
    a. True
    b. False
    c. Uncertain

11. **Generate most nearly means**

    a. imagine
    b. create
    c. project
    d. lose

12. **Juanita finished the race before Lucy. Mary finished the race after Lucy. Mary finished the race before Juanita. If the first two statements are true, the third is**

    a. True
    b. False
    c. Uncertain

13. **Labor most nearly means**

    a. give
    b. animal
    c. work
    d. science

14. **Which word does *not* belong with the others?**

    a. touch
    b. sight
    c. sense
    d. hearing

15. **Abundant means the *opposite* of**

    a. meager
    b. honest
    c. foolish
    d. tame

16. **Morose most nearly means**

    a. content
    b. new
    c. flexible
    d. sad

17. **Which word does *not* belong with the others?**

    a. feather
    b. bird
    c. beak
    d. wing

18. **Robert read his paper before Weston. Abigail read her paper after Tyrone. Robert read his paper before Tyrone. If the first two statements are true, the third is**

    a. True
    b. False
    c. Uncertain

19. **Portrait most nearly means**

    a. history
    b. picture
    c. investigation
    d. device

20. **Cage is to bird as jail is to**

    a. cell
    b. crime
    c. prisoner
    d. warden

21. **Strive most nearly means**

    a. follow
    b. dive
    c. try hard
    d. divide

22. Which word does *not* belong with the others?

a. water
b. ocean
c. lake
d. river

23. Sentence is to paragraph as verse is to

a. rhyme
b. line
c. novel
d. poem

24. Valid most nearly means

a. possible
b. forgotten
c. old-fashioned
d. true

25. Ruthless means the *opposite* of

a. protective
b. merciful
c. small
d. healthy

26. Quest most nearly means

a. search
b. discovery
c. plan
d. talent

27. Which word does *not* belong with the others?

a. yard
b. length
c. mile
d. foot

28. Colleague most nearly means

a. cook
b. coworker
c. criminal
d. teacher

29. Chaos means the *opposite* of

a. act
b. motion
c. order
d. gravity

30. Which word does *not* belong with the others?

a. sandal
b. slipper
c. shoe
d. glove

31. Vacant most nearly means

a. future
b. open
c. empty
d. circular

32. Bread is to grain as jam is to

a. bread
b. fruit
c. knife
d. jar

33. Hat is to cap as shoe is to

a. sneaker
b. foot
c. lace
d. race

34. Prevalent means the *opposite* of

a. common

b. thick

c. subtle

d. rare

35. Which word does *not* belong with the others?

a. tool

b. hammer

c. knife

d. screwdriver

36. Contort most nearly means

a. polish

b. touch

c. sprint

d. twist

37. Which word does *not* belong with the others?

a. pear

b. apple

c. fruit

d. orange

38. Reprimand means the *opposite* of

a. praise

b. steal

c. give

d. forbid

39. Agnes can count faster than Louis and Jeremy. Lisa can count faster than Agnes. Jeremy can count faster than Lisa. If the first two statements are true, the third is

a. True

b. False

c. Uncertain

40. Tree is to trunk as flower is to

a. bee

b. stem

c. leaf

d. pollen

41. Which word does *not* belong with the others?

a. dog

b. mammal

c. cat

d. rabbit

42. Culpable most nearly means

a. guilty

b. careful

c. honest

d. skilled

43. Which word does *not* belong with the others?

a. peanut

b. cashew

c. shell

d. walnut

44. **Mile is to distance as pound is to**

a. weight
b. ounce
c. food
d. kilogram

45. **Ray, Eric, and Steve have the same number of baseball cards. Carl has fewer baseball cards than Eric. Steve has fewer baseball cards than Carl. If the first two statements are true, the third is**

a. True
b. False
c. Uncertain

46. **Erratic means the *opposite* of**

a. abrupt
b. stable
c. jealous
d. upset

47. **Conspicuous most nearly means**

a. optional
b. new
c. obvious
d. expected

48. **Mayville has more inhabitants than Suntown, but fewer than Lanville. Pinton has fewer inhabitants than Suntown. Lanville has more inhabitants than Pinton. If the first two statements are true, the third is**

a. True
b. False
c. Uncertain

49. **Esteem means the *opposite* of**

a. respect
b. dislike
c. debate
d. certainty

50. **Which word does *not* belong with the others?**

a. speak
b. yell
c. sound
d. whisper

51. **Indifferent means the *opposite* of**

a. concerned
b. soft
c. casual
d. clever

52. **Which word does *not* belong with the others?**

a. flute
b. violin
c. orchestra
d. cello

53. Ollie is older than Quinn and Joseph. Sally is older than Steven and Joseph. Ollie is younger than Sally. If the first two statements are true, the third is

a. True
b. False
c. Uncertain

54. Cook is to kitchen as doctor is to

a. patient
b. hospital
c. medicine
d. needle

55. Which word does *not* belong with the others?

a. theater
b. stadium
c. arena
d. crowd

56. Howard can sing more songs than Bill but fewer than Enid. Adam can sing more songs than Becky and Enid. Adam can sing fewer songs than Howard. If the first two statements are true, the third is

a. True
b. False
c. Uncertain

57. Which word does *not* belong with the others?

a. book
b. cover
c. page
d. spine

58. Penelope has more cats than Uma but fewer than Michael. Michael has fewer cats than Petra. Penelope has more cats than Petra. If the first two statements are true, the third is

a. True
b. False
c. Uncertain

59. Tree is to forest as star is to

a. sun
b. sky
c. planet
d. constellation

60. Intentional means the *opposite* of

a. distracted
b. unhappy
c. accidental
d. hungry

Quantitative Skills

Questions 1-52, 30 Minutes

1. **What number should come next in this series: 4, 12, 20, 28, ____?**

   a. 32
   b. 34
   c. 36
   d. 38

2. **Examine the rectangle below and find the best answer.**

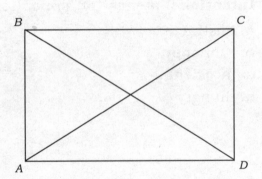

   a. *AC* is bigger than *BD* and bigger than *AB*
   b. *AC* is equal to *BD* and bigger than *AB*
   c. *BC* is bigger than AB and bigger than *BD*
   d. *AB* is equal to *CD* and equal to *BD*

3. **What number divided by 2 is $\frac{2}{3}$ of 39?**

   a. 13
   b. 26
   c. 39
   d. 52

4. **Examine the following to find the best answer.**

   1. $\frac{1}{4}$ of 84
   2. $\frac{1}{2}$ of 48
   3. $\frac{1}{2}$ of 42

   a. 1 > 2 > 3
   b. 1 = 2 = 3
   c. 2 > 1 = 3
   d. 2 > 1 > 3

5. **What number should come next in this series: 3, 6, 12, 24, ____?**

   a. 27
   b. 30
   c. 36
   d. 48

6. **Examine (A), (B), and (C) to find the best answer.**

(A)   (B)   (C)

   a. (A) has as many squares as (B) and fewer than (C)

   b. (A) has more squares than (B) and fewer than (C)

   c. (B) and (C) each have more squares than (A)

   d. (A), (B), and (C) each have the same number of squares

7. **What number should come next in this series: 4, 8, 12, 16, ____?**

   a. 18
   b. 20
   c. 22
   d. 24

8. **Examine the following to find the best answer.**

1. 20% of 60
2. 60% of 20
3. 200% of 6

   a. 1 is greater than 2 or 3
   b. 1, 2, and 3 are equal
   c. 1 is equal to 2 and greater than 3
   d. 2 is less than 1 and 3

9. **20% of what number is 5 times 3?**

   a. 15
   b. 25
   c. 50
   d. 75

10. **What number should come next in this series: 5, 8, 12, 15, 19, ____?**

   a. 21
   b. 22
   c. 23
   d. 24

11. **Examine the following to find the best answer.**

1. 3^2
2. 4^2
3. 5^1

   a. 1 > 2 > 3
   b. 1 = 2 = 3
   c. 2 > 1 = 3
   d. 2 > 1 > 3

12. **What number should come next in this series: 8, 5, 9, 6, 10, ____?**

   a. 7
   b. 8
   c. 9
   d. 14

13. **$\frac{2}{3}$ of what number is $\frac{1}{2}$ of 24?**

   a. 36
   b. 18
   c. 12
   d. 6

14. **What number should come next in this series: 4, 7, 9, 12, 14, 17, ___?**

   a. 18
   b. 19
   c. 20
   d. 21

15. **What number is $\frac{3}{4}$ of the product of 3, 4, and 5?**

   a. 45
   b. 60
   c. 75
   d. 240

16. **Examine the following to find the best answer.**

   1. $\frac{5}{10}$

   2. $\frac{70}{100}$

   3. $\frac{8}{100}$

   a. 1 > 2 > 3
   b. 1 = 2 = 3
   c. 2 > 1 = 3
   d. 2 > 1 > 3

17. **What number is 200% of the difference between 12 and 3?**

   a. 3
   b. 9
   c. 12
   d. 18

18. **Examine the following to find the best answer.**

   1. $3(5 \times 9)$
   2. $(3 \times 5) \times 9$
   3. $3 \times 5 \times 9$

   a. 1 is greater than 2 and 3
   b. 1 is equal to 2 and less than 3
   c. 2 and 3 are equal and greater than 1
   d. 1, 2, and 3 are equal

19. **What number should fill the blank in this series: 12, 18, 22, 28, ___, 38?**

   a. 28
   b. 30
   c. 32
   d. 34

20. **$\frac{5}{100}$ of the product of 5 and 4 is**

   a. 1
   b. $\frac{1}{4}$
   c. 4
   d. 5

21. Below is a circle with center *O*. Find the best answer.

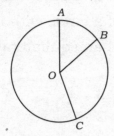

a. *OA > OB > OC*
b. *OA = OB > OC*
c. *OA = OB < OC*
d. *OA = OB = OC*

22. What number divided by 4 is 15% of 90?

a. 42
b. 48
c. 52
d. 54

23. What number should fill the blank in this series: 4, 8, 10, 20, 22, ____, 46?

a. 44
b. 42
c. 36
d. 32

24. Examine the following to find the best answer.

1. the smallest prime number bigger than 4
2. the square root of 25
3. 75% of 8

a. 1 is greater than 2 and 3
b. 1 is equal to 2 and less than 3
c. 2 and 3 are equal and greater than 1
d. 1, 2, and 3 are equal

25. The sum of 20 and what number is equal to the product of 6 and 8?

a. 22
b. 24
c. 28
d. 32

26. What number should fill the blank in this series:

$2, \frac{1}{2}, 3, \frac{1}{3}$____$, \frac{1}{4}$?

a. $\frac{1}{5}$

b. 3

c. 4

d. 5

27. Below is a square and a equilateral triangle. Find the best answer.

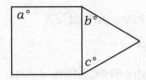

a. *a* is greater than *b* + *c*
b. *a* is less than *b* + *c*
c. *a* is equal to *b* + *c*
d. *a*, *b*, and *c* are all equal

28. What number should come next in this series: 30, 28, 25, 21, ____?

a. 18
b. 17
c. 16
d. 15

29. What number is 140% of 40?

a. 16
b. 32
c. 56
d. 64

30. What number should come next in this series: 2, 4, 3, 5, 4, 6, 5, ____?

a. 6
b. 7
c. 8
d. 9

31. Examine the following to find the best answer.

1. the area of a square with side 3
2. the area of a circle with radius 3
3. the area of an equilateral triangle with side 3

a. 1 > 2 > 3
b. 1 = 3 < 2
c. 3 < 1 < 2
d. 3 < 1 = 2

32. What number is 2 more than the difference of 3^3 and 3^4?

a. 3
b. 5
c. 29
d. 56

33. Examine the figure below and find the best answer.

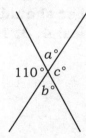

a. *a* + *c* = *b* + *c* = *a* + *b*
b. *a* + *c* = *b* + *c* > *a* + *b*
c. *a* + *b* > *a* + *c* > *b* + *c*
d. *a* + *b* > *a* + *c* = *b* + *c*

34. What number should come next in this series: 11, 22, 44, 88, ___?

   a. 122
   b. 124
   c. 144
   d. 176

35. What number should fill the blank in this series: 15, 30, 35, 50, 55, ___, 75?

   a. 70
   b. 65
   c. 60
   d. 55

36. 75% of 20% of 200 is

   a. 30
   b. 40
   c. 45
   d. 50

37. Examine (A), (B), and (C) to find the best answer.

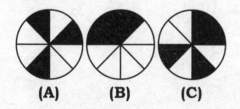

(A)   (B)   (C)

   a. (A) is more shaded than (B)
   b. (A) is less shaded than (B) and more shaded than (C)
   c. (C) is more shaded than both (A) and (B)
   d. (A), (B), and (C) are equally shaded

38. $\frac{3}{5}$ of the average of 20, 25, and 45 is

   a. 14
   b. 18
   c. 22
   d. 24

39. What number should fill the blank in this series: 20, 30, 45, 65, ___, 120?

   a. 70
   b. 80
   c. 90
   d. 110

40. Examine the following to find the best answer.

1. 6.5×10^{-3}
2. 0.0065
3. 650×10^{-4}

   a. 1 is greater than 2 and 3
   b. 1 is equal to 2 and less than 3
   c. 2 and 3 are equal and greater than 1
   d. 1, 2, and 3 are equal

41. **What number should come next in this series: 1, 1, 2, 4, 3, 9, 4, ____?**

    a. 12
    b. 14
    c. 16
    d. 18

42. **Examine the following to find the best answer if $x = 2$.**

    1. $2x^2$
    2. $(2x)^2$
    3. $2^2 \times x^2$

    a. 1 is greater than 2 and 3
    b. 1 is equal to 3 and less than 2
    c. 2 and 3 are equal and greater than 1
    d. 1, 2, and 3 are equal

43. **What is 40% of 20% of 600?**

    a. 24
    b. 48
    c. 60
    d. 120

44. **What number leaves a remainder of 3 when divided by 4?**

    a. 25
    b. 31
    c. 33
    d. 37

45. **What number should come next in this series: 15, 20, 18, 23, 21, 26, 24, ____?**

    a. 22
    b. 26
    c. 28
    d. 29

46. **Examine the following to find the best answer.**

    1. the area of a square with side 2
    2. the area of a square with side 3
    3. the area of half of a square with side 4

    a. 2 > 1 > 3
    b. 3 > 1 > 2
    c. 3 > 2 > 1
    d. 2 > 3 > 1

47. **What number is 5 greater than the product of 15 and $\frac{1}{3}$?**

    a. 5
    b. 10
    c. 15
    d. 20

48. What number should fill the blank in this series: 56, 51, 48, 43, 40, ____, 32?

   a. 37
   b. 36
   c. 35
   d. 34

49. Examine the following to find the best answer.

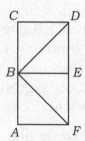

1. the perimeter of square *BCDE*
2. the perimeter of triangle *BDF*
3. the perimeter of rectangle *ACDF*

   a. 2 > 1 > 3
   b. 3 > 1 > 2
   c. 3 > 2 > 1
   d. 2 > 3 > 1

50. What number is $\frac{1}{6}$ of the average of 18, 24, 25, and 29?

   a. 4
   b. 5
   c. 6
   d. 7

51. What number should come next in this series: 110, 55, 50, 25, 20, ____?

   a. 15
   b. 10
   c. 5
   d. 0

52. What number is 16 more than 6^2?

   a. 22
   b. 36
   c. 48
   d. 52

Reading
Questions 1-62, 25 Minutes

Questions 1–8 refer to the following passage.

Passage 1 - Westward Journey

I do not remember crossing the Missouri River, or anything about the long day's journey through Nebraska. Probably by that time I had crossed so many rivers that I was dull to them. The only thing very noticeable about Nebraska was that it was still, all day long.

I had been sleeping, curled up in a red plush seat, for a long while when we reached Black Hawk. Jake <u>roused</u> me and took me by the hand. We stumbled down from the train to a wooden siding, where men were running about with lanterns. I couldn't see any town, or even distant lights; we were surrounded by utter darkness. The engine was panting heavily after its long run. In the red glow from the firebox, a group of people stood huddled together on the platform, encumbered by bundles and boxes.

I knew this must be the immigrant family the conductor had told us about. The woman wore a fringed shawl tied over her head, and she carried a little tin trunk in her arms, hugging it as if it were a baby. There was an old man, tall and stooped. Two half-grown boys and a girl stood holding oilcloth bundles, and a little girl clung to her mother's skirts. Presently a man with a lantern approached them and began to talk, shouting and exclaiming. I pricked up my ears, for it was positively the first time I had ever heard a foreign <u>tongue</u>.

1. **When the story begins, the narrator is on a**
    a. plane
    b. ship
    c. rooftop
    d. train

2. **The narrator finds the rivers in Nebraska "dull" probably because**
    a. the narrator has never liked rivers
    b. the narrator has seen too many rivers
    c. the rivers in Missouri were much more interesting
    d. they were all too small to be interesting

3. **The word <u>roused</u>, as used in the passage, most nearly means**

   a. woke
   b. saw
   c. ran
   d. told

4. **The narrator finds Nebraska remarkable for its**

   a. cows
   b. interesting scenery
   c. silence
   d. fields of corn

5. **The word <u>tongue</u>, as used in the passage, most nearly means**

   a. song
   b. mouth
   c. language
   d. handle

6. **The people described in the second paragraph are carrying "bundles and boxes" probably because they**

   a. are farmers taking their goods to market
   b. are coming back from a shopping trip
   c. have recently arrived in this country from elsewhere
   d. are paid to move other people's things

7. **The narrator "stumbled down from the train" probably because the narrator**

   a. was still sleepy
   b. was not wearing shoes
   c. wore a cast on one leg
   d. was very hungry

8. **Which of the following is true of the family described in the final paragraph?**

   a. The family has four children—three boys and a girl.
   b. The family has four children—two boys and two girls.
   c. The family has three children—two boys and a girl.
   d. The family has three children—all boys.

Questions 9–16 refer to the following passage.

Passage 2 - The Evolution of Electricity

Though electricity has only recently been used to drive machines, people have known about electricity for thousands of years. The ancient Greeks discovered that they could make objects cling together by rubbing cloth against amber. This, we now know, is due to static electricity.

Benjamin Franklin was one of the earliest people to investigate this curious phenomenon. His curiousity in electricity was sparked when he began to play with an electricity tube that was given to him by his friend Peter Collinson.

Franklin is widely regarded as the first person to realize that lightning was made of electrically charged air. As a way of testing his theory, he attempted to discover whether lightning would pass through a metal object. To show this, he used a kite to raise a key into the air on a stormy night. From this experiment, Franklin realized that this electricity could be guided to the ground by a metal wire or rod, thereby protecting houses, people, and ships from being hurt.

Many other people in the late 1700s to mid-1800s worked to discover more of the laws and uses of electricity. In 1779 Allesandro Volta, an Italian inventor, created the first battery. For the first time, a controlled and regular stream of electricity could be used. For his discovery, the volt was named after him.

Perhaps the most <u>significant</u> development was made by Michael Faraday. He discovered that when you move a magnet back and forth inside a wire coil, you will generate electricity inside the wire. With this knowledge he was able to build the first electric generator and the first electric motor (which is essentially an electric generator in reverse). Even today, the generators that we use to make electricity in our hydroelectric dams are almost identical to the one he created well over a century ago.

Later, Thomas Edison and Nikola Tesla improved the generator and created transformers, which change the voltage of an electrical current to adapt it to a particular purpose. While Edison <u>advocated</u> direct current (DC), Tesla argued for alternating current (AC), which we use today in our homes.

Without the hard work and intelligence of these people, we never would have developed the use of electricity. Almost our whole modern world—computers, radios, even lights—depends on their discoveries.

9. **One of Franklin's discoveries was**

    a. how to protect houses from lightning
    b. the battery
    c. the electric generator
    d. a hydroelectric dam

10. **This passage is mostly about**

    a. what lightning really is
    b. how a battery works
    c. the early scientists who investigated electricity
    d. how much the Greeks knew about electricity

11. **With which of the following would the author probably agree?**

    a. The electric generator was the most important discovery of all time.
    b. Modern electric motors are very different from Faraday's generator.
    c. The discovery of electricity was very important to the development of the modern world.
    d. Benjamin Franklin was a better writer than a scientist.

12. **According to the passage, which of the following is true?**

    a. Thomas Edison was a good friend of Benjamin Franklin's.
    b. The word volt is named after Michael Faraday.
    c. Benjamin Franklin was the first person to know about the existence of electricity.
    d. Faraday built the first electric generator.

13. **The word significant, as used in the passage, most nearly means**

    a. readable
    b. important
    c. well-known
    d. accidental

14. **According to the passage, Edison and Tesla disagreed about**

    a. whether hydroelectric dams should be built
    b. whether to use direct or alternating current
    c. how a transformer should be designed
    d. how to create electricity

15. **According to the passage, what device can change the voltage of an electric current?**

    a. a generator
    b. a transformer
    c. an electric motor
    d. a battery

16. **The word <u>advocated</u>, as used in the passage, most nearly means**

    a. disagreed
    b. promoted
    c. imagined
    d. threw away

Questions 17–24 refer to the following passage.

Passage 3 - The Flight of Amelia Earhart

After Charles Lindbergh made history with his flight across the Atlantic Ocean, New York publisher George Putnam wanted to have a woman make the same flight. He found Amelia Earhart.

At first, Putnam didn't trust her to fly the plane. Earhart made the transatlantic flight as a passenger with two male <u>colleagues</u> at the controls. However, Amelia decided that she wanted to be the pilot. She began to improve her flight skills, breaking record after record in speed and number of miles flown by a woman.

Finally in 1932, she decided that she wanted to make a solo transatlantic flight. She wanted to do it not only for herself, but to show that <u>aviation</u> was not exclusive to men. When she touched down in Ireland, she became an instant hero. She was showered with awards and attention from the international press.

Amelia began flying greater and greater distances. She flew across America, and then across the Pacific Ocean. Finally, she decided that she wanted to fly around the world at its widest point: the equator. This would be a journey longer than anyone had ever made.

On May 20, 1937, she took off from Oakland, California, with her navigator, Fred Noonan, in an attempt to fly around the globe. At that time, airplanes could not go very far on a tank of fuel. Moreover, her small Lockheed Electra 10E could not carry enough fuel to fly more than 6,000 miles. Therefore she had to make several small flights, stopping every few thousand miles in order to refuel.

After flying more than half the distance around the world, Amelia's plane was lost. Ten ships searched for more than two weeks, but no trace of the plane could be found. To this day, nobody is sure what became of Amelia Earhart.

17. According to the passage, who was the first person to make a transatlantic flight?

a. Fred Noonan

b. Charles Lindbergh

c. George Putnam

d. Amelia Earhart

18. The word <u>colleagues</u>, as used in the passage, most nearly means

a. coworkers

b. brothers

c. students

d. mechanics

19. What would be the best title for this passage?

a. "How to Make a Transatlantic Flight"

b. "The Amazing Story of Amelia Earhart"

c. "Modern American Airplanes"

d. "The Life of George Putnam"

20. The word <u>aviation</u>, as used in the passage, most nearly means

a. birdwatching

b. the flying of airplanes

c. airplane repair

d. going on vacation

21. You would probably find this article in

a. an encyclopedia

b. a science textbook

c. a book on European history

d. a book on the Lockheed Electra 10E

22. Which of the following can be inferrred from the passage?

a. The Lockheed Electra 10E was the best airplane available in 1937.

b. Charles Lindbergh taught Earhart how to fly.

c. Amelia was never afraid of flying.

d. The equator represents the largest path around the earth.

23. With which of the following would the author probably agree?

    a. The U.S. government should have looked harder for Earhart's plane.

    b. Nobody is certain what happened to Earhart's plane.

    c. Earhart could have flown around the world without stopping.

    d. Earhart's plane must have run out of fuel and crashed into the Pacific Ocean.

24. Fred Noonan was Earhart's

    a. teacher

    b. sponsor

    c. navigator

    d. mechanic

Questions 25–32 refer to the following passage.

Passage 4 - Louis Pasteur vs The Germs

Louis Pasteur, born in 1822, is perhaps best known for having discovered the role of germs in disease. Before Pasteur, nobody was certain what caused most illnesses. Nobody thought that small creatures, invisible to the naked eye, could be the cause of so many dangerous diseases.

Pasteur, however, after spending many hours looking through a microscope, discovered that germs could reproduce very rapidly and be very dangerous to humans. This led him to conclude that doctors—who, up until that time, did not always wash their hands or their instruments—were spreading disease and that they needed to <u>sterilize</u> their equipment and scrub their hands. People began for the first time to use antiseptics, and this helped to greatly reduce the number of infections in hospitals.

Pasteur also discovered that heat could kill bacteria. He discovered this one day while experimenting with chickens. He realized that a certain bacteria, called anthrax, could live in sheep but could not live in chickens. The reason for this, he discovered, was that chickens had a body temperature of 44 degrees Celsius, or more than 100 degrees Fahrenheit. Today, we heat our dairy products to kill the germs, a process that we call pasteurization.

Finally, and most important, Pasteur discovered the principle of vaccination. Pasteur realized that animals could make defenses against diseases such as anthrax. The problem was to find a way to help their bodies make these defenses without making them sick. He realized that he could kill the anthrax germs by injecting them into chickens and then take those dead germs and inject them into sheep. Since the germ was dead, it would not make the sheep sick; but it still allowed the animal to make <u>antibodies</u> to protect it if it ever came into contact with live anthrax.

Today, people all over the world get vaccines and are free from dangerous diseases such as polio, thanks to Louis Pasteur.

25. This passage is mostly about

    a. Louis Pasteur's childhood

    b. the important discoveries of Louis Pasteur

    c. how to make a vaccine

    d. why it is important to wash your hands

26. It can be inferred from the passage that an antiseptic is

    a. something that kills germs

    b. a machine used to heat milk

    c. a kind of bacteria

    d. a kind of microscope

27. Pasteur's advice for doctors was that they should

    a. read more books

    b. wash their hands and equipment

    c. begin to use anesthetics

    d. be nicer to their patients

28. It can be inferred from the passage that sheep

    a. have a body temperature of less than 44 degrees Celsius

    b. are not as smart as chickens

    c. could pass diseases on to other kinds of animals

    d. often became ill with polio

29. The word <u>sterilize</u>, as used in the passage, most nearly means

    a. rebuild

    b. sell

    c. check for safety

    d. kill the germs

30. **According to the facts in the passage, which of these might be pasteurized?**

   a. beef
   b. cheese
   c. broccoli
   d. apples

31. **With which of the following would the author probably agree?**

   a. 44 degrees Celsius is hot enough to kill any germ.
   b. Receiving a vaccine is usually very painful.
   c. Polio was the most dangerous disease of all time.
   d. Pasteur made many important contributions to good health.

32. **The word <u>antibodies</u>, as used in the passage, most nearly means**

   a. holes
   b. defenses
   c. wool
   d. shepherds

Questions 33–40 refer to the following passage.

Passage 5 - A Chocolate-Covered History

The cocoa plant, from which chocolate is made, is native to Central and South America. Many of the native cultures—most notably the Aztecs, but even the ancient Mayans—cultivated and ate the fruit of the cocoa plant. In certain cultures, cocoa beans were even used as a form of money. The Aztecs made cocoa beans into a hot drink with no sugar at all. In fact, the Aztecs used chili peppers to make it spicy. It was bitter and strong, and they called it xocoatl.

When Spanish explorers arrived in South America, they discovered the cocoa bean and brought it back to Europe in huge quantities. This was how chocolate was introduced to Europeans. At the beginning, the Europeans drank it in the Aztec <u>fashion</u>—hot, spicy, and unsweetened.

It wasn't until the seventeenth century that Europeans began to add sugar instead of chili peppers to their cocoa, and chocolate became a sweet drink. At first, when cocoa was rare, chocolate was considered a delicacy; as trade with the Americas became more regular, chocolate became accessible to almost everyone.

The last step in the evolution of chocolate was its <u>transformation</u> from a drink to a solid bar. In the 1820s, a process was developed to press out some of the fat (the "butter") in the cocoa bean. The resulting powder could be mixed with sugar, recombined with the cocoa butter, and formed into solid bars. By the 1850s, what we know today as chocolate was finally available.

33. This story is mostly about

a. the evolution of chocolate

b. the importance of cocoa beans to the Aztecs

c. how to make xocoatl

d. when chocolate arrived in Europe

34. The word <u>fashion</u>, as used in the passage, most nearly means

a. clothes

b. way

c. house

d. cup

35. The people who brought chocolate to Europe were the

a. Mayans

b. Aztec

c. Spanish

d. Dutch

36. It can be inferred from the passage that

a. cocoa plants have never been grown in Europe

b. the Aztecs did not have sugar

c. Europeans began to add sugar to their chocolate in the fifteenth century

d. one ingredient in solid chocolate is cocoa butter

37. The author says that when it first arrived in Europe, chocolate was a "delicacy" because it was

a. very sweet

b. rare

c. difficult to make

d. inexpensive

38. According to the passage, which of the following is true?

a. Cocoa beans have been used as a form of money.

b. The Aztecs put sugar in their chocolate drink.

c. The first Europeans to discover the cocoa bean were the Germans.

d. The cocoa plant was originally grown in Asia.

39. Which of the following can be inferred from the passage?

   a. Most Europeans didn't like chocolate until it was sweetened with sugar.

   b. Chocolate was the most important discovery of European explorers in the Americas.

   c. When chocolate first arrived in Europe, it was not available to everyone.

   d. The Aztecs were the first people to drink chocolate.

40. The word <u>transformation</u>, as used in the passage, most nearly means

   a. discussion

   b. melting

   c. change

   d. cooking

Vocabulary

41. Choose the best definition of the underlined word.

a **malleable** substance

a. slimy
b. soft
c. interesting
d. bumpy

42. Choose the best definition of the underlined word.

an **impartial** jury

a. fair
b. whole
c. new
d. thankful

43. Choose the best definition of the underlined word.

a **meritorious** act

a. quick
b. silent
c. unknown
d. noble

44. Choose the best definition of the underlined word.

to **abdicate** the throne

a. seize
b. give up
c. envy
d. control

45. Choose the best definition of the underlined word.

a large **receptacle**

a. picture
b. table
c. container
d. tool

46. Choose the best definition of the underlined word.

an **inquisitive** mind

a. curious
b. normal
c. distracted
d. entertained

47. Choose the best definition of the underlined word.

a **cynical** attitude

a. silly
b. remarkable
c. distrustful
d. loyal

48. Choose the best definition of the underlined word.

the **dominant** part

a. youngest
b. largest
c. intelligent
d. hopeful

49. Choose the best definition of the underlined word.

a **tactful** remark

a. probable
b. crude
c. steady
d. polite

50. Choose the best definition of the underlined word.

a **thorough** investigation

a. complete
b. late
c. official
d. thoughtless

51. Choose the best definition of the underlined word.

an unintended **consequence**

a. interruption
b. result
c. discovery
d. section

52. Choose the best definition of the underlined word.

a **mediocre** performance

a. excellent
b. public
c. lengthy
d. average

53. Choose the best definition of the underlined word.

an **elaborate** project

a. original
b. complex
c. expensive
d. ordinary

54. Choose the best definition of the underlined word.

a recently discovered **paradox**

a. treasure
b. puzzle
c. witness
d. map

55. Choose the best definition of the underlined word.

the **pinnacle** of his career

a. peak
b. end
c. study
d. talent

56. Choose the best definition of the underlined word.

to **guarantee** a victory

a. dream
b. avoid
c. desire
d. promise

57. Choose the best definition of the underlined word.

a **grave** situation

a. serious
b. honorable
c. poor
d. customary

58. Choose the best definition of the underlined word.

to **imply** something else

a. add
b. reply
c. suggest
d. see

59. Choose the best definition of the underlined word.

a **sedate** individual

a. famous
b. calm
c. picky
d. dry

60. Choose the best definition of the underlined word.

to require great **exertion**

a. audience
b. preparation
c. effort
d. money

61. Choose the best definition of the underlined word.

a **mobile** home

a. popular
b. small
c. movable
d. country

62. Choose the best definition of the underlined word.

an **equitable** settlement

a. closed
b. fair
c. proud
d. lost

Mathematics

Questions 1-64, 45 Minutes

Mathematical Concepts

1. Which can be divided by 8 with no remainder?

   a. 38
   b. 56
   c. 65
   d. 81

2. Which of the following is the largest?

   a. $\frac{2}{3}$
   b. $\frac{1}{4}$
   c. $\frac{1}{3}$
   d. $\frac{2}{5}$

3. If you add two even whole numbers, the result will be

   a. odd
   b. prime
   c. even
   d. odd and positive

4. How many distinct prime factors does the number 18 have?

   a. 1
   b. 2
   c. 3
   d. 4

5. The radius of a circle with a circumference of 16π is

   a. 4π
   b. 4
   c. 8
   d. 16

6. Which of the following is the least common multiple of 3 and 9?

   a. 3
   b. 9
   c. 18
   d. 27

7. What is 3.096 + 2.85 rounded to the nearest tenth?

   a. 5.95
   b. 5.94
   c. 5.946
   d. 5.9

8. What is the greatest integer less than –2.4?

   a. –3
   b. –2.5
   c. –2
   d. –1

9. Which of the following is equal to 3.21×10^2?

    a. 0.0321

    b. 0.321

    c. 32.1

    d. 321

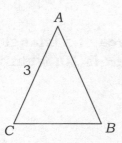

10. What is the perimeter of equilateral triangle *ABC*?

    a. 3

    b. 4.5

    c. 6

    d. 9

11. Which of the following is closest in value to –4?

    a. –3.8

    b. –4.01

    c. –4.078

    d. –4.101

12. The ratio of 3.5 to 2 is the same as the ratio of

    a. 14 to 8

    b. 7 to 6

    c. 350 to 20

    d. 6 to 4

13. Two positive integers have a sum of 18 and a product of 72. Which of the following could be one of the two numbers?

    a. 6

    b. 8

    c. 10

    d. 14

14. At Davis Junior High the ratio of students to teachers in each classroom is 18:1. What fractional part of the people in the classroom are teachers?

    a. $\frac{1}{19}$

    b. $\frac{1}{18}$

    c. $\frac{18}{19}$

    d. $\frac{18}{1}$

15. If –5.2 < *x* < 3.4, how many possible integer values for *x* are there?

    a. 6

    b. 7

    c. 8

    d. 9

16. What is the perimeter of a square with an area of 36?

    a. 12

    b. 18

    c. 24

    d. 36

17. **3³ =**
    a. 91
    b. 92
    c. 27
    d. 272

18. **Which of the following is a pair of reciprocals?**

    a. $\left(\dfrac{1}{3}, \dfrac{9}{3}\right)$

    b. $\left(1, \dfrac{1}{2}\right)$

    c. $\left(\dfrac{1}{3}, -\dfrac{1}{3}\right)$

    d. $\left(3, \dfrac{3}{3}\right)$

19. **Which of the following is equal to 0.16?**

    a. $\dfrac{4}{25}$

    b. $\dfrac{16}{10}$

    c. $\dfrac{8}{5}$

    d. $\dfrac{4}{10}$

20. **Which of the following is equal to $2\sqrt{2^3}$?**
    a. 24
    b. $2\sqrt{3}$
    c. $4\sqrt{2}$
    d. 2

21. **If the area of a triangle is 30, and its height is 10, what is its base?**
    a. 3
    b. 5
    c. 6
    d. 9

22. **The ratio of piano students to guitar students at a certain music school is 2:4. If 80 students are learning the guitar, how many students are learning the piano?**
    a. 10
    b. 20
    c. 30
    d. 40

23. **How many 1-inch cubes can fit into a cube with side 3?**
    a. 3
    b. 6
    c. 9
    d. 27

24. In Amy's bag are three cans of cola and one can of lemon-lime soda. If Amy randomly takes one can at a time out of her bag, what is the greatest number of cans she must take out of her bag to make sure that she gets a can of cola?

a. 1
b. 2
c. 3
d. 4

Problem Solving

25. $\dfrac{5}{0.25} =$

a. 0.2
b. 2
c. 20
d. 200

26. Mary went shopping one day. She spent \$8 on a hat, \$12 on a dress, and \$2 on a scarf. If she had \$30 to spend, how much money did she have left at the end of the day?

a. \$8
b. \$20
c. \$22
d. \$52

27. If $5x + 3 = 21$, then $x =$

a. $\dfrac{18}{5}$
b. $\dfrac{5}{18}$
c. $\dfrac{24}{5}$
d. $\dfrac{5}{24}$

28. What percent of 96 is 8?

a. $1\dfrac{1}{2}$
b. $8\dfrac{1}{3}$
c. $8\dfrac{3}{8}$
d. 12

29. $7\dfrac{2}{5} - 3\dfrac{2}{3} =$

a. $4\dfrac{11}{15}$ $7\dfrac{6}{15} - 3\dfrac{10}{15}$
b. $4\dfrac{4}{15}$
c. $3\dfrac{4}{15}$ $6\dfrac{21}{15}$
d. $3\dfrac{11}{15}$ $3\dfrac{11}{15}$

30. Annie buys 1 pack of gum every day of the week, except for Saturday, when she buys 2 packs of gum. If a pack of gum costs 75 cents, how much does Annie spend on gum every week?

    a. $5.75
    b. $6.00
    c. $6.25
    d. $2.25

31. On a certain map, 1 mile is represented by 2.5 inches. How long is a road that has a length of 12.5 inches on the map?

    a. 0.2 miles
    b. 5 miles
    c. 7.5 miles
    d. 10 miles

32. During a special sale, a dress originally priced for $80 was marked down by 30%. What was the price of the dress during the sale?

    a. $79
    b. $67
    c. $56
    d. $50

33. $\dfrac{16}{5} \times \dfrac{15}{8} =$

    a. 6
    b. 8
    c. 9
    d. 11

34. If $x^2 + 4 = 20$, then x could be

    a. 3
    b. 4
    c. 5
    d. 6

35. $5.2 \times 2.1 =$

    a. 10.92
    b. 10.22
    c. 7.3
    d. 3.1

36. Molly scored 86, 87, 93, and x on her four history tests. If her average for the four tests was 91, what is the value of x?

    a. 91
    b. 93
    c. 96
    d. 98

37. 25% of 80 is equal to 10% of what number?

    a. 200
    b. 2,000
    c. 400
    d. 4,000

38. Which of the following is equal to $\dfrac{1}{3} \div \dfrac{3}{7}$?

   a. $\dfrac{1}{7}$

   b. $\dfrac{7}{3}$

   c. $\dfrac{7}{9}$

   d. $\dfrac{9}{7}$

39. At a birthday party, there were 3 boxes of doughnuts. Each box contained 14 doughnuts. If the 12 party guests ate 3 doughnuts each, how many doughnuts were left over at the end of the party?

   a. 4

   b. 6

   c. 8

   d. 10

40. How many minutes will it take for an airplane traveling 400 miles per hour to travel 6,000 miles?

   a. 15

   b. 90

   c. 900

   d. 1,200

41. $4 - (5 - 2) + 3 \times 5 =$

   a. 12

   b. 16

   c. 20

   d. 23

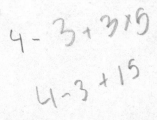

42. Albert is twice as old as Bert, and Bert is 7 years younger than Carl. If Albert is 12 years old, how old will Carl be in 8 years?

   a. 21

   b. 18

   c. 13

   d. 6

43. If $4^x = 16^3$, then $x =$

   a. 4

   b. 5

   c. 6

   d. 8

44. If the ratio of tomatoes to cucumbers in David's garden is 2:6, and there are 72 cucumbers in the garden, how many tomatoes are there?

   a. 6

   b. 12

   c. 18

   d. 24

45. $6\dfrac{1}{4} \div 12\dfrac{1}{2} =$

   a. $\dfrac{3}{4}$

   b. $\dfrac{2}{3}$

   c. $\dfrac{1}{2}$

   d. $1\dfrac{1}{3}$

46. If $5x + 5 = 3x - 9$, then $x =$

   a. −7

   b. −5

   c. 5

   d. 7

(handwritten at top of page)

1.25
15
625
1250

18.75

21.25
18
1000
1250

22.50

47. Tabatha decided to save money to buy a plant. If the plant costs $20, and Tabatha saves $1.25 per day, how many days will she have to save in order to have enough money to buy the plant?

  a. 16
  b. 18
  c. 22
  d. 24

(handwritten: 1.25⟌20)

48. Alex has three times as many cards as David. If the average number of cards that Alex and David have is 20, how many cards does Alex have?

  a. 30
  b. 25
  c. 20
  d. 10

49. If a square has a perimeter of 40 feet, what is its area?

  a. 16 ft²
  b. 64 ft²
  c. 100 ft²
  d. 124 ft²

50. If $-5x - 1 < 9$, which of the following is true?

  a. $x < -2$

  b. $x > -2$

  c. $x < -\dfrac{1}{2}$

  d. $x > -\dfrac{1}{2}$

(handwritten: $-5x < 10$)

51. If a bus leaves city A at 9:45 A.M. and arrives in city B at 4:05 P.M. how long did it take the bus to travel from city A to city B?

  a. 5 hours 40 minutes
  b. 6 hours 20 minutes
  c. 6 hours 40 minutes
  d. 7 hours 20 minutes

52. If the average of 3, 8, and x is equal to the average of 7 and x, what is the value of x?

  a. 1
  b. 2
  c. 3
  d. 4

53. Kim put 40 blue beads and 20 red beads on a necklace. Approximately what percent of the beads on the necklace were red?

  a. 25%
  b. 30%
  c. 33%
  d. 40%

54. How many times greater is $2\dfrac{1}{4}$ than $\dfrac{3}{4}$?

  a. 3
  b. 5
  c. 6
  d. 8

55. If $\dfrac{1}{4x} + 3 = 6$, then $x =$

    a. 12

    b. 6

    c. $\dfrac{1}{12}$

    d. $\dfrac{1}{6}$

56. The price of a toy is reduced by $15. If the new price of the toy is 80% of the original price, what was the original price of the toy?

    a. $30

    b. $45

    c. $75

    d. $80

57. $\dfrac{.08 + .08 + .08 + .08}{4} =$

    a. 0.08

    b. 0.16

    c. 0.02

    d. 0.2

58. If Leslie can run 2 miles in 35 minutes, how long will it take her to run 16 miles at the same rate?

    a. 3 hours 50 minutes

    b. 4 hours 40 minutes

    c. 5 hours 50 minutes

    d. 6 hours 20 minutes

59. $2\sqrt{12} \times 2\sqrt{3} =$

    a. 12

    b. $2\sqrt{12}$

    c. $4\sqrt{12}$

    d. 24

60. $(55 - 62) \times 4 - 2^3 =$

    a. −36

    b. −28

    c. 28

    d. 36

61. Jason gets 35 cents for every weed he pulls from his neighbor's yard. He wants to earn enough money to buy a game that costs $52.50. How many weeds must he pull in order to earn enough money to buy the game?

    a. 80

    b. 100

    c. 120

    d. 150

62. At Davis High, 150 students take biology and 120 take physics. Of these students, 30 take both biology and physics. How many students take biology but do not take physics?

    a. 20

    b. 30

    c. 120

    d. 130

63. If $2(2x + 2) = 16$, then $x =$

    a. 2

    b. 3

    c. 4

    d. 5

64. Which of the following is not the product of two distinct prime numbers?

    a. 3

    b. 6

    c. 10

    d. 15

Language

Questions 1–60, 25 minutes

For questions 1–40, check the sentences for errors of usage, capitalization, or punctuation. If there is no error, choose (D).

1. Choose the sentence with the correct grammar.

   a. Supermarkets try to make their food look as appetizing as possible.

   b. The Tower of London is the city's most popular tourist attraction.

   c. Many people enjoy listening to quiet music while they work.

   d. No mistake.

2. Choose the sentence with the correct grammar.

   a. There are three kinds of rooms at the Main Street Hotel.

   b. Today's cars are most more powerful than cars of the past.

   c. It is always important to read the directions very careful.

   d. No mistake.

3. Choose the sentence with the correct grammar.

   a. Lisa bought a silk dress from a store at the mall.

   b. Jason left the cake in the oven and burned it.

   c. Most seashells are made from calcium.

   d. No mistake.

4. Choose the sentence with the correct punctuation.

   a. I know some words, that my friends don't know.

   b. Camels can travel for days, without stopping to drink.

   c. My three favorite vegetables are carrots, spinach, and onions.

   d. No mistake.

5. Choose the sentence with the correct capitalization.

   a. Most of the food we eat is grown in Foreign Countries.

   b. If you paint indoors, make sure that Your room is well ventilated.

   c. Last year I saw an exhibition of modern American art at the museum.

   d. No mistake.

6. Choose the sentence with the correct punctuation.

   a. I jumped, when I heard a loud knock on the door.

   b. "That's interesting," he said. "I never knew that."

   c. There is more than one correct answer to Lukes question.

   d. No mistake.

7. Choose the sentence with the correct grammar.

   a. Jeff visited a cheese factory and learned how cheese is made.

   b. I forgot to invite my brother's best friend to the party.

   c. Though Mark is not a doctor, he knows a great deal about medicine.

   d. No mistake.

8. Choose the sentence with the correct grammar.

   a. Many people don't not know that snakes are reptiles.

   b. He gave my brother and me a book.

   c. Max go to the museum last week with his mother.

   d. No mistake.

9. Choose the sentence with the correct punctuation.

   a. Frogs lay their egg's in the water.

   b. Julie had a hard time reading her sister's handwriting.

   c. Franklin D Roosevelt was an expert politician.

   d. No mistake.

10. Choose the sentence with the correct punctuation.

   a. Everyone should read Shakespeare's play's.

   b. The dog licked its paw after stepping on a sharp rock.

   c. Since I didnt have enough money, I couldnt buy the book.

   d. No mistake.

11. Choose the sentence with the correct grammar.

   a. Martina are a naturally optimistic person.

   b. David say, "I hope we find her soon."

   c. My brother has a large number of baseball cards.

   d. No mistake.

12. Choose the sentence with the correct grammar.

    a. Some animals sleeps all winter.

    b. My father take some great pictures of me.

    c. Amy saw the cat and showed it to her sister.

    d. No mistake.

13. Choose the sentence with the correct capitalization.

    a. Peter is always late for School.

    b. My doctor recommends that I eat more fruit.

    c. Carpentry and Cabinetmaking are very different skills.

    d. No mistake.

14. Choose the sentence with the correct punctuation.

    a. David greatly enjoyed the new opera, that he saw last night.

    b. "Isn't it beautiful?" asked Laurie when she saw her sister's new pet.

    c. Pavlov won a Nobel Prize for his work with dog's.

    d. No mistake.

15. Choose the sentence with the correct grammar.

    a. I always wash my hands before eating.

    b. Some people mistakenly believe that he knows how to fly an airplane.

    c. After winning the race, the runner began to cry.

    d. No mistake.

16. Choose the sentence with the correct grammar.

    a. My father gave the car to my brother and me.

    b. We never thought that they will arrive on time.

    c. When it rains, the roads are become very slippery and dangerous.

    d. No mistake.

17. Choose the sentence with the correct grammar.

    a. Unless you finished your spinach, you won't be allowed to have cake.

    b. Troy played the most brilliant game of his life last night.

    c. Tom holded his breath and hoped that his brother would score a goal.

    d. No mistake.

18. **Choose the sentence with the correct punctuation.**

    a. Even after losing, David refused to give up hope.
    b. Manny warmly greeted his guests at the door.
    c. "Penelope," Jason replied, "I don't think you're ready."
    d. No mistake.

19. **Choose the sentence with the correct grammar.**

    a. They weren't sure of the address, so they ask for directions.
    b. Paul is a man who loves to play baseball in the park.
    c. Abigail thank her teacher at the end of the school year.
    d. No mistake.

20. **Choose the sentence with the correct grammar.**

    a. Everyone thinks that he or she has the right answer.
    b. When Ines arrived at school, she didn't not know which classes to take.
    c. Jan suddenly become very pale.
    d. No mistake.

21. **Choose the sentence with the correct grammar.**

    a. Jackson is born in a log cabin in North Carolina.
    b. The audience, was obviously very pleased, with the performance.
    c. The birds in the park by the lake sing beautifully.
    d. No mistake.

22. **Choose the sentence with the correct grammar.**

    a. Any citizen over 18 year old can vote in the election.
    b. It is always important to read every pages of the book.
    c. It is easier to learn to walk than to dance.
    d. No mistake.

23. **Choose the sentence with the correct grammar.**

    a. I am very worried about his failing health.
    b. The most easiest way to move heavy cargo is by ship.
    c. I would much rather take the bus to work than driving.
    d. No mistake.

24. **Choose the sentence with the correct grammar.**

    a. You need to try a mango to know whether you like it.

    b. The jugglers attracted a large crowd.

    c. Kim realized that she had forgotten to bring her lunch and her homework.

    d. No mistake.

25. **Choose the sentence with the correct grammar.**

    a. After beginning her career as a schoolteacher, Ida Tarbell became a writer.

    b. Airplanes require frequent inspections to ensure that they are safe.

    c. Early ice skates were made of wood and leather.

    d. No mistake.

26. **Choose the sentence with the correct grammar.**

    a. This puzzle is one of the more complicated ever made.

    b. The fruit I ate yesterday was much better than the fruit I ate today.

    c. Jack keep his trophies on a shelf in the basement.

    d. No mistake.

27. **Choose the sentence with the correct grammar.**

    a. While hiking in the forest, we eaten lunch near a small creek.

    b. The greatest book I have ever read was written by Ernest Hemingway.

    c. The mayor of the town is very concerned for pollution.

    d. No mistake.

28. **Choose the sentence with the correct grammar.**

    a. Matt wash the dishes while Alex dried them.

    b. Tomorrow, Richard and his sister will go to the amusement park.

    c. Woodrow, my pet hamster, escapes from his cage last night.

    d. No mistake.

29. **Choose the sentence with the correct grammar.**

    a. I was very impressed to seen him lift that heavy weight.

    b. Nathan always carry a leather wallet in his back pocket.

    c. I hardly ever drink coffee before noon.

    d. No mistake.

30. Choose the sentence with the correct grammar.

a. It has been so long since I have seen them that I have forgotten what they look like.

b. Owen thought that his brother was not very nice toward his mother.

c. I need to buy some new strings for my guitar.

d. No mistake.

31. Choose the sentence with the correct grammar.

a. When I seen him again, I'll give him the message.

b. I have seen that book on the shelf just behind the counter.

c. Tammy plays the violin, but she prefer the flute.

d. No mistake.

32. Choose the sentence with the correct grammar.

a. Building a treehouse can be a very educational experience.

b. While chasing a squirrel, my cat bumped into the wall.

c. My parents told me that I am mature enough to have my own bank account.

d. No mistake.

33. Choose the sentence with the correct grammar.

a. Anis goes to Brattleborough every summers to study physics.

b. How many languages do Mr. Ferral speak?

c. I think that Ms. Walton is the most intelligent of all my teachers.

d. No mistake.

34. Choose the sentence with the correct grammar.

a. Barry was so impressed by the book that he decided to become a cook.

b. The Constitution of the United States was signed in September 1787.

c. The human body stores excess energy in the form of fat.

d. No mistake.

35. Choose the sentence with the correct grammar.

a. My mother said she thinks that I should drink more milk.

b. My friend Jim find a snake hiding in the grass behind his house.

c. Anna return her books to the library yesterday.

d. No mistake.

36. Choose the sentence with the correct punctuation.

a. Max did not respond to Davids letter.

b. "Can you bring me a chair?" asked my sister.

c. The river, is on the other side of the hill.

d. No mistake.

37. Choose the sentence with the correct grammar.

a. Most people do not think of fish as dangerous, but the barracuda is an exception.

b. Each of the guests at the party was a professor.

c. Walter was excited to hear that his mother had gotten a promotion.

d. No mistake.

38. Choose the sentence with the correct grammar.

a. David will arrive at the airport sometime next week.

b. Vivian told me that she had never gone so far in the wood alone.

c. Everyone at the party received a note from the father of the bride.

d. No mistake.

39. Choose the sentence with the correct grammar.

a. The marbles, are in a jar, on the top shelf, of the closet.

b. Most of the people at the party think that he is 15 years old.

c. Sarah thinks her father's job wasn't very dull.

d. No mistake.

40. Choose the sentence with the correct grammar.

a. Yesterday my best friend David said he wants to be a policeman someday.

b. Harriet Tubman made nineteen trips to the South and guides more than 300 slaves to freedom.

c. Few people know that Massachusetts has the countries biggest crop of cranberries.

d. No mistake.

Spelling

For questions 41–50, look for errors in spelling.

41. Choose the incorrect spelling.

    a. Martin was very happy with the toy he purchased.

    b. Early automobiles had headlights made of brass.

    c. He complemented her on her pretty dress.

    d. No mistake.

42. Choose the incorrect spelling.

    a. Some films are serious while others are merely for entertainment.

    b. Lawrence walked for eight days in the dessert without finding any water.

    c. Mr. Carter tried to improve the working conditions in his factory.

    d. No mistake.

43. Choose the incorrect spelling.

    a. Jennifer was a vigorous and effective public speaker.

    b. There was very little difference between their two positions.

    c. Most nations switched from sail to steam power at the turn of the century.

    d. No mistake.

44. Choose the incorrect spelling.

    a. Patrick thinks that he made the wrong descision the other day.

    b. It is never easy to choose between two people who are so similar.

    c. John has been a student of political science for over five years.

    d. No mistake.

45. Choose the incorrect spelling.

    a. Lonny likes to read magazines on the weekends.

    b. Everyone can benefit from improvements in transportation.

    c. The people cheered when the war was finally over.

    d. No mistake.

46. Choose the incorrect spelling.

    a. Last week Sally's father took her to the aquarium.

    b. My essay was supposed to be fifty sentenses long.

    c. Lindsay was the best musician of the group.

    d. No mistake.

47. Choose the incorrect spelling.

    a. Tina was worried that she could not pay off her debts.

    b. The sun was shinning brightly and the birds were singing.

    c. David's parents sat down and waited for the concert to begin.

    d. No mistake.

48. Choose the incorrect spelling.

    a. Modern farmers make good use of agricultural technology.

    b. Our history teacher sent David to the principle's office.

    c. There are several advantages to his method.

    d. No mistake.

49. Choose the incorrect spelling.

    a. Carol accomplished much less than she promised.

    b. Many disasters are caused by poor management.

    c. Both candidates agreed on most of the important political issues.

    d. No mistake.

50. Choose the incorrect spelling.

    a. Mr. Bowles helped to put these historical events into perspective for us.

    b. Amelia is an ambitious woman who wants to become a lawyer someday.

    c. The British goverment was unhappy with her performance.

    d. No mistake.

Composition

51. Choose the sentence that is correct and most clearly written.

a. Yesterday five miles Alex ran around the track.

b. Around the track, yesterday Alex ran five miles.

c. Five miles was how far Alex ran around the track yesterday.

d. Alex ran five miles around the track yesterday.

52. Choose the sentence that is correct and most clearly written.

a. 21 years old was the age when Jonathan decided that he wanted to become a linguist.

b. Jonathan decided, at the age of 21 years old, that a linguist was what he wanted to become.

c. Jonathan decided to become a linguist when he was 21 years old.

d. When he was 21 years old, Jonathan decided that a linguist was what to be.

53. Choose the sentence that is correct and most clearly written.

a. To read the works of Shakespeare was what Dr. Thornton recommended to his students.

b. The works of Shakespeare was what Dr. Thornton recommended to his students to read.

c. Dr. Thornton suggested that his students read the works of Shakespeare.

d. The works of Shakespeare, suggested Dr. Thornton, were what his students should read.

54. **Where should the following sentence be placed in the paragraph below?**

Her career as an activist began when she was a schoolteacher.

1) Susan B. Anthony, born in 1820, was one of the strongest advocates for women's rights in America. 2) She was filled with horror when she realized that the male schoolteachers were being paid much more for performing the same job. 3) Shortly after that she began to fight for equality and for women's suffrage, or the right to vote. 4) She was never deterred by her many traditionalist opponents. 5) Before she died in 1906, Susan B. Anthony addressed the women's suffrage convention. 6) She urged them to fight on and not to surrender. 7) Just over ten years later, women were finally given the right to vote.

   a. After sentence 1
   b. After sentence 2
   c. After sentence 3
   d. After sentence 4

55. **Where should the following sentence be placed in the paragraph below?**

Nonetheless, they are powerful animals and some of the fastest birds in the air.

1) Hummingbirds are most commonly found in South America, but can be found in other parts of the Western Hemisphere. 2) They are extremely small in size, as small as 3 inches in length. 3) They can reach speeds of up to 60 miles per hour, and can beat their wings up to 75 times every second. 4) They expend so much energy that they have to constantly eat. 5) At night, when they cannot feed, they fall into a deep sleep similar to hibernation.

   a. After sentence 1
   b. After sentence 2
   c. After sentence 3
   d. After sentence 4

56. Fill in the blank.

Many dogs have natural hunting instincts; _____ retrievers enjoy fetching and carrying things in their mouths.

a. in contrast,
b. for example,
c. because,
d. likewise

57. Fill in the blank.

I was not able to go to the concert last week _____ I could not get tickets.

a. therefore
b. nevertheless
c. moreover
d. because

58. Fill in the blank.

Picking apples off the tree too early is not good for the tree; _____ the apples won't taste very good either.

a. however,
b. for example,
c. furthermore,
d. but,

59. Which sentence does not belong in the following paragraph?

1) My paternal grandfather worked for many years as a photographer's assistant. 2) In the evenings, he gave private dance lessons to actors. 3) Since he didn't have a lot of money, the apartment his family lived in was very small. 4) But he earned enough to send my father to college. 5) There were not many colleges in rural America in the 1950s. 6) It was very important to my grandfather to see that his son had a good education.

a. Sentence 2
b. Sentence 3
c. Sentence 4
d. Sentence 5

60. Which sentence does not belong in the following paragraph?

1) A few years ago, I was looking through some old photographs that my parents kept in the attic. 2) I uncovered pictures of my family as they stood in line at Ellis Island and looked at the Statue of Liberty. 3) The Statue of Liberty was a gift from the French government. 4) My grandparents spent a few days in a shelter that overlooked the Hudson River. 5) However, they did not stay in New York for long. 6) Thankfully their cousins in Chicago gave them jobs and so they moved to the Midwest to begin their new lives. 7) This is the story of how my family arrived in America.

a. Sentence 2
b. Sentence 3
c. Sentence 4
d. Sentence 5

Chapter 20
HSPT
Practice Test 1:
Answers and
Explanations

ANSWER KEY

Verbal Skills

1.	A	38.	A
2.	B	39.	B
3.	B	40.	B
4.	C	41.	B
5.	B	42.	A
6.	D	43.	C
7.	B	44.	A
8.	C	45.	B
9.	D	46.	B
10.	C	47.	C
11.	B	48.	A
12.	B	49.	B
13.	C	50.	C
14.	C	51.	A
15.	A	52.	C
16.	D	53.	C
17.	B	54.	B
18.	C	55.	D
19.	B	56.	B
20.	C	57.	A
21.	C	58.	B
22.	A	59.	D
23.	D	60.	C
24.	D		
25.	B		
26.	A		
27.	B		
28.	B		
29.	C		
30.	D		
31.	C		
32.	B		
33.	A		
34.	D		
35.	A		
36.	D		
37.	C		

Quantitative Skills

1.	C	38.	B
2.	B	39.	C
3.	D	40.	B
4.	C	41.	C
5.	D	42.	C
6.	A	43.	B
7.	B	44.	B
8.	B	45.	D
9.	D	46.	D
10.	B	47.	B
11.	A	48.	C
12.	A	49.	C
13.	B	50.	A
14.	B	51.	B
15.	A	52.	D
16.	D		
17.	D		
18.	D		
19.	C		
20.	A		
21.	D		
22.	D		
23.	A		
24.	B		
25.	C		
26.	C		
27.	B		
28.	C		
29.	C		
30.	B		
31.	C		
32.	D		
33.	B		
34.	D		
35.	A		
36.	A		
37.	C		

Reading

1.	D	38.	A
2.	B	39.	C
3.	A	40.	C
4.	C	41.	B
5.	C	42.	A
6.	C	43.	D
7.	A	44.	B
8.	B	45.	C
9.	A	46.	A
10.	C	47.	C
11.	C	48.	B
12.	D	49.	D
13.	B	50.	A
14.	B	51.	B
15.	B	52.	D
16.	B	53.	B
17.	B	54.	B
18.	A	55.	A
19.	B	56.	D
20.	B	57.	A
21.	A	58.	C
22.	D	59.	B
23.	B	60.	C
24.	C	61.	C
25.	B	62.	B
26.	A		
27.	B		
28.	A		
29.	D		
30.	B		
31.	D		
32.	B		
33.	A		
34.	B		
35.	C		
36.	D		
37.	B		

Mathematics

1.	B	38.	C
2.	A	39.	B
3.	C	40.	C
4.	B	41.	B
5.	C	42.	A
6.	B	43.	C
7.	D	44.	D
8.	A	45.	C
9.	D	46.	A
10.	D	47.	A
11.	B	48.	A
12.	A	49.	C
13.	A	50.	B
14.	A	51.	B
15.	D	52.	A
16.	C	53.	C
17.	C	54.	A
18.	A	55.	C
19.	A	56.	C
20.	C	57.	A
21.	C	58.	B
22.	D	59.	D
23.	D	60.	A
24.	B	61.	D
25.	C	62.	C
26.	A	63.	B
27.	A	64.	A
28.	B		
29.	D		
30.	B		
31.	B		
32.	C		
33.	A		
34.	B		
35.	A		
36.	D		
37.	A		

Language Skills

1.	D	38.	D
2.	A	39.	B
3.	D	40.	A
4.	C	41.	C
5.	C	42.	B
6.	B	43.	D
7.	D	44.	A
8.	B	45.	D
9.	B	46.	B
10.	B	47.	B
11.	C	48.	B
12.	C	49.	D
13.	B	50.	C
14.	B	51.	D
15.	D	52.	C
16.	A	53.	C
17.	B	54.	A
18.	D	55.	B
19.	B	56.	B
20.	A	57.	D
21.	C	58.	C
22.	C	59.	D
23.	A	60.	B
24.	D		
25.	D		
26.	B		
27.	B		
28.	B		
29.	C		
30.	D		
31.	B		
32.	D		
33.	C		
34.	D		
35.	A		
36.	B		
37.	D		

ANSWERS AND EXPLANATIONS

Verbal Skills

1. **A**

2. **B**   The U.S. as a country is led by a president; the army as a whole is led by a general.

3. **B**   To fortify means to strengthen, so the opposite is weaken.

4. **C**   Sad, lonely, and upset are all types of feelings.

5. **B**

6. **D**   Gigantic means very large; hilarious means very funny.

7. **B**   Opaque means hard to see or understand; the opposite is clear.

8. **C**   Oregano, parsley, and pepper are all types of spices.

9. **D**

10. **C**   We can diagram this as follows: $J > A$, $K > A$. We know that John and Kenny each have more than Alice, but we don't know whether John has more than Kenny.

11. **B**

12. **B**   We can diagram this as follows: $J > L$, $L > M$. We know that Juanita finished before Lucy, so Lucy did not finish the race before Juanita.

13. **C**

14. **C**   Touch, sight, and hearing are all types of senses.

15. **A**   Abundant means plentiful; the opposite is meager.

16. **D**

17. **B**   Feathers, beaks, and wings are all parts of a bird.

18. **C**   We can diagram this as follows: $R > W$, $T > A$. We have no idea how Robert and Weston relate to Abigail and Tyrone, so we can't know whether Robert or Tyrone read first.

19. **B**

20. **C**   A bird is kept in a cage; a prisoner is kept in a jail.

21. **C**

22. **A**   Oceans, lakes, and rivers are all bodies of water.

23. **D**   A paragraph is made up of sentences; a poem is made up of verses.

24. **D**

25. **B**   Ruthless means without mercy; the opposite is merciful.

26. **A**

27. **B**   Yard, mile, and foot are all measurements of length.

28. **B**

29. **C**   Chaos means disorder, so the opposite is order.

30. **D**   Sandal, slipper, and shoe are all worn on the foot; a glove is worn on the hand.

31. **C**

32. **B**   Bread is made from grain; jam is made from fruit.

33. **A**   A hat and a cap are both worn on the head; a shoe and a sneaker are both worn on the foot.

34. **D**   Prevalent means common; the opposite is rare.

35. **A**   Hammer, knife, and screwdriver are all types of tools.

36. **D**

37. **C**   Pear, apple, and orange are all forms of fruit.

38. **A**   Reprimand means to scold; the opposite is to praise.

39. **B**   We can diagram this as follows: $A >$ Louise, Lisa $> A > J$. Since Lisa counts faster than Agnes, and Agnes can count faster than Jeremy, we know that Jeremy does not count faster than Lisa.

40. **B**   A trunk is the base of a tree; a stem is the base of a flower.

41. **B**   Dog, cat, and rabbit are all kinds of mammals.

42. **A**

43. **C**   Peanuts, cashews, and walnuts all have shells.

44. **A**   Mile is a measure of distance; pound is a measure of weight.

45. **B**   We can diagram this as follows: $R\ E\ S > C$. Since Eric has the same number of cards as Steve, they both have more than Carl. Therefore it is false, that Steve has fewer cards than Carl.

46. **B**   Erratic means unstable; the opposite is stable.

47. **C**

48. **A**   We can diagram this as follows: $L > M > S$, $S > P$. Since Lanville has more inhabitants than Samtown, and Samtown has more than Pinton, we know that Lanville has more inhabitants than Pinton.

49. **B** Esteem means admiration or respect; the opposite is dislike.

50. **C** Speak, yell, and whisper all describe ways of making sounds.

51. **A** Indifferent means unconcerned; the opposite is concerned.

52. **C** Flute, violin, and cello are all instruments in an orchestra.

53. **C** We can diagram this as follows: $O > Q$, $O > J$, Sally > Stephen, Sally > J. All we know about Ollie and Sally is that they are each older than Joseph. But we don't know whether Ollie or Sally is older.

54. **B** A cook works in a kitchen; a doctor works in a hospital.

55. **D** Theater, stadium, and arena are all places where crowds gather.

56. **B** We can diagram this as follows: $E > H >$ Bill, $A >$ Becky, $A > E$. Since Adam can sing more songs than Enid, and Enid can sing more songs than Howard, we know that Adam cannot sing fewer songs than Howard.

57. **A** Cover, page, and spine are all parts of a book.

58. **B** We can diagram this as follows: $M >$ Penelope $> U$, Petra $> M$. Since Petra has more cats than Michael, and Michael has more than Penelope, we know that Penelope does not have more cats than Petra.

59. **D** A group of trees is a forest; a group of stars is a constellation.

60. **C** Intentional means done on purpose; the opposite is accidental.

Quantitative Skills

1. **C** The series goes 4 (+ 8) 12 (+ 8) 20 (+ 8) 28 (+ 8) **36**.

2. **B** In a rectangle, the diagonals are always equal, and they are the longest lines.

3. **D** Divide 39 by 3 to get 13. That's $\frac{1}{3}$ of 39, so $\frac{2}{3}$ of 39 = 26. Divide each answer choice by 2 to see which one gives you 26.

4. **C** $\frac{1}{4}$ of 84 = 21. $\frac{1}{2}$ of 48 = 24. $\frac{1}{2}$ of 42 = 21. Therefore (1) and (3) are identical and smaller than (2).

5. **D** The series goes 3 ($\times$ 2) 6 ($\times$ 2) 12 ($\times$ 2) 24 ($\times$ 2) **48**.

6. **A** If we count the squares, we find that (A) has 12 squares, (B) has 12 squares, and (C) has 20 squares.

7. **B** The series goes 4 (+ 4) 8 (+ 4) 12 (+ 4) 16 (+ 4) 20.

8. **B** 20% of 60 is the same as $\frac{20}{100} \times 60$, or 12. 60% of 20 is the same as $\frac{60}{100} \times 20$, or 12. 200% of 6 is the same as $\frac{200}{100} \times 6$, or 12.

9. **D** $5 \times 3 = 15$. Try taking 20% of each of the choices to see which gives you 15. When you get to D, you'll see that 20% of 75 = $\frac{20}{100} \times 75$.

10. **B** The series goes 5 (+ 3) 8 (+ 4) 12 (+ 3) 15 (+ 4) 19 (+ 3) **22**.

11. **A** $3^3 = 3 \times 3 \times 3 = 27$. $4^2 = 4 \times 4 = 16$. $5^1 = 5 \times 1 = 5$.

12. **A** The series goes 8 (− 3) 5 (+ 4) 9 (− 3) 6 (+ 4) 10 (− 3) **7**.

13. **B** $\frac{1}{2}$ of 24 = 12. Try taking $\frac{2}{3}$ of each answer choice to see which equals 12.

14. **B** The series goes 4 (+ 3) 7 (+ 2) 9 (+ 3) 12 (+ 2) 14 (+ 3) 17 (+ 2) **19**.

15. **A** The product of 3, 4, and 5 is 60. $\frac{3}{4} \times 60 = 45$.

16. **D** $\frac{5}{10} = 0.5$. $\frac{70}{100} = 0.7$. $\frac{8}{100} = 0.08$.

17. **D** The difference between 12 and 3 is 9. 200% of 9 = $\frac{200}{100} \times 9 = 18$.

18. **D** If you carry out the multiplications in (1), (2), and (3), you'll get 135 for each one. All three are equal, which makes (D) the answer.

19. **C** The series goes 12 (+ 6) 18 (+ 4) 22 (+ 6) 28 (+ 4) **32** (+ 6) 38.

20. **A** The product of 5 and 4 is 20. $\frac{5}{100} \times 20 = \frac{5}{5} = 1$.

21. **D** Since O is the center of the circle, OA, OB, and OC are all radii. All radii of a circle have the same lengths.

22. **D** 15% of 90 is the same as $\frac{15}{100} \times 90 = 13.5$. Try each answer choice to see which number divided by 4 is 13.5.

23. **A** The series goes 4 (× 2) 8 (+ 2) 10 (× 2) 20 (+ 2) 22 (× 2) **44** (+ 2) 46.

24. **B** The smallest prime number bigger than 4 is 5. The square root of 25 is 5. 75% of 8 is $\frac{75}{100} \times 8 = 6$.

25. **C** The product of 6 and 8 is 48. Add 20 to each of the choices to see which number gives you 48.

26. **C** Each number in the series is followed by its reciprocal.

27. **B** Each of the angles in a square is 90°, and each of the angles in an equilateral triangle is 60°. Therefore a = 90°, b = 60°, and c = 60°.

28. **C** The series goes 30 (− 2) 28 (− 3) 25 (− 4) 21 (− 5) **16**.

29. **C** Translate 140% of 40 as $\frac{140}{100} \times 40 = 56$.

30. **B** The series goes 2 (+ 2) 4 (− 1) 3 (+ 2) 5 (− 1) 4 (+ 2) 6 (− 1) 5 (+ 2) **7**.

31. **C** The area of a square with sides 3 is $3 \times 3 = 9$. The area of a circle with radius 3 is 9π. You may not know how to solve for the area of an equilateral triangle with side 3, but you know that its area is smaller than that of a square with side 3.

32. **D** $3^3 = 3 \times 3 \times 3 = 27$. $3^4 = 3 \times 3 \times 3 \times 3 = 81$. The difference between 27 and 81 is 54. Two more than this is 56.

33. **B** Since angle a is on the same line with the angle 110°, we know that a must be 70°. Angle c must also be 110°, since it is across from 110°; angle b must be 70°, since it is across from angle a. Therefore $a + c$ and $b + c$ are each 180°, and are bigger than $a + c$, which is 70°.

34. **D** The series goes 11 (× 2) 22 (× 2) 44 (× 2) 88 (× 2) **176**.

35. **A** The series goes 15 (+ 15) 30 (+ 5) 35 (+ 15) 50 (+ 5) 55 (+ 15) **70** (+ 5) 75.

36. **A** Don't make this one too complicated; just translate this as $\frac{75}{100} \times \frac{20}{100} \times 200$. Once you cancel out all the zeros, you get $\frac{75}{10} \times 2 \times 2 = 30$.

37. **C** Choices (A) and (B) each have three parts shaded, while (C) has four parts shaded.

38. **B** Use the average formula to figure out this problem and find the average of 20, 25, and 45. The sum of these numbers is 90. Divide the sum by the number of items: $90 \div 3 = 30$. $\frac{3}{5}$ of 30 is 18.

39. **C** The series goes 20 (+ 10) 30 (+ 15) 45 (+ 20) 65 (+ 25) **90** (+ 30) 120.

40. **B** To figure out 6.5×10^{-3}, move the decimal 3 places to the left, and get 0.0065. Likewise, to solve 650×10^{-4}, move the decimal 4 places to the left, and get 0.065. Since (3) has a 6 in the hundredths place, it is the largest.

41. **C** The series goes $1^{(2)} = 1$, $2^{(2)} = 4$, $3^{(2)} = 9$, $4^{(2)} = \mathbf{16}$.

42. **C** If $x = 2$, then (1) = 8, (2) = 16, and (3) = 16.

43. **B** Translate this question as $\frac{40}{100} \times \frac{20}{100} \times 600$. If you cancel all the zeros, you get $4 \times 2 \times 6$, or 48.

44. **B** Plug in each answer choice. 25 divided by 4 is 6 with a remainder of 1, so cross off (A). 31 divided by 4 is 7 with a remainder of 3.

45. **D** The series goes 15 (+ 5) 20 (− 2) 18 (+ 5) 23 (− 2) 21 (+ 5) 26 (− 2) 24 (+ 5) **29**.

46. **D** The area of any rectangle is equal to its length × width. Since a square has equal sides, we use the same number for each. (1) is therefore 4, (2) is 9, and (3) is $4 \times 4 = 16$, but half of that is 8.

47. **B** The product of 15 and $\frac{1}{3}$ is 5, and 5 more than 5 is 10.

48. **C** The series goes 56 (− 5) 51 (− 3) 48 (− 5) 43 (− 3) 40 (− 5) **35** (− 3) 32.

49. **C** One diagonal of a square is always longer than one side of a square. But a diagonal is always shorter than two sides of a square. (Try measuring this if you want to prove it to yourself.) Since BD and BF are longer than CD and CB, we know that (2) is larger than (1). Since BD and BF are less than the sum of $BC + CD$ and $BA + AF$ we know that (3) is larger than (2).

50. **A** First we need to find the average of 18, 24, 25, and 29. To do this, we add them to get 96, and then divide by 4 to get 24. $\frac{1}{6}$ of 24 is 4.

51. **B** The series goes 110 (÷ 2) 55 (– 5) 50 (÷ 2) 25 (– 5) 20 (÷ 2) **10**.

52. **D** 6^2 is 6 × 6 = 36. 16 more is 52.

Reading

Comprehension

1. **D** The third sentence of the second paragraph states, "We stumbled down from the train...."

2. **B** The first paragraph says, "I had crossed so many rivers that I was dull to them." The best paraphrase of the idea is (B).

3. **A** Just before the word *roused*, we see that the narrator "had been sleeping."

4. **C** At the end of the first paragraph, the narrator says that Nebraska is remarkable because "it was still, all day long."

5. **C** In the sentences before the word *tongue*, the narrator hears people talking, shouting, and exclaiming.

6. **C** According to the last paragraph, the people were immigrants.

7. **A** Just before mentioning that he "stumbled down from the train," the narrator "had been sleeping."

8. **B** The last paragraph says that they had "two half-grown boys and a girl, and a little girl clung to her mother's skirts."

9. **A** The third paragraph says that he discovered something to help protect "houses, people, and ships."

10. **C** Choices (A), (B), and (D) are too narrow to be the main idea. The passage discusses Franklin, Volta, Faraday, and Edison. This makes (C) the best choice.

11. **C** Choice (A) is extreme, and there is no evidence to support (B) or (D) in the passage. The author does say in the last sentence, however, that electricity is important to the modern world.

12. **D** According to the fifth paragraph, Faraday invented the generator.

13. **B** The fifth paragraph says that Faraday's discovery helped create the first electric motor, and that today's generators are almost identical to his.

14. **B** According to the sixth paragraph, Edison and Tesla disagreed about whether to use direct or alternating current.

15. **B** The sixth paragraph states that the transformer can "change the voltage of an electrical current."

16. **B** In the sixth paragraph, the word *advocated* is used with the same meaning as argued for.

17. **B** The first sentence says that Lindbergh was the first person to make a transatlantic flight.

18. **A** The second paragraph says that Earhart was in a plane with two people "at the controls," who would be her colleagues or coworkers.

19. **B** The passage mostly talks about Amelia Earhart.

20. **B** The third paragraph says that Earhart wanted to fly "to show that aviation was not exclusive to men."

21. **A** This story is mostly about a person, Amelia Earhart, so (A) is the most logical choice.

22. **D** According to the fourth paragraph, the "widest point" of the world is the equator.

23. **B** The final sentence of the story says that "nobody is sure what became of Amelia Earhart."

24. **C** The fifth paragraph says that Fred Noonan was "her navigator."

25. **B** Choices (A), (C), and (D) are only details of the story.

26. **A** The second paragraph says that Pasteur encouraged people to use antiseptics, which reduced infection caused by germs.

27. **B** The second paragraph says that Pasteur wanted doctors to "wash their hands [and] their instruments."

28. **A** The third paragraph says that anthrax could live in sheep but not in chickens, whose body temperature is above 44 degrees Celsius. Therefore, the body temperature of sheep must be less than 44 degrees Celsius.

29. **D** In the second paragraph, the word *sterilize* is used to describe a cleaning process to eliminate germs.

30. **B** The third paragraph says that pasteurization refers to the process of heating "dairy products." The only choice that is a dairy product is cheese.

31. **D** The final sentence of the passage says that Pasteur helped to free people from diseases.

32. **B** In the fourth paragraph, the word *antibodies* is used to refer to something that can protect the body from disease.

33. **A** Choices (B), (C), and (D) are details of the story. The main idea discusses chocolate from the time it was used by the Aztecs through its use in Europe.

34. **B** The word *fashion* is used to describe how European's drank chocolate, which was using the same method that the Aztec's use ("hot, spicy, and unsweetened").

35. **C** According to the second paragraph, it was the Spanish who brought chocolate to Europe.

36. **D** Choice (A) is extreme, so it can be eliminated. There is no evidence in the passage to support (B) or (C). However, the final paragraph says that cocoa butter is part of solid chocolate.

37. **B** The third paragraph says, "At first, when cocoa was rare, chocolate was considered a delicacy."

38. **A** The first paragraph says that "cocoa beans were even used as a form of money."

39. **C** The third paragraph says that later, "chocolate became accessible to almost everyone." Therefore, at first, it must not have been available to everyone.

40. **C** The final paragraph discusses how chocolate was changed from a drink to solid form.

Vocabulary

41. **B**

42. **A**

43. **D**

44. **B**

45. **C**

46. **A**

47. **C**

48. **B**

49. **D**

50. **A**

51. **B**

52. **D**

53. **B**

54. **B**

55. **A**

56. **D**

57. **A**

58. **C**

59. **B**

60. **C**

61. **C**

62. **B**

Mathematics

Mathematical Concepts

1. **B**   Try dividing each answer choice by 8. All of the choices except 56 leave a remainder.

2. **A**   Use the Bowtie to see which fraction is largest. You can also Ballpark—only (A) and (D) are more than $\frac{1}{2}$.

3. **C**   Try adding any two even whole numbers. 2 + 2 = 4, which is an even number.

4. **B**   First, factor 18, which can be written as 1×18, 2×9, and 3×6. Of these, only 2 and 3 are prime.

5. **C**   The circumference of a circle is equal to $2\pi r$. Since the circumference is equal to 16π, we know that $16\pi = 2\pi r$.

6. **B**   Plug in the answer choices one at a time. Is 3 a multiple of 3 and 9? No. Is 9 a multiple of 3 and 9? Yes.

7. **D**   3.096 + 2.85 = 5.946, but don't forget to round to the nearest tenth.

8. **A**   Draw a number line and find –2.4 on it. Now move to the left (less than –2.4), and find the largest integer.

9. **D** 10^2 means that you move the decimal two places to the right.

10. **D**   All sides of an equilateral triangle are equal, and the perimeters for a triangle is the sum of all sides. Therefore, 3 + 3 + 3 = 9.

11. **B**   You can either plot these points on a number line or find the difference between each and –4, –4.01 is only 0.01 away from –4.

12. **A**   One easy way to test ratios is to try either reducing or expanding each number by the same power. For instance, if we test 3.5 and 2, we get 7 and 4. Now we can see that (B) and (D) won't work. If we double again, we get 14 and 8.

13. **A**   Plug in the answers one at a time. If one of the numbers is 6, then the other must be 12, so that their sum is 18. Is their product also 72? Yes.

14. **A**   The fractional part is always the part over the whole. Since there is one teacher, but a total of 19 people, the fractional part that represents teachers is $\frac{1}{19}$.

15. **D**   Draw a number line and count the integer numbers between –5.2 and 3.4. You have –5, –4, –3, –2, –1, 0, 1, 2, and 3.

16. **C**   If a square has an area of 36, each of its sides is 6. So its perimeter is 6 + 6 + 6 + 6 = 24.

17. **C** $3^3 = 3 \times 3 \times 3 = 27$. $9^1 = 9$, so cross off (A). $9^2 = 9 \times 9 = 81$, so cross off (B). $27^1 = 27$.

18. **A** Since reciprocals are numbers that when multiplied together become 1, try multiplying together the numbers in each choice: $\dfrac{1}{3} \times \dfrac{9}{3} = 1$.

19. **A** 0.16 is the same as $\dfrac{16}{100}$, which can be reduced to $\dfrac{4}{25}$.

20. **C** We can change this expression to $2\sqrt{4 \times 2}$ and take the square root of 4 out from under the root sign.

21. **C** The formula for the area of a triangle is area $= \dfrac{(\text{base} \times \text{height})}{2}$. We know the area is 30 and the height is 10, so we can plug these values into the equation to get $30 = \dfrac{(\text{base} \times 10)}{2}$. The base must be 6.

22. **D** We can multiply 4 by 20 to get 80. This means that there must be $2 \times 20 = 40$ piano students.

23. **D** The volume of a cube with side 3 is $3 \times 3 \times 3 = 27$. The volume of a cube with side 1 is $1 \times 1 \times 1$. Therefore we can fit 27 of the smaller cubes into the larger cube.

24. **B** To make *sure* she gets a can of cola, she will have to remove all of the lemon-lime soda first. This means if on the first try she pulls out a can of lemon-lime soda, she will be certain to pull out a can of cola on the next try.

Problem Solving

25. **C** This is the same as $\dfrac{5}{\frac{1}{4}}$. To divide fractions, we flip and multiply: $5 \times \dfrac{4}{1} = 20$.

26. **A** Mary spent $8 + $12 + $2 = $22. Since she started with $30, she had $8 left at the end of the day.

27. **A** First subtract 3 from both sides of the equation, which becomes $5x = 18$. Now divide each side by 5.

28. **B** Translate this as $\dfrac{x}{100} \times 96 = 8$. Then solve for x.

29. **D** First, turn these into ordinary fractions. To solve the first fraction, multiply 5 times 7 and add two to get the numerator (37) and keep the same denominator (5). To solve the second fraction, multiply 3 times 3 and add 2 to get the numerator (11) and keep the same denominator (3). Then the problem becomes $\dfrac{37}{5} - \dfrac{11}{3}$. Now use the Bowtie to subtract them: $\dfrac{111}{15} - \dfrac{55}{15} = \dfrac{56}{15} = 3\dfrac{11}{15}$.

30. **B** If she buys 1 pack of gum every day except Saturday, that makes 6 packs of gum. If we add the 2 she buys on Saturday, we get a total of 8 packs for the week. Now we multiply by 75 cents to find out the total cost for the week.

31. **B** We can set up this problem as a ratio. If 1 mile = 2.5 inches, we want to know how many miles is shown by 12.5 inches: $\dfrac{1}{2.5} = \dfrac{x}{12.5}$. Cross-multiply, and we get 5 miles.

32. **C** First, take 30% of $80: $\dfrac{30}{100} \times 80 = 24$. So the dress will be marked down by $24. $80 − $24 = $56.

33. **A** It will be easier if we reduce before we multiply. If we cross-reduce, the problem becomes 2 × 3 = 6.

34. **B** If we subtract 4 from each side of the equation, we get $x^2 = 16$. Now try plugging in the answer choices. Which choice squared equals 16? Choice (B) does.

35. **A** To multiply decimals, multiply the numbers without decimals: 52 × 21 = 1092. Now we put back the two decimal places.

36. **D** Since her average on 4 tests was 91, her total score on those four tests must have been 4 × 91 = 364. The sum of the other three tests is 86 + 87 + 93 = 266. The last test must be 364 − 266 = 98. You can also plug in the answer choices to get the same answer.

37. **A** Translate this as $\dfrac{25}{100} \times 80 = \dfrac{10}{100} x$. Now solve for x.

38. **C** To divide fractions, flip and multiply: $\dfrac{1}{3} \div \dfrac{3}{7} = \dfrac{1}{3} \times \dfrac{7}{3} = \dfrac{7}{9}$.

39. **B** If 3 boxes contained 14 doughnuts each, that makes 3 × 14 = 42 total doughnuts. If 12 guests ate 3 doughnuts each, there were 12 × 3 = 36 doughnuts eaten. 42 − 36 = 6 doughnuts left over.

40. **C** If the airplane goes 400 miles per hour, we divide 6,000 total miles by 400 to find out how many hours it will take. This makes 15 hours to complete the trip. But the answer asks for the number of minutes! Since 1 hour = 60 minutes, we need to multiply 15 by 60 to get the number of minutes.

41. **B** Remember order of operations! First, do the parentheses (5 − 2) = 3. Then multiply 3 × 5 = 15. Now it reads 4 − 3 + 15, which equals 16.

42. **A** If Albert is 12, and he is twice as old as Bert, then Bert is 6. We also know that Bert is 7 years younger than Carl, so Carl is 13. In 8 years, then, Carl will be 21.

43. **C** Try plugging in the answer choices. Could x be 4? Does $4^4 = 16^3$? The easy way to find out is to write it out longhand: $4^4 = 4 \times 4 \times 4 \times 4$. $16^3 = 16 \times 16 \times 16$, which is the same as $4 \times 4 \times 4 \times 4 \times 4 \times 4$. Therefore, (A) can't be right. But we've made an interesting discovery. We know that $16^3 = 4 \times 4 \times 4 \times 4 \times 4 \times 4$. Therefore we need a total of six 4s on the left side of the equation. This means the answer is (C).

44. **D** We can set up a proportion: $\dfrac{2}{6} = \dfrac{x}{72}$. Cross-multiply to find that $x = 24$.

45. **C** First let's convert these to normal fractions. This gives us $\dfrac{\frac{25}{4}}{\frac{25}{2}}$. To divide these fractions, we need to flip the second one and multiply: $\dfrac{25}{4} \div \dfrac{25}{2} = \dfrac{25}{4} \times \dfrac{2}{25} = \dfrac{1}{2}$.

46. **A**   To solve for x, begin by getting the x's on one side of the equation. To do this, subtract $3x$ from each side, and get $2x + 5 = -9$. Now subtract 5 from each side, which gives us $2x = -14$. Now divide each side by 2.

47. **A**   To find out how many days she will need to save $20, we divide $\dfrac{\$20}{\$1.25}$, which gives us 16.

48. **A**   The easiest way to solve this is by plugging in the answer choices. Let's try (A). If Alex has 30 cards, and has three times as many as David, then David has 10 cards. Do their cards average 20? Yes.

49. **C**   If the perimeter of a square is 40 feet, its sides are 10 (the perimeter of a square equals four times the length of one side). To find the area, square the length (s^2) of the sides: $10^2 = 10 \times 10 = 100$ ft^2.

50. **B**   Let's try solving for x. If we add 1 to each side, we get $-5x < 10$. Now divide each side by -5. Remember that when dividing by a negative number, you have to change the direction of the inequality sign, changing the $<$ into a $>$ sign. So we get $x > -2$.

51. **B**   From 9:45 A.M. to 10:05 A.M. is 20 minutes. From 10:05 A.M. to 4:05 P.M. is 6 hours.

52. **A**   The easiest way to solve this is by plugging in the answer choices. Let's try (A) first. Could x be 1? Is the average of 3, 8, and 1 equal to the average of 7 and 1? Yes.

53. **C**   There are a total of 60 beads on the necklace, and 20 of them are red. Therefore the percentage of red beads on the necklace is $\dfrac{20}{60} = 33\%$.

54. **A**   To see how many times greater one number is than another, you divide: $\dfrac{2\frac{1}{4}}{\frac{3}{4}}$. If we change the fractions into normal fraction form, we get $\dfrac{\frac{9}{4}}{\frac{3}{4}}$. To divide, flip and multiply: $\dfrac{9}{4} \times \dfrac{4}{3} = 3$.

55. **C**   First, move the numbers to the other side of the equation by subtracting 3 from each side. This gives us $\dfrac{1}{4x} = 3$. To get the x on top, we can invert both sides of the equation, which gives us $4x = \dfrac{1}{3}$. Now divide each side by 4.

56. **C**   Since $15 is equal to 20% off the original price, we can translate: 15 is 20% of what number? $15 = \dfrac{20}{100}x$. If we solve for x, we get $x = 75$. You can also plug in the answer choices to get the same answer.

57. **A**   Add the decimals on top to get 0.32 and divide by 4, or see that the fraction could be changed to $\dfrac{4 \times 0.08}{4}$ and cancel the 4s. Divide this, and we get 0.08.

58. **B**   Let's set up a proportion: $\dfrac{2\ miles}{35\ minutes} = \dfrac{16\ miles}{x\ minutes}$. Cross-multiply to get 280 minutes, which is the same as 4 hours 40 minutes.

59. **D** If we multiply these together, we get $4\sqrt{36}$. Since $\sqrt{36} = 6$, this becomes $4 \times 6 = 24$.

60. **A** Remember order of operations. We do parentheses and exponents first, to get $-7 \times 4 - 8$. Then, we do multiplication to get $-28 - 8 = -36$.

61. **D** To see how many 35-cent weeds he needs to pull, we can divide $\dfrac{\$52.50}{.35}$. To make this easier to divide, move the decimal point two places to the right: $\dfrac{5250}{35} = 150$.

62. **C** We know that 150 students take biology, but 30 of them take physics as well. To see how many take biology without taking physics, subtract 30 from 150.

63. **B** Try plugging in the answer choices. Let's start with (A). Could x be 2? Does $2(2(2) + 2) = 16$? No. Try (B). Could x be 3? Does $2(2(3) + 2) = 16$? Yes.

64. **A** $6 = 2 \times 3$, $10 = 5 \times 2$, and $15 = 5 \times 3$. Only 3 is not the product of two distinct prime numbers. (Remember that 1 is not prime!)

Language

Usage

1. **D**

2. **A** Since "three kinds" is plural, the sentence needs to begin "There are."

3. **D**

4. **C** Items in a list should be separated by commas.

5. **C** Adjectives that refer to nationalities should be capitalized.

6. **B** When someone is speaking, a comma should be placed before the closed quotation marks, when the sentence will continue after the person is done speaking.

7. **D**

8. **B** Since the book was given to me, "me" becomes the object pronoun.

9. **B** The word *sister's* is possessive and needs an apostrophe.

10. **B** The word *it's* is not possessive and should be spelled *its*.

11. **C** Since baseball cards are countable, we use the word "number."

12. **C** The sentence begins in the past tense with the verb *saw*. It should continue in the past tense with the verb *showed*.

13. **B** The word *doctor* is not a proper name and should not be capitalized.

14. **B** The sentence begins with a direct quotation, which requires quotation marks.

15. **D**

16. **A** "Me" is in the correct form because it's an indirect object.

17. **B** We are talking about the game, so we use the adjective *brilliant*.

18. **D**

19. **B** Since we are referring to a person, we use *who*.

20. **A** "Everyone" is singular, so it needs the singular: "he or she has the right answer."

21. **C** "The birds" is plural, so it needs the plural verb *sing*.

22. **C** The sentence maintains parallel form.

23. **A** The correct idiom is *worried about*.

24. **D**

25. **D**

26. **B** To keep the comparisons in this sentence parallel, we use the past tense, "ate."

27. **B** "Greatest" is the correct superlative form.

28. **B** Since the sentence discusses tomorrow, it should use the future tense *will go*.

29. **C** The adverbial phrase "hardly ever" describes how often I drink coffee before noon.

30. **D**

31. **B** "Seen" is an invalid verb form, the sentence should read "I have seen" or "I saw."

32. **D**

33. **C** Since Ms. Walton is being compared to all the other teachers, you use the superlative form "most intelligent."

34. **D**

35. **A** "She thinks" creates correct subject/verb agreement.

36. **B** A direct question should end with a question mark.

37. **D**

38. **D**

39. **B** "Most of the people" is plural and requires the plural verb form "think."

40. **A** "Yesterday" requires the past tense "said."

Spelling

41. **C** The word *complimented* is misspelled.

42. **B** The word *desert* is misspelled.

43. **D**

44. **A** The word *decision* is misspelled.

45. **D**

46. **B** The word *sentences* is misspelled.

47. **B** The word *shining* is misspelled.

48. **B** The word *principal's* is misspelled.

49. **D**

50. **C** The word *government* is misspelled.

Composition

51. **D** (A), (B), and (C) separate "five miles" and "around the track," which should be together.

52. **C** (A), (B), and (D) are wordy and awkward.

53. **C** (A), (B), and (D) are wordy and awkward.

54. **A** The sentence we need to place introduces the idea of her working as a schoolteacher.

55. **B** The sentence we need to place introduces a contrast by saying that they are powerful animals. Therefore it should follow a sentence that implies they are not powerful.

56. **B** Since the second phrase continues the idea of the first, we need a same-direction word such as (B) or (C). Choice (C), however, is not logical in this context.

57. **D** Since the second phrase continues the idea of the first, we need a same-direction word such as (A) or (D). When a second phrase explains the first, because is the best choice. Choice (D) is your answer.

58. **C** The second phrase continues the idea of the first, so we need a same-direction word such as (B) or (C). Since the second phrase gives additional information and not an example, (C) is best.

59. **D** The rest of the paragraph is about the narrator's grandfather.

60. **B** While the rest of the paragraph is about the arrival of a family in America, sentence 3 is only about the Statue of Liberty.

Chapter 21
HSPT
Practice Test 2

Verbal Skills

1. **Diligent most nearly means**

    a. stable
    b. lost
    c. hardworking
    d. original

2. **Severe means the *opposite* of**

    a. buried
    b. informative
    c. historic
    d. mild

3. **Candle is to wax as tire is to**

    a. road
    b. car
    c. rubber
    d. tread

4. **Which word does *not* belong with the others?**

    a. spoon
    b. food
    c. knife
    d. fork

5. **Horse is to stable as chicken is to**

    a. farm
    b. coop
    c. sty
    d. rooster

6. **Which word does not belong with the others?**

    a. winter
    b. season
    c. fall
    d. summer

7. **Prohibit most nearly means**

    a. punish
    b. disallow
    c. locate
    d. paint

8. **Which word does *not* belong with the others?**

    a. shirt
    b. dress
    c. clothes
    d. shorts

9. **Famished is to hungry as arid is to**

    a. dry
    b. desert
    c. water
    d. heat

10. **Biased means the *opposite* of**

    a. original
    b. neutral
    c. merciful
    d. closed

11. **Suitcase is to clothes as briefcase is to**

   a. papers
   b. business
   c. leather
   d. handle

12. **Hinder means the *opposite* of**

   a. help
   b. gather
   c. decrease
   d. blame

13. **Content most nearly means**

   a. able to be heard
   b. satisfied
   c. precise
   d. courteous

14. **Rachel finished the test before Alice. Barry finished the test after Richard. Rachel finished the test before Richard. If the first two statements are true, the third is**

   a. True
   b. False
   c. Uncertain

15. **Container is to lid as house is to**

   a. door
   b. people
   c. roof
   d. window

16. **Credible most nearly means**

   a. edible
   b. lazy
   c. believable
   d. drinkable

17. **Sincere means the *opposite* of**

   a. final
   b. dishonest
   c. common
   d. complete

18. **Ines stood ahead of Marcus in line. Larry stood after Marcus in line. Larry stood before Ines in line. If the first two statements are true, the third is**

   a. True
   b. False
   c. Uncertain

19. **Contaminate most nearly means**

   a. infect
   b. produce
   c. learn
   d. suggest

20. **Bink had more balloons than David. David had fewer balloons than Alex and Carol. Alex had more balloons than Bink. If the first two statements are true, the third is**

   a. True
   b. False
   c. Uncertain

21. **Which word does *not* belong with the others?**

   a. sail
   b. mast
   c. rudder
   d. ship

22. **Fortunate most nearly means**

   a. proud
   b. hopeful
   c. late
   d. lucky

23. **Zoologist is to animal as botanist is to**

   a. rock
   b. plant
   c. ocean
   d. book

24. **Which word does *not* belong with the others?**

   a. fruit
   b. apple
   c. peach
   d. pear

25. **John is taller than Bart and Evelyn. Mark is taller than John. Mark is taller than Evelyn. If the first two statements are true, the third is**

   a. True
   b. False
   c. Uncertain

26. **Which word does *not* belong with the others?**

   a. water
   b. liquid
   c. oil
   d. vinegar

27. **Frank most nearly means**

   a. clean
   b. honest
   c. light
   d. annoying

28. **Famine is to food as drought is to**

   a. water
   b. sound
   c. bread
   d. room

29. **Olivia ate more apples than Jennifer. Jennifer ate fewer apples than Nancy. Nancy ate more apples than Olivia. If the first two statements are true, the third is**

   a. True
   b. False
   c. Uncertain

30. **Which word does *not* belong with the others?**

   a. tree
   b. trunk
   c. branch
   d. leaf

31. **Immune means the *opposite* of**

   a. shared
   b. complex
   c. vulnerable
   d. learned

32. **Which word does *not* belong with the others?**

    a. tea
    b. coffee
    c. water
    d. cereal

33. **Elude most nearly means**

    a. escape
    b. show
    c. remain
    d. shout

34. **Frank has seen more films than Jonathan and Nicholas. Jonathan has seen the same number of films as Manny. Manny has seen fewer films than Frank. If the first two statements are true, the third is**

    a. True
    b. False
    c. Uncertain

35. **Which word does *not* belong with the others?**

    a. sole
    b. shoe
    c. lace
    d. heel

36. **Mimic most nearly means**

    a. talk
    b. study
    c. imitate
    d. search

37. **Counterfeit means the *opposite* of**

    a. genuine
    b. amusing
    c. young
    d. loose

38. **Felix walked farther than Danielle but not as far as Kate. Amanda walked farther than Kate. Amanda walked farther than Felix. If the first two statements are true, the third is**

    a. True
    b. False
    c. Uncertain

39. **Barbaric means the *opposite* of**

    a. equal
    b. popular
    c. civilized
    d. embarrassed

40. **Which word does *not* belong with the others?**

    a. dog
    b. fish
    c. hamster
    d. pet

41. **Conventional means the *opposite* of**

    a. usual
    b. boring
    c. strange
    d. rough

42. **Inspect most nearly means**

a. practice

b. jump

c. stretch

d. examine

43. **Varied means the *opposite* of**

a. similar

b. finished

c. ironic

d. simple

44. **Which word does *not* belong with the others?**

a. milk

b. goat

c. cow

d. horse

45. **Maple is to tree as apple is to**

a. fruit

b. leaf

c. green

d. seed

46. **Diminish most nearly means**

a. announce

b. please

c. discover

d. reduce

47. **Mindy read fewer books than Mike, but more than Walter. Rochelle read fewer books than Mike. Mindy read more books than Rochelle. If the first two statements are true, the third is**

a. True

b. False

c. Uncertain

48. **Which word does *not* belong with the others?**

a. movie

b. book

c. fiction

d. play

49. **Unbiased most nearly means**

a. weak

b. neutral

c. helpful

d. realistic

50. **Criticize means the *opposite* of**

a. stare

b. praise

c. read

d. catch

51. **Which word does *not* belong with the others?**

a. mop

b. floor

c. broom

d. vacuum

52. **Bird is to wing as fish is to**

a. water

b. fin

c. salmon

d. gill

53. **Permanent most nearly means**

a. active

b. proud

c. unchanging

d. difficult

54. Sergio has more badges than Terence, but fewer than Wendy. Zack has fewer badges than Terence. Wendy has fewer badges than Zack. If the first two statements are true, the third is

a. True
b. False
c. Uncertain

55. Serene most nearly means

a. peaceful
b. tired
c. clever
d. thoughtful

56. Enlarge means the *opposite* of

a. greet
b. enjoy
c. reduce
d. expand

57. Which word does *not* belong with the others?

a. wind
b. rain
c. snow
d. coat

58. Hour is to day as month is to

a. year
b. time
c. week
d. calendar

59. Which word does *not* belong with the others?

a. brick
b. stone
c. house
d. wood

60. Authentic most nearly means

a. valuable
b. genuine
c. sharp
d. gradual

Quantitative Skills

1. What number should come next in this series: 2, 4, 8, 16, ____?

a. 18
b. 24
c. 32
d. 36

2. Examine (A), (B), and (C) to find the best answer.

(A)   (B)   (C)

a. (A) is more shaded than (B)
b. (A) is less shaded than (B) and more shaded than (C)
c. (B) and (C) are both more shaded than (a)
d. (A), (B), and (C) are equally shaded

3. What number should come next in this series: 6, 15, 24, 33, ____?

a. 42
b. 4
c. 38
d. 36

4. 25% of what number is 3 times 5?

a. 15
b. 25
c. 50
d. 60

5. What number should come next in this series: 1, 3, 9, 27, ____?

a. 24
b. 36
c. 66
d. 81

6. Examine the following and find the best answer.

1. 40% of 80
2. 50% of 64
3. 150% of 16

a. 1 is greater than 2 or 3
b. 1, 2, and 3 are equal
c. 1 is equal to 2 and larger than 3
d. 2 is less than 1 and 3

7. What number divided by 3 is $\frac{1}{4}$ of 24?

a. 18
b. 14
c. 12
d. 6

8. What number should come next in this series: 100, 99, 97, 94, ____?

    handwritten: 1 2 3

    a. 90
    b. 89
    c. 88
    d. 86

9. Examine the following to find the best answer.

    1. $\frac{1}{4}$ of 96 *handwritten: 24*
    2. 2×48 *handwritten: 96*
    3. $\frac{1}{2}$ of 192 *handwritten: 96*

    handwritten computations: 3⟌96 .25 480 1920 24.00 96 2⟌192 10

    a. 1 > 2 > 3
    b. 1 = 2 = 3
    c. 2 = 3 > 1
    d. 2 > 1 > 3

10. What number should come next in this series: 5, 8, 13, 16, 21, ____?

    handwritten: 3 5 3 5

    a. 22
    b. 23
    c. 24
    d. 26

11. Examine the following and find the best answer.

    1. 32^1 *handwritten: 32*
    2. 2^5 *handwritten: 32*
    3. 3^3 *handwritten: 27*

    a. 1 > 2 > 3
    b. 1 = 2 > 3
    c. 2 > 1 = 3
    d. 2 > 1 > 3

12. What number should come next in this series: 10, 7, 8, 5, 6 ____?

    a. 2
    b. 3
    c. 5
    d. 9

13. $\frac{4}{5}$ of what number is 10% of 40?

    a. 3
    b. 4
    c. 5
    d. 8

    handwritten: (c) circled

14. What number should come next in this series: 6, 9, 13, 16, 20, ____?

    a. 21
    b. 22
    c. 23
    d. 24

15. Examine the following and find the best answer.

    1. 0.008
    2. 0.0088
    3. 0.08

    a. 1 > 2 > 3
    b. 3 > 1 > 2
    c. 3 > 2 > 1
    d. 2 > 1 > 3

16. What number should fill in the blank in this series: 2, 6, 12, 16, 22 ____?

    a. 26
    b. 28
    c. 32
    d. 34

17. What number is $\frac{1}{4}$ of the difference between 80 and 64?

a. 4
b. 8
c. 12
d. 16

18. Examine the following and find the best answer.

1. 3(4 + 9)   39
2. 12 + 27   39
3. 34 + 9   43

a. 1 is greater than 2 and 3
b. 1 is equal to 2 and less than 3
c. 2 and 3 are equal and greater than 1
d. 1, 2, and 3 are equal

19. What number is 18 more than $\frac{1}{5}$ of 15?

a. 18
b. 21
c. 23
d. 25

20. Look at the rectangles below. Find the best answer.

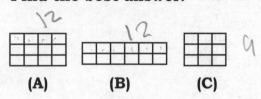

(A)   (B)   (C)

a. the perimeter of (A) < the perimeter of (B) < the perimeter of (C)
b. the perimeter of (C) < the perimeter of (A) < the perimeter of (B)
c. the perimeter of (A) < the perimeter of (C) < the perimeter of (B)
d. the perimeter of (A) = the perimeter of (C) < the perimeter of (B)

21. What number is 10% of 20% of 300?

a. 6
b. 9
c. 60
d. 90

22. What number should come next in this series: 8, 9, 16, 17, 24, 25, _____?

a. 31
b. 32
c. 33
d. 34

23. Examine the following and find the best answer.

1. 3.02×10^3 *3020* *3000*
2. 32×10^2 *3000*
3. 302×10^0 *0*

   a. 1 is greater than 2 and 3

   b. 2 is larger than 1, which is larger than 3

   c. 2 and 3 are equal and greater than 1

   d. 1, 2, and 3 are equal

24. What number leaves a remainder of 2 when divided by 7?

   a. 24

   b. 51

   c. 60

   d. 64

25. The figure below is a circle with center O. Find the best answer.

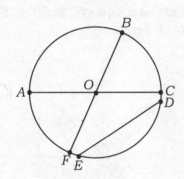

   a. *AC* is equal to *FB* and larger than *ED*

   b. *AC* is larger than *FB* and *ED*

   c. *AC* is equal to *FB* and smaller than *ED*

   d. *AC*, *FB*, and *ED* are equal

26. What number should fill the blank in this series: 1, 7, 3, 21, ____, 35?

$\times 6 \quad -4 \quad +18$

   a. 4

   b. 5

   c. 7

   d. 28

27. Look at the rectangle below. Find the best answer.

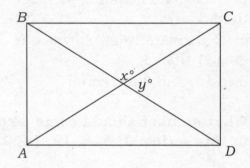

   a. $x < y < 90°$

   b. $x > 90° > y$

   c. $x + y = 90°$

   d. $90° > x > y$

28. Examine the following and find the best answer.

1. $\dfrac{7}{100} + \dfrac{6}{10} + 3$ $3\dfrac{67}{100}$

2. $\dfrac{3}{100} + \dfrac{7}{10} + 6$ $6\dfrac{73}{100}$

3. $\dfrac{6}{100} + \dfrac{3}{10} + 7$ $7\dfrac{36}{100}$

    a. 1 is greater than 2 and 3

    b. 1 is greater than 2 and less than 3

    c. 3 is greater than 2, which is greater than 1

    d. 1, 2, and 3 are equal

29. What number should come next in this series: 2, 4, 6, 12, 14, 28, ____?

    a. 30

    b. 32

    c. 48

    d. 56

30. What number is 9 times more than 20% of 60?

    a. 21

    b. 63

    c. 108

    d. 180

31. What number should fill the blank in this series: 9, 7, 5, 9, 7, ____, 9?

    a. 5

    b. 7

    c. 9

    d. 11

32. What is 17 more than twice the difference between 15 and 17?

    a. 19

    b. 20

    c. 21

    d. 22

33. What number should come next in this series: 9, 20, 31, 42, ____?

    a. 52

    b. 53

    c. 61

    d. 84

34. Look at the square below. Find the best answer.

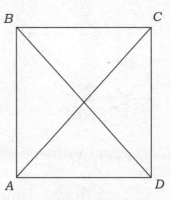

    a. $AC = BC > AD$

    b. $AC > AB > BD$

    c. $AC > AB = BC$

    d. $AC = BD = BC$

35. What number should come next in this series: 7, 14, 13, 26, 25, ___?

a. 32
b. 37
c. 42
d. 50

36. The sum of 8 and what number is equal to $\frac{1}{11}$ of 121?

a. 2
b. 3
c. 5
d. 7

(handwritten: 11 | 121, 11, 11/11)

37. Examine the following and find the best answer.

1. the perimeter of a square with side 4 *(handwritten: 16)*
2. the area of a square with side 4 *(handwritten: 16)*
3. the area of half of a square with side 8 *(handwritten: 32)*

a. 2 > 1 > 3
b. 3 > 1 > 2
c. 3 > 2 = 1
d. 2 = 3 > 1

38. What number should fill the blank in this series: 2, 4, 6, 4, 6, 8, ___, 8, 10?

a. 2
b. 4
c. 6
d. 10

39. Examine the figure below and find the best answer.

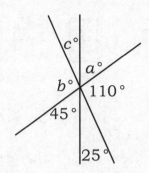

a. $b > a > c$
b. $c > a > b$
c. $c > b > a$
d. $b > c > a$

40. What is the difference between 23 and the average of 42, 45, and 39?

a. 17
b. 19
c. 21
d. 23

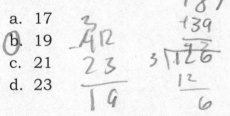

41. What number is $\frac{1}{4}$ the product of 8 and 18?

a. 6
b. 12
c. 18
d. 36

(handwritten: 6, 18, 8, 2)144, .25, 720, 2880, 3600)

42. **Examine (A), (B), and (C) and find the best answer.**

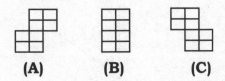

    (A)   (B)   (C)

   a. the area of (A) > the area of (B) = the area of (C)

   b. the area of (B) > the area of (C) = the area of (A)

   c. the area of (C) < the area of (A) = the area of (B)

   d. the area of (A) = the area of (B) = the area of (C)

43. **What number should come next in this series: 88, 85, 83, 80, 78, ____?**

   a. 77
   b. 76
   c. 75
   d. 74

44. **Examine the following and find the best answer.**

   1. −(8 − 10) 2
   2. 8 − 10 -2
   3. −8 − 10 -18

   a. 1 is bigger than 2, which is bigger than 3
   b. 2 is bigger than 3, which is bigger than 1
   c. 1 and 2 are equal and bigger than 3
   d. 1 and 3 are equal and bigger than 2

45. **What number should fill the blank in this series: 49, 7, 81, ____, 121, 11?**

   a. 8
   b. 9
   c. 10
   d. 79

46. **What number is 50% greater than the product of 6 and 3?**

   a. 9
   b. 14
   c. 18
   d. 27

47. **What is the difference between 10% of 50 and 20% of 100?**

   a. 5
   b. 10
   c. 15
   d. 20

   5 + 20

48. **What number should fill the blank in this series: 6, 8, 7, 9, ____, 10, 9, 11?**

   a. 7
   b. 8
   c. 9
   d. 11

49. What is 4 less than $\frac{5}{3}$ of 9?

    a. 5
    b. 9
    c. 11
    d. 13

50. What number is 18 more than half the sum of 4, 9, and 11?

    a. 12
    b. 20
    c. 30
    d. 34

51. What number is 2 more than the average of 10, 15, and 8?

    a. 9
    b. 11
    c. 13
    d. 15

52. What number should come next in this series: 41, 11, 52, 22, 63, ____?

    a. 27
    b. 33
    c. 37
    d. 44

Reading

Questions 1–62, 25 minutes

Questions 1–8 refer to the following passage.

Passage 1 - Reminiscence on the River

This was our last watch fire of the year, and there were reasons why I should remember it better than any of the others. Next week the other boys were to file back to their old places in Sandtown High School, but I was to go up to the divide to teach my first country school in the Norwegian district. I was already homesick at the thought of <u>quitting</u> the boys with whom I had always played, of leaving the river and going up into a windy plain that was all windmills and cornfields and big pastures, where there was nothing willful or unmanageable in the landscape, no new island, and no chance of unfamiliar birds—such as often followed the watercourses.

Other boys came and went and used the river for fishing or skating, but we six were sworn to the spirit of the stream, and we were friends mainly because of the river. There were the two Hassler boys. Fritz and Otto, sons of the little German tailor. They were the youngest of us—ragged boys of ten and twelve, with sunburned hair, weather-strained faces, and pale blue eyes. Otto, the elder, was the best mathematician in school and clever at his books, but he always dropped out in the spring term as if the river could not get on without him. He and Fritz caught the fat, horned catfish and sold them about the town, and they lived so much in the water that they were as brown and sandy as the river itself.

There was Percy Pound, a fat, freckled boy with chubby cheeks, who took half a dozen 'boys' storypapers and was always being kept in for reading detective stories behind his desk. There was Tip Smith, destined by his freckles and red hair to be the buffoon in all our games, though he walked like a timid little old man and had a funny, cracked laugh. Tip worked hard at his father's grocery store every afternoon, and swept it out before school in the morning.

1. **The word <u>quitting</u>, as used in the passage, most nearly means**
   a. leaving
   b. cheating
   c. playing with
   d. feeding

2. **According to the story, the narrator belonged to a group that gathered**
   a. in the narrator's backyard
   b. in the gym after school
   c. near the river
   d. at Percy Pound's house

3. **It can be inferred from the passage that the narrator is**
   a. younger than 10 years old
   b. between 10 and 20 years old
   c. between 20 and 30 years old
   d. more than 30 years old

4. **This story mostly describes**
   a. the narrator's friends
   b. the narrator's teachers
   c. Otto Hassler
   d. the parents of the students at Sandtown High

5. **Why will the narrator remember this watch fire better than others?**
   a. It is the narrator's birthday.
   b. The narrator is going away soon.
   c. The narrator has just been born.
   d. The narrator has recently gotten a new job.

6. **It can be inferred from the passage that the narrator has recently become**
   a. a parent
   b. a police officer
   c. a teacher
   d. a journalist

7. **According to the passage, who caught and sold catfish?**

   a. Otto and Tip
   b. Otto and Fritz
   c. Fritz and the narrator
   d. Fritz and Percy

8. **Tip's father was**

   a. a tailor
   b. a grocer
   c. a teacher
   d. a fish merchant

Questions 9–17 refer to the following passage.

Passage 2 - Illuminating the Electric Eel

The electric eel is one of the most curious animals on the planet. It is found in the marshes of the Amazon Basin, and can grow up to almost eight feet in length— as long as some crocodiles. As the name implies, the electric eel has the ability to generate a strong electric field.

The electric eel uses this special ability in several ways. Mild electrical impulses can help the eel to sense different objects around it and to navigate the waters in which it lives. The eel can send out mild electrical signals, in much the same way as a bat uses sound waves, in order to find its way around.

When it comes time to feed, the eel relies on its electrical system for hunting. Because small animals have a different electrical "signature" than do plants or rocks, the electric eel effectively has a kind of radar that allows it to find fish. When the eel finds its prey, it delivers a strong electric current that can instantly kill smaller animals such as fish. The force of the charge is often strong enough to kill or stun even larger animals. A human could survive one or two shocks, but would probably not survive several. Eels, however, do not hunt humans and will only shock a human in self-defense.

How does the eel avoid hurting itself? The eel has evolved with a kind of insulation that protects its nervous system. This insulation acts as a buffer against the electricity that it generates.

There may be one more way in which the electric eel uses electricity. Some scientists believe that eels can communicate among themselves using electrical signals akin to the clicks and whistles of other animals such as dolphins. As this point, however, this theory has not yet been proven.

9. **The word <u>generate</u>, as used in the passage, most nearly means**

    a. examine
    b. create
    c. protect
    d. catch

10. **The author of the passage is probably**

    a. a marine biologist
    b. an electrician
    c. a history teacher
    d. a fisherman

11. **The word <u>current</u>, as used in the passage, most nearly means**

    a. modern
    b. charge
    c. vision
    d. river

12. **Which of the following can be inferred from the passage?**

    a. Bats use electricity to help them see in the dark.
    b. Electric eels are more like crocodiles than like fish.
    c. Without electricity, electric eels would have a hard time feeding.
    d. Electric eels kill many people each year.

13. **The word <u>buffer</u>, as used in the passage, most nearly means**

    a. cleaner
    b. protection
    c. poison
    d. source

14. **Which of the following does the author probably believe?**

    a. Electric eels are the most dangerous creatures on earth.
    b. Electric eels have as many teeth as do crocodiles.
    c. We are not yet certain whether electric eels use electricity to communicate.
    d. Bats can also generate electric fields.

15. **The author uses each of the following animals to help describe the electric eel except**

    a. the bat
    b. the dolphin
    c. the crocodile
    d. the horse

16. **It can be inferred from the passage that the electricity is dangerous because it**

    a. damages the nervous system
    b. interferes with breathing
    c. deprives animals of food
    d. causes animals to bleed

17. **You could probably find this article in**

    a. a dictionary
    b. a guide to an aquarium
    c. a chemistry textbook
    d. a photography magazine

Questions 18–24 refer to the following passage.

Passage 3 - Pavlov and His Reaction

Ivan Pavlov was a Russian physiologist born in 1849. Instead of becoming a doctor, he chose to work in a medical laboratory, where he worked on the function of the nervous system. It is said that his salary was so meager that he and his family had to live in an unheated apartment in St. Petersburg. Nonetheless, Pavlov was so dedicated to his work that he remained at the laboratory almost all his life.

Pavlov was best known for his research on conditioned reflexes. While some reflexes are innate, such as the knee-jerk response when a doctor strikes with a mallet just below the kneecap, Pavlov showed that other reflexes can be acquired through experience or training. To demonstrate this, Pavlov performed a series of experiments on dogs. For several days in a row, one of Pavlov's assistants rang a bell just before feeding his dogs. The dogs learned to associate the bell with food. Pavlov discovered that afterward, when he rang the bell, the dogs would begin to salivate in anticipation of a meal. Pavlov argued that humans, just like dogs, have many conditioned reflexes.

Following Pavlov's idea, a school of psychology called behaviorism arose. Behaviorists such as B. F. Skinner believe that almost all animal (including human) behavior could be explained in terms of conditioning. Though behaviorism cannot plausibly explain all of human behavior, it has deepened our understanding of the way in which we react to events in the world. For his work, Pavlov received the Nobel Prize in 1904.

18. **The word <u>meager</u>, as used in the passage, most nearly means**
    a. funny
    b. small
    c. late
    d. critical

19. **It can be inferred from Pavlov's experiment that conditioned reflexes**
    a. can only be learned when hungry
    b. depend on repeated experiences
    c. can be found mostly in dogs
    d. are stronger than innate reflexes

20. **According to the passage, the knee-jerk response is**
    a. conditioned
    b. innate
    c. partially conditioned and partially innate
    d. neither conditioned nor innate

21. **The word <u>innate</u>, as used in the passage, most nearly means**
    a. violent
    b. inborn
    c. puzzling
    d. large

22. **The author mentions B. F. Skinner as someone who**
    a. disagreed with Pavlov's findings
    b. gave Pavlov the Nobel Prize
    c. believed in Pavlov's work and continued it
    d. was one of Pavlov's students

23. **According to what the author says in the passage, the author would probably agree that behaviorism**

    a. can explain all of human behavior

    b. is an interesting but limited way of explaining behavior

    c. was criticized by Pavlov

    d. was wrong and should be forgotten about

24. **The word <u>conditioned</u>, as used in the passage, most nearly means**

    a. electrical

    b. unknown

    c. mild

    d. learned

Questions 25–29 refer to the following passage.

Passage 4 - Cousin Fanny

She was extraordinarily <u>credulous</u>—would believe anything on earth anyone told her—because, although she had plenty of humor, she herself never would deviate from the absolute truth a moment, even in jest. I do not think she would have told an untruth to save her life. Well, of course we used to play on her to tease her. Frank would tell her the most unbelievable and impossible lies such as that he thought he saw a mouse yesterday on the back of the sofa she was lying on (this would make her bounce up like a ball), or that he believed he heard—he was not sure—that Mr. Scroggs (the man who had rented her old home) had cut down all the old trees in the yard and pulled down the house because he wanted the bricks to make brick ovens. This would worry her excessively (she loved every brick in the old house, and often said she would rather live in the kitchen there than in a palace anywhere else), and she would get into such a state of depression that Frank would finally have to tell her that he was just "fooling" her.

She used to make him do a good deal of waiting on her in return, and he was the one she used to get to dress old Fashion's back when it was raw and to put drops in her eyes. He got quite expert at it. She said it was a penalty for his worrying her so.

She was a great musician of the connection. This is in itself no mean praise, for it was the fashion for every musical gift among the girls to be <u>cultivated</u> and every girl played or sang more or less, some of them very well. But cousin Fanny was not only this. She had a way of playing that used to make the old piano sound different from itself, and her voice was almost the sweetest I ever heard except one or two on the stage.

25. **We can infer from the passage that the reason Fanny would "bounce up like a ball" is that**

    a. she is very energetic
    b. she is afraid of mice
    c. she likes to play games
    d. her couch had very powerful springs

26. **The word <u>credulous</u>, as used in the passage, most nearly means**

    a. dependable
    b. trusting
    c. intelligent
    d. lazy

27. **According to the passage, Fanny's musical talents include**

    a. the piano and the violin
    b. her voice and the piano
    c. the violin and the flute
    d. her voice and the violin

28. **The word <u>cultivated</u>, as used in the passage, most nearly means**

    a. beautiful
    b. planted
    c. encouraged
    d. lonely

29. **Which of the following can be inferred from the passage?**

    a. Fanny lived in a palace.
    b. Mr. Scroggs's first name is Frank.
    c. Frank liked to tease Fanny.
    d. Fanny was often worried about her children.

Questions 30–35 refer to the following passage.

Passage 5 - Life of Caesar

Julius Caesar was perhaps the most important politician's leader of all time. It was his military and political genius that created the Roman Empire, a civilization so large and powerful that no other Western government could be considered its equal until the 1700s. Caesar's historical influence was so great that the German and Russian words for emperor (Kaiser and Czar) are derived from his name.

Caesar belonged to a family of many senators and other politicians. In spite of this, Caesar did not simply act in the interest of his family. Early in his life, Caesar not only championed the Roman people but also fought against abuse and corruption in the senate.

For ten years, between 58 and 49 B.C.E., Caesar led a series of <u>campaigns</u> known as the Gallic Wars. His armies conquered the Gauls in France, and he marched as far north as England. Thanks to Caesar's military skill, almost all of Europe was under Roman control. These battles showed Caesar to be one of the greatest military strategists of all time.

Around 50 B.C.E., Caesar's popularity and strength began to frighten Pompey, who used to be his friend and colleague. Pompey tried to convince the senate to disband Caesar's army. In response, Caesar marched his army into Rome, defeated Pompey, and declared himself dictator.

Caesar was famously killed on the Ides of March (March 15) by a band of conspirators including Brutus, whom Caesar had considered a friend.

30. **The author gives us the German and Russian words for emperor to demonstrate**
    a. the similarities between the German and Russian languages
    b. how words can change over time
    c. the importance of Julius Caesar in Western history
    d. that Julius Caesar spoke German and Russian

31. **The author would probably agree that the Roman Empire**
    a. was one of the most powerful civilizations of the ancient world
    b. was not as important as modern historians think it is
    c. ended in the 1700s
    d. was led by Pompey

32. **It is somewhat surprising that Caesar was a champion of the people because he**

    a. did not like the Roman people

    b. was too busy fighting

    c. came from a family of senators and politicians

    d. was not a very nice person

33. **The word <u>campaigns</u>, as used in the passage, most nearly means**

    a. wars

    b. stories

    c. studies

    d. games

34. **According to the passage, Pompey became afraid of Caesar because Caesar**

    a. had a famous father

    b. was rich

    c. was powerful and popular

    d. had a very big army

35. **Which of the following is true based on the passage?**

    a. Caesar fought Pompey in the Gallic Wars.

    b. The Gallic Wars took place in 58 to 49 B.C.E.

    c. Caesar never left the city of Rome.

    d. Caesar died in the month of May.

Questions 36–40 refer to the following passage.

Passage 6 - A Short History of Mary Shelley

Mary Shelley was born in 1797. Her parents, Mary Wollstonecraft and William Godwin, were both writers; Wollstonecraft's *A Vindication of the Rights of Woman* made her one of the most important early feminist thinkers. Shelley was surrounded as a child by some of the greatest literary figures of her day, including Samuel Coleridge and Charles Lamb. Her parents introduced her to these people because they believed that every child had the potential to develop a great intellect.

Shelley wrote her best-known work, *Frankenstein,* at the age of 19. She wrote it while staying at Lake Geneva with a group of young poets that included Lord Byron and Percy Shelley, whom she would later marry.

Frankenstein is not merely a horror story, but a brillant work of art. The dark, gloomy imagery in *Frankenstein* was probably in part a reflection of the <u>calamities</u> taking place in Mary Shelley's life, which included several suicides in her extended family. Certain feminist ideas inherited from her mother are also included, as is a romantic mistrust of modern technology.

Shelley's bad luck continued. Her first child died shortly after birth. Later, Percy drowned when Mary was just 24 years old. She continued to write and lived among other artists and literary figures for the rest of her life.

36. With which of the following would the author probably agree?

   a. Mary Shelley was too young to be a writer.

   b. Mary Shelley was the best writer of the nineteenth century.

   c. Frankenstein is one of the great works of modern literature.

   d. Shelley would never have written Frankenstein had it not been for Coleridge.

37. According to the passage, which one of the following influenced the way Shelley wrote *Frankenstein*?

   a. the birth of her first child

   b. her mother's feminist ideas

   c. the works of Samuel Coleridge

   d. a bad dream she had as a child

38. What is this passage mostly about?

   a. the relationship between Mary Shelley and Lord Byron

   b. a gathering of poets at Lake Geneva

   c. Mary Shelley's life and work

   d. why Frankenstein is so scary

39. In approximately what year did Shelley write *Frankenstein*?

   a. 1805

   b. 1811

   c. 1816

   d. 1820

40. The world <u>calamities</u>, as used in the passage, most nearly means

   a. feelings

   b. tragedies

   c. suggestions

   d. questions

Vocabulary

41. Choose the best definition of the underlined word.

an important <u>era</u>

a. place
b. time
c. story
d. person

42. Choose the best definition of the underlined word.

a <u>concise</u> explanation

a. pleasant
b. famous
c. short
d. proud

43. Choose the best definition of the underlined word.

to show great <u>compassion</u>

a. strength
b. interest
c. dislike
d. sympathy

44. Choose the best definition of the underlined word.

a dangerous <u>felon</u>

a. criminal
b. sport
c. vacation
d. shark

45. Choose the best definition of the underlined word.

a <u>mythical</u> creature

a. farm
b. surprising
c. imaginary
d. muscular

46. Choose the best definition of the underlined word.

a <u>weary</u> traveler

a. busy
b. difficult
c. famous
d. tired

47. **Choose the best definition of the underlined word.**

    an <u>unorthodox</u> approach

    a. happy
    b. violent
    c. unusual
    d. marvelous

48. **Choose the best definition of the underlined word.**

    to <u>conceal</u> the truth

    a. sing
    b. study
    c. hide
    d. display

49. **Choose the best definition of the underlined word.**

    to <u>tremble</u> with joy

    a. shake
    b. skip
    c. sit
    d. pounce

50. **Choose the best definition of the underlined word.**

    a dangerous <u>epidemic</u>

    a. idea
    b. flight
    c. disease
    d. package

51. **Choose the best definition of the underlined word.**

    a museum <u>exhibition</u>

    a. visitor
    b. display
    c. building
    d. box

52. **Choose the best definition of the underlined word.**

    to <u>reinforce</u> a building

    a. decorate
    b. examine
    c. strengthen
    d. project

53. **Choose the best definition of the underlined word.**

    a <u>crucial</u> part

    a. important
    b. difficult
    c. magnetic
    d. wasted

54. **Choose the best definition of the underlined word.**

    a <u>tedious</u> speech

    a. loud
    b. boring
    c. received
    d. sparse

55. Choose the best definition of the underlined word.

to **endorse** a candidate

a. write
b. criticize
c. plead
d. support

56. Choose the best definition of the underlined word.

the **arduous** task

a. school
b. finished
c. difficult
d. adult

57. Choose the best definition of the underlined word.

a **qualified** person

a. sick
b. capable
c. interesting
d. older

58. Choose the best definition of the underlined word.

to **decline** an invitation

a. refuse
b. send
c. paint
d. dream

59. Choose the best definition of the underlined word.

a **potent** chemical

a. strong
b. common
c. illegal
d. mixed

60. Choose the best definition of the underlined word.

to **perturb** someone

a. please
b. bother
c. introduce
d. hire

61. Choose the best definition of the underlined word.

rapid **respiration**

a. running
b. selling
c. breathing
d. change

62. Choose the best definition of the underlined word.

a moving **oration**

a. injury
b. decision
c. meal
d. speech

Mathematics

Questions 1-64, 45 Minutes

Mathematical Concepts

1. Which of the following is greatest?

   a. 0.1042
   b. 0.1105
   c. 0.0288
   d. 0.0931

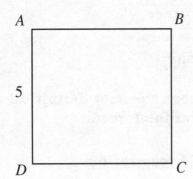

2. What is the area of the square *ABCD*?

   a. 5
   b. 20
   c. 25
   d. 50

3. What is the least positive integer divisible by 3, 4, and 5?

   a. 30
   b. 40
   c. 50
   d. 60

4. The decimal representation of $5 + 60 + \dfrac{5}{100}$ is

   a. 65.05
   b. 65.5
   c. 56.05
   d. 56.5

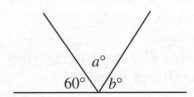

5. What is the sum of *a* + *b*?

   a. 60°
   b. 100°
   c. 120°
   d. 160°

6. The product of 0.28 and 100 is approximately

   a. 0.3
   b. 2.8
   c. 2
   d. 30

7. What is the greatest prime factor of 45?

    a. 2
    b. 3
    c. 5
    d. 9

8. A store normally sells a certain dress for $160. During a special sale, the store reduces the price of the dress to $120. By what percent is the price of the dress reduced for the sale?

    a. 20%
    b. 25%
    c. 30%
    d. 40%

9. $10^3 \times 10^5 =$

    a. 10^8
    b. 10^{15}
    c. 100^8
    d. 100^{15}

10. All of the following are multiples of 8 except

    a. 24
    b. 96
    c. 178
    d. 192

11. What is the volume of a box with length 6, width 8, and height $\frac{1}{2}$?

    a. 96
    b. 48
    c. 24
    d. $14\frac{1}{2}$

12. If the ratio of boys to girls in a class is 3:4 and there are 124 girls in the class, how many boys are there in the class?

    a. 33
    b. 93
    c. 103
    d. 109

13. $(4^2)^3 =$

    a. 4^5
    b. 4^6
    c. 5^4
    d. 3^{16}

14. In the number 365, the product of the digits is how much greater than the sum of the digits?

    a. 76
    b. 54
    c. 36
    d. 14

15. What is 2,847 rounded to the nearest tenth?

 a. 2.84

 b. 2.9

 c. 2.8

 d. 2.85

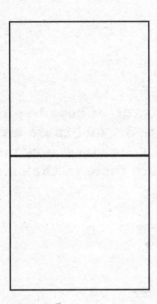

16. Each of the squares in the figure above has an area of 16. What is the perimeter of the figure?

 a. 16

 b. 24

 c. 28

 d. 32

17. If one of the angles inside a triangle measures 85 degrees, what could the other two angles measure?

 a. 45° and 55°

 b. 45° and 50°

 c. 35° and 50°

 d. 50° and 60°

18. $\sqrt{2^2}$

 a. 1

 b. 2

 c. 4

 d. 16

19. Juan has 5 blue marbles, 9 green marbles, and 3 red marbles. What fractional part of his marbles is blue?

 a. $\frac{5}{9}$

 b. $\frac{5}{17}$

 c. $\frac{17}{5}$

 d. $\frac{9}{5}$

20. Which of the following is true?

 a. $2\sqrt{2} + 3\sqrt{3} = 5\sqrt{5}$

 b. $2\sqrt{2} \times 3\sqrt{3} = 5\sqrt{5}$

 c. $2\sqrt{2} + 3\sqrt{2} = 5\sqrt{2}$

 d. $2\sqrt{2} \times 3\sqrt{2} = 6\sqrt{2}$

21. What is the smallest common multiple of 6 and 4?

 a. 4

 b. 6

 c. 12

 d. 24

22. Which of the following leaves a remainder of 4 when divided by 6?

 a. 18

 b. 22

 c. 26

 d. 32

23. If you multiply a negative even number by a positive odd number, the result will be
    a. negative and even
    b. negative and odd
    c. positive and even
    d. positive and odd

24. How many prime numbers are there between 0 and 10?
    a. 3
    b. 4
    c. 5
    d. 6

Problem Solving

25. $\dfrac{5}{15} + \dfrac{6}{13} =$
    a. $\dfrac{11}{28}$
    b. $\dfrac{31}{39}$
    c. $\dfrac{6}{39}$
    d. $\dfrac{13}{15}$

26. Maxine scored 42, 45, and 46 on her first three history tests. What score would she need on her fourth test to raise her average to 48?
    a. 50
    b. 55
    c. 59
    d. 62

27. 20% of 40% of 500 is
    a. 20
    b. 30
    c. 40
    d. 60

28. $6 - 3(2 - 4) + 5 =$
    a. 9
    b. 11
    c. 17
    d. 19

29. $\dfrac{20}{.02} =$
    a. 0.1
    b. 10
    c. 100
    d. 1,000

30. The price of a $25 comic book is decreased by 5%. What is the new price of the comic book?
    a. $23.75
    b. $22.75
    c. $20.25
    d. $20.00

31. On a certain map, 8 miles is represented by 1 inch. If two cities are 3.5 inches apart on the map, what is the distance between these two cities?
    a. 8 miles
    b. 16 miles
    c. 24 miles
    d. 28 miles

32. Which of the following is equal to 0.24?

    a. $\dfrac{12}{5}$

    b. $\dfrac{24}{10}$

    c. $\dfrac{12}{50}$

    d. $\dfrac{4}{10}$

33. Alice's Emporium discounts the price of a shirt by 20%, and then discounts it again by an additional 10%. The final price represents what percent decrease from the original price of the shirt?

    a. 15%

    b. 18%

    c. 28%

    d. 30%

34. Two positive integers have a ratio of 6:9. If the smaller of the two numbers is 18, what is the average of the two numbers?

    a. 15

    b. 22.5

    c. 24

    d. 27

35. $11 + 5 \times 6 \div 3 - (2 - 5) =$

    a. 47

    b. 41

    c. 96

    d. 102

36. A swimming pool has dimensions 4 feet by 10 feet by 12 feet. If the pool can be filled at a rate of 8 cubic feet per minute, how many minutes will it take to fill the pool?

    a. 20

    b. 24

    c. 48

    d. 60

37. At Joe's Burger Shop, two hamburgers and an order of french fries cost $3.55. If three hamburgers cost $4.05, what is the price of an order of french fries?

    a. $0.50

    b. $0.65

    c. $0.85

    d. $1.15

38. In a certain classroom, the ratio of boys to girls is 3:5. If there are 32 students in the class, how many girls are in the class?

    a. 12

    b. 14

    c. 16

    d. 20

39. The area of a circle with radius 8 is how much greater than its circumference?

    a. 8π

    b. 16π

    c. 24π

    d. 48π

40. $4^4 =$
   a. 16^2
   b. 31^1
   c. 32^2
   d. 64^2

41. If two-thirds of the 660 students at Middleburg Junior High attend the school dance, how many students do not atttend?
   a. 220
   b. 240
   c. 400
   d. 440

42. Which of the following is equal to $2\sqrt{2} \times 3\sqrt{2}$?
   a. 24
   b. $5\sqrt{2}$
   c. $6\sqrt{2}$
   d. 12

43. $18 + \dfrac{3}{4} + \dfrac{3}{6} + \dfrac{1}{4} =$
   a. 19
   b. $19\dfrac{1}{2}$
   c. 20
   d. $20\dfrac{1}{6}$

44. If $3x + 5 = 23$, then $x =$
   a. 3
   b. 4
   c. 5
   d. 6

45. $\dfrac{1}{2} \div \dfrac{1}{10} =$
   a. 5
   b. $\dfrac{1}{5}$
   c. $\dfrac{1}{20}$
   d. 20

46. If $zy + 18 = 36$, and $x = 2$, then $y =$
   a. 6
   b. 7
   c. 8
   d. 9

47. What is the area of a rectangle with length 15 feet and width 24 feet?
   a. 240 ft^2
   b. 280 ft^2
   c. 320 ft^2
   d. 360 ft^2

48. $\left(7 \times \dfrac{1}{100}\right) + \left(2 \times \dfrac{1}{10}\right) + \left(6 \times \dfrac{1}{1000}\right) + 4 =$
   a. 4.267
   b. 4.276
   c. 4.726
   d. 5.627

49. A pound of onions costs $3.25 at the supermarket. What is the maximum number of pounds of onions that Larry can buy with $13?
   a. 4
   b. 5
   c. 6
   d. 7

50. $5.5 \div 0.2 =$

    a. 11

    b. 13.5

    c. 23.5

    d. 27.5

51. Four years ago, Alex was half as old as he is now. How old is Alex now?

    a. 4

    b. 5

    c. 6

    d. 8

52. $5\frac{1}{2} \times 2\frac{1}{3} =$

    a. $10\frac{1}{6}$

    b. $12\frac{5}{6}$

    c. $7\frac{1}{5}$

    d. $5\frac{1}{3}$

53. If one gallon of paint can cover $2\frac{1}{2}$ square feet, how many gallons of paint will be needed to cover a rectangular wall that measures 20 feet by 12 feet?

    a. 48

    b. 64

    c. 72

    d. 96

54. If $2x^2 + y = 55$ and $y = 5$, what could x be?

    a. 3

    b. 5

    c. 6

    d. 7

55. $4\sqrt{18} \times 3\sqrt{2} =$

    a. 72

    b. $12\sqrt{18}$

    c. $4\sqrt{32}$

    d. 36

56. How many seconds are there in 4 hours?

    a. 240

    b. 2,400

    c. 3,600

    d. 14,400

57. In a group of 100 children, there are 24 more girls than boys. How many girls are in the group?

    a. 62

    b. 50

    c. 38

    d. 24

58. If $-4x - 3 < x + 2$, what is the range of possible values of x?

    a. $x < -1$

    b. $x < 1$

    c. $x > -1$

    d. $x > 1$

59. How many multiples of 5 and 6 are there between 1 and 100?

a. 3
b. 5
c. 7
d. 9

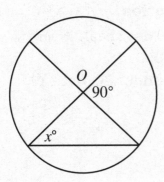

60. The figure above is a circle with center *O*. What is the value of *x*?

a. 30°
b. 45°
c. 60°
d. 90°

61. Emil can shape two cookies every minute. How long will it take him to shape 150 cookies?

a. 1 hour 15 minutes
b. 1 hour 25 minutes
c. 3 hours 15 minutes
d. 5 hours

62. Carl is twice as old as his brother Jim, who is five years older than Liz. If Carl is 15 years older than Liz, how old is Jim?

a. 20
b. 15
c. 10
d. 8

63. The diameter of a circle with a circumference of 8π is

a. 2
b. 8
c. 16
d. 64

64. Alex buys a gallon of soda for $8.50, and wants to split the cost among 5 people. How much will each person pay?

a. $1.70
b. $1.65
c. $1.50
d. $0.65

Language

Questions 1–60, 25 minutes

For questions 1–40, check the sentences for errors of usage, capitalization, or punctuation. If there is no error, choose (D).

1. **Choose the sentence with the correct capitalization.**

   a. David studied French for many years but could not speak it very well.
   b. Ophelia was a great singer as well as a gifted poet.
   c. Some of the world's greatest chess players are under 30 years old.
   d. No mistake

2. **Choose the sentence with the correct grammar.**

   a. If I had a telescope, I will be able to see that planet.
   b. Steve ran very quickly around the track.
   c. We are all going to sing a songs after dinner.
   d. No mistake

3. **Choose the sentence with the correct punctuation.**

   a. The first typewriters were huge machines, that were difficult to operate.
   b. I went home to help clean my parent's room.
   c. We followed the river for three mile's before eating lunch.
   d. No mistake

4. **Choose the sentence with the correct grammar.**

   a. My uncle lived in houston while he was in college.
   b. Belgium was neutral for years, but then it decided to join the war.
   c. There are few things more enjoyable than a walk through the Park.
   d. No mistake

5. **Choose the sentence with the correct capitalization.**

   a. Last year we spent our vacation near Lake Michigan.
   b. Alicia's Teacher is very well educated.
   c. How many times have you seen Martin's Father?
   d. No mistake

6. **Choose the sentence with the correct grammar.**

    a. We were all so scared that nobody said a word.

    b. "I don't know how you can eat that," said Ms. Carroll.

    c. Each of us has at least three hundred baseball cards.

    d. No mistake

7. **Choose the sentence with the correct capitalization.**

    a. My Mother found a cat behind the grocery store.

    b. I broke my arm on New Year's Eve.

    c. How many times have you been to the Coast of California?

    d. No mistake

8. **Choose the sentence with the correct grammar.**

    a. Mary was an imaginative child who reads many books.

    b. My teacher asked me if I knew whose backpack was left on the bus.

    c. Cathryn spent her summer working with chimpanzees.

    d. No mistake

9. **Choose the sentence with the correct punctuation.**

    a. Jane sat at the front of the boat; and tried to catch a fish.

    b. My brother, and I are going fishing this weekend.

    c. Many great battles of the American Revolution took place around Boston, Massachusetts.

    d. No mistake

10. **Choose the sentence with the correct capitalization.**

    a. The Blueberries in Kai's backyard are always delicious.

    b. I have never seen so many People at once.

    c. My book report is due on Monday.

    d. No mistake

11. **Choose the sentence with the correct grammar.**

    a. The eruption of a volcano is a violent and frightening event.

    b. Since the end of the school year, I have had little to do.

    c. Do you think I should bring flowers to the party?

    d. No mistake

12. Choose the sentence with the correct punctuation.

 a. Nitrogen and oxygen, are the most common gases in our atmosphere.

 b. The book was so popular, that the author became famous.

 c. Sally asked, "Have you seen the new park?"

 d. No mistake

13. Choose the sentence with the correct punctuation.

 a. Annie's letter was dated Saturday, July 5.

 b. We were very impressed, by his playing.

 c. Manny's brother left for college, last week.

 d. No mistake

14. Choose the sentence with the correct grammar.

 a. Jane's cat ran away two weeks ago, but it finally came back.

 b. Mrs. Hendon greet her daughter and nephew when they arrived.

 c. The Pulitzer Prize are named after the newspaper reporter Joseph Pulitzer.

 d. No mistake

15. Choose the sentence with the correct grammar.

 a. Dorothea Dix helps to change the way that ill prisoners were treated.

 b. The story was written by my friend and me.

 c. Graphs are useful tools to help organized and display information.

 d. No mistake

16. Choose the sentence with the correct capitalization.

 a. marion and I have not seen each other for months.

 b. How many times have you seen this Movie?

 c. My father and I went to see Chief Stanley at the firehouse.

 d. No mistake

17. Choose the sentence with the correct grammar.

 a. Alison had already taken her bath by the time I arrived.

 b. There will be enough wind to fly a kites today.

 c. Almost every culture has it's own special kind of music.

 d. No mistake

18. **Choose the sentence with the correct grammar.**

    a. Paul went to the park after dinner to play with his Friends.

    b. Everyone appreciated julia's hard work.

    c. We went to the store together.

    d. No mistake

19. **Choose the sentence with the correct grammar.**

    a. The driver the only witness to the crime.

    b. Paula is serving dinner on the patio.

    c. Archaeology the study of early civilizations.

    d. No mistake

20. **Choose the sentence with the correct grammar.**

    a. Many of Picasso paintings were based on photographs of his friends.

    b. Rachel's family is very happy for her.

    c. I like white papers better then blue papers.

    d. No mistake

21. **Choose the sentence with the correct punctuation.**

    a. The cat was searching for its water dish.

    b. Patricia want's to work for herself.

    c. Laura has seen more films' than Jackie has.

    d. No mistake

22. **Choose the sentence with the correct grammar.**

    a. Each of my friends has a toy car.

    b. Sarah was fascinate by the pictures.

    c. Jason knows the names of almost all the instrument in a orchestra.

    d. No mistake

23. **Choose the sentence with the correct grammar.**

    a. Sarah is probably, very hungry.

    b. She is not ready to finish the job.

    c. Martins mother gave him two days to clean his room.

    d. No mistake

24. Choose the sentence with the correct grammar.

    a. I saw several stars in the sky, but my sister saw hardly any.

    b. Charles go to the pool to practice every day after school.

    c. Some believe that the helicopter is first drawn by Leonardo da Vinci.

    d. No mistake

25. Choose the sentence with the correct grammar.

    a. Libby begged her parents to let her go to the concert on a weeknight.

    b. Alice and her parents are going to visit their friends at the beach.

    c. Kathy grabbed her books and ran out the door.

    d. No mistake

26. Choose the sentence with the correct grammar.

    a. This box contains fewer cookies than the other box.

    b. In my very first game I hit three home run.

    c. David leave his notebook on the kitchen counter.

    d. No mistake

27. Choose the sentence with the correct grammar.

    a. Lidia's mother have a frown on her face.

    b. The new librarian are very friendly.

    c. Michael has as many pictures as his brother.

    d. No mistake

28. Choose the sentence with the correct grammar.

    a. Peter's cookies are better than Steve's.

    b. She have no reason to be afraid.

    c. Lisa's brother win the first race of the day.

    d. No mistake

29. Choose the sentence with the correct grammar.

    a. Unlike animals, plant can make their own food.

    b. Mr. Jones is a intelligent and caring teacher.

    c. My mother divided the sandwich between my sister and me.

    d. No mistake

30. **Choose the sentence with the correct grammar.**

    a. Paper make up almost half of the garbage in America.

    b. My brother is heavier than I am.

    c. I would rather seen a movie than go to the opera.

    d. No mistake

31. **Choose the sentence with the correct punctuation.**

    a. It is impossible to travel faster than the speed of light.

    b. I was invited to his party, but I caught the flu and could not attend.

    c. Frank is not only a great writer, but he can also draw cartoons.

    d. No mistake

32. **Choose the sentence with the correct punctuation.**

    a. Most bees live in hive's, but some live alone.

    b. The member's of our team sold candy to raise money for a trip.

    c. That collar belongs to my friend's dog Spot.

    d. No mistake

33. **Choose the sentence with the correct capitalization.**

    a. Alex and I played in the park after school the other day.

    b. The punch served at Anna's party was delicious.

    c. The dwarf planet Pluto is named after a Greek god.

    d. No mistake

34. **Choose the sentence with the correct capitalization.**

    a. Women played a very important role in the American Revolution.

    b. Computers are now found in almost every home in the United States.

    c. The first westerner to discover Hawaii was Captain James Cook.

    d. No mistake

35. **Choose the sentence with the correct grammar.**

    a. My teacher looked at my homework very closely and found several mistakes.

    b. Penny looked out the window and seen a rainbow.

    c. Martin was so worry that he couldn't sleep.

    d. No mistake

36. **Choose the sentence with the correct grammar.**

   a. There were fewer houses in my neighborhood than I remembered.

   b. The ship was so bad damaged by the iceberg that it had to return to port.

   c. Katrina give a presentation to the class on the origins of ballet.

   d. No mistake

37. **Choose the sentence with the correct grammar.**

   a. The greatest singer of the twentieth century was Frank Sinatra.

   b. William the Conqueror invading England in 1066.

   c. After hurting his knee, David begin to groan.

   d. No mistake

38. **Choose the sentence with the correct grammar.**

   a. Neither gunpowder nor the compass was invented in Europe.

   b. Janet would believe almost anything that anyone told her.

   c. Missy fell off her horse, but she was not injured.

   d. No mistake

39. **Choose the sentence with the correct grammar.**

   a. The computer is one of our most importantest educational tools.

   b. The giant mouse ran through the house and escaped from the cat.

   c. Did you know that Julie is an experience guide and mountaineer?

   d. No mistake

40. **Choose the sentence with the correct grammar.**

   a. Our parents often help us with our math homework.

   b. Wallace has always wanted to visit Paris, but he has never has the time.

   c. Rick go to the library every day after school to study.

   d. No mistake

Spelling

For questions 41–50, look for errors in spelling.

41. Choose the incorrect spelling.

   a. Everyone should have a good dictionary and thesaurus in the house.

   b. He admited that he had never seen the play.

   c. After years of neglect, the building finally collapsed.

   d. No mistake

42. Choose the incorrect spelling.

   a. Terry considered joining a traveling circus.

   b. Drew usually exaggerates a bit when he tells a story.

   c. He was seldom late to a party.

   d. No mistake

43. Choose the incorrect spelling.

   a. Many great discoveries happen entirely by accident.

   b. If we don't show up on time, they're going to be very angry.

   c. Winning the scholarship was a great oportunity for John.

   d. No mistake

44. Choose the incorrect spelling.

   a. His messy handwriting made his letter nearly illegible.

   b. I think he was sincerely sorry for what he did.

   c. We have a rehersal for the play almost every night.

   d. No mistake

45. Choose the incorrect spelling.

   a. His teacher was awed and very impressed by his artistic ability.

   b. Mr. Worthington thought that Kathy looked upset.

   c. I tried to learn to sew, but I wasn't very good at it.

   d. No mistake

46. Choose the incorrect spelling.

   a. The play was so long that it required two intermissions.

   b. Uma prefered to sit on the couch.

   c. Each tribe has a cloth with a distinctive pattern.

   d. No mistake

47. Choose the incorrect spelling.

   a. My sister practises the piano two hours a day.

   b. John told me that he wants to be an astronaut.

   c. His article was misleading, even if true.

   d. No mistake

48. Choose the incorrect spelling.

   a. The sheriff's deputy caught the thief later that night.

   b. Paul was surprized to hear that he had won the award.

   c. Agnes was very fond of her stuffed bear named Edward.

   d. No mistake

49. Choose the incorrect spelling.

   a. Justin was confused by the strange behavior of his pet frog.

   b. Many people enjoy the challenge of an outdoor adventure.

   c. Linus Pauling received the Nobel Prize for his many scientific accomplishments.

   d. No mistake

50. Choose the incorrect spelling.

   a. Ms. Davis teaches mathmatics and physics.

   b. Cecil did not intend to insult his friend.

   c. George was not sure how his friends would react to his talent.

   d. No mistake

Composition

51. Choose the sentence that is correct and most clearly written.

a. Martin decided on the blue suit after several days.

b. The blue suit was decided upon by Martin after several days.

c. After several days, the blue suit was decided upon by Martin.

d. The blue suit, after several days, was what Martin decided on.

52. Choose the sentence that is correct and most clearly written.

a. Importantly, occasions such as birthdays should not be forgotten.

b. Occasions, such as birthdays, which are important, should not be forgotten.

c. Birthdays are important occasions which should not be forgotten.

d. Occasions should not be forgotten when they are as important as birthdays.

53. Choose the sentence that is correct and most clearly written.

a. Spinach is my favorite food it goes well with almost anything.

b. Spinach is my favorite food; it goes well with almost anything.

c. Spinach is my favorite food and spinach goes well with almost anything.

d. Spinach is my favorite food to go well with almost anything.

54. Where should the following sentence be placed in the paragraph below?

She was responsible for promoting sanitary surgical methods, a pure water supply, and other hygienic measures.

1) Born in Italy and raised in England, Florence Nightingale is recognized universally as the person who established the principles of modern nursing. 2) In 1854, Nightingale assembled a team of women to care for British soldiers during the Crimean War. 3) During her nearly two years of service, Nightingale stressed cleanliness and good medical care. 4) These measures led to a drop in the mortality rate from 60% to 2%, saving countless British lives. 5) When she returned from the war, she founded the Nightingale School to train the next generation of professional nurses.

a. After sentence 2

b. After sentence 3

c. After sentence 4

d. After sentence 5

55. Where should the following sentence be placed in the paragraph below?

The ash spread over hundreds of square miles, making the sky look black as night.

1) In 1980, Mount Saint Helens, in the state of Washington, became a volcano. 2) It exploded for the first time in thousands of years. 3) The explosion was felt as far north as Seattle and as far south as Los Angeles. 4) The mountain threw tons of ash into the air before it stopped exploding a few days later. 5) There was, however, no lava. 6) Most geologists believe that Mount Saint Helens will not explode again for many thousands of years to come. 7) But they admit that another explosion might occur at any time.

a. After sentence 2
b. After sentence 3
c. After sentence 4
d. After sentence 5

56. Fill in the blank.

Jason thought that he found a lump of gold, _____ it turned out to be a painted rock.

a. because
b. moreover
c. but
d. or

57. Fill in the blank.

Most people feel that it is worthwhile to buy a better product, _____ it might cost a little more.

a. therefore
b. even though
c. in fact
d. despite

58. **Fill in the blank.**

Brushing your teeth every day is important to prevent cavities; _____ it helps your gums stay healthy and prevents bad breath.

a. moreover,
b. nonetheless,
c. yet,
d. in contrast,

59. **Which sentence does not belong in the following paragraph?**

1) Many people think that rabbits are rodents, like rats and mice. 2) In fact, rabbits are not rodents at all. 3) Rodents scare many people because they have sharp teeth and claws. 4) Rabbits, along with hares, belong to a class of animals called lagomorphs. 5) Lagomorph is a Greek word that means "rabbit-shaped."

a. Sentence 2
b. Sentence 3
c. Sentence 4
d. Sentence 5

60. **Which sentence does not belong in the following paragraph?**

1) Of all the animals on earth, the one most suited to its environment is probably the camel. 2) Camels live in the desert, where water is scarce and breathing is difficult due to the sand in the air. 3) To cope with these conditions, camels can store several days' worth of water in their humps. 4) There are no higher animals on earth that can live without water. 5) Camels also have extra-long eyelashes and hairs that cover their noses to keep the sand out. 6) Furthermore, their large feet help them walk on the sand, which is difficult terrain for most other pack animals.

a. Sentence 2
b. Sentence 3
c. Sentence 4
d. Sentence 5

Chapter 22
HSPT
Practice Test 2:
Answers and
Explanations

ANSWER KEY

	Verbal Skills				Quantitative Skills				Reading		
1.	C	38.	A	1.	C	38.	C	1.	A	38.	C
2.	D	39.	C	2.	D	39.	A	2.	C	39.	C
3.	C	40.	D	3.	A	40.	B	3.	B	40.	B
4.	B	41.	C	4.	D	41.	D	4.	A	41.	B
5.	B	42.	D	5.	D	42.	D	5.	B	42.	C
6.	B	43.	A	6.	C	43.	C	6.	C	43.	D
7.	B	44.	A	7.	A	44.	A	7.	B	44.	A
8.	C	45.	A	8.	A	45.	B	8.	B	45.	C
9.	A	46.	D	9.	C	46.	D	9.	B	46.	D
10.	B	47.	C	10.	C	47.	C	10.	A	47.	C
11.	A	48.	C	11.	B	48.	B	11.	B	48.	C
12.	A	49.	B	12.	B	49.	C	12.	C	49.	A
13.	B	50.	B	13.	C	50.	C	13.	B	50.	C
14.	C	51.	B	14.	C	51.	C	14.	C	51.	B
15.	C	52.	B	15.	C	52.	B	15.	D	52.	C
16.	C	53.	C	16.	A			16.	A	53.	A
17.	B	54.	B	17.	A			17.	B	54.	B
18.	B	55.	A	18.	B			18.	B	55.	D
19.	A	56.	C	19.	B			19.	B	56.	C
20.	C	57.	D	20.	B			20.	B	57.	B
21.	D	58.	A	21.	A			21.	B	58.	A
22.	D	59.	C	22.	B			22.	C	59.	A
23.	B	60.	B	23.	B			23.	B	60.	B
24.	A			24.	B			24.	D	61.	C
25.	A			25.	A			25.	B	62.	D
26.	B			26.	B			26.	B		
27.	B			27.	B			27.	B		
28.	A			28.	C			28.	C		
29.	C			29.	A			29.	C		
30.	A			30.	C			30.	C		
31.	C			31.	A			31.	A		
32.	D			32.	C			32.	C		
33.	A			33.	B			33.	A		
34.	A			34.	C			34.	C		
35.	B			35.	D			35.	B		
36.	C			36.	B			36.	C		
37.	A			37.	C			37.	B		

Mathematics

1.	B	38.	D
2.	C	39.	D
3.	D	40.	A
4.	A	41.	A
5.	C	42.	D
6.	D	43.	B
7.	C	44.	D
8.	B	45.	A
9.	A	46.	D
10.	C	47.	D
11.	C	48.	B
12.	B	49.	A
13.	B	50.	D
14.	A	51.	D
15.	C	52.	B
16.	B	53.	D
17.	B	54.	B
18.	B	55.	A
19.	B	56.	D
20.	C	57.	A
21.	C	58.	C
22.	B	59.	A
23.	A	60.	B
24.	B	61.	A
25.	B	62.	C
26.	C	63.	B
27.	C	64.	A
28.	C		
29.	D		
30.	A		
31.	D		
32.	C		
33.	C		
34.	B		
35.	A		
36.	D		
37.	C		

Language Skills

1.	D	38.	D
2.	B	39.	B
3.	B	40.	A
4.	B	41.	B
5.	A	42.	D
6.	D	43.	C
7.	B	44.	C
8.	B	45.	D
9.	C	46.	B
10.	C	47.	A
11.	D	48.	B
12.	C	49.	D
13.	A	50.	A
14.	A	51.	A
15.	B	52.	C
16.	C	53.	B
17.	A	54.	B
18.	C	55.	C
19.	B	56.	C
20.	B	57.	B
21.	A	58.	A
22.	A	59.	B
23.	B	60.	C
24.	A		
25.	D		
26.	A		
27.	C		
28.	A		
29.	C		
30.	B		
31.	D		
32.	C		
33.	D		
34.	D		
35.	A		
36.	A		
37.	A		

ANSWERS AND EXPLANATIONS

Verbal Skills

1.   **C**   Diligent means hardworking.

2.   **D**   Severe means serious; the opposite is mild.

3.   **C**   A candle is made of wax; a tire is made of rubber.

4.   **B**   A spoon, a knife, and a fork are utensils used to eat food.

5.   **B**   A horse lives in a stable; a chicken lives in a coop.

6.   **B**   Winter, fall, and summer are seasons of the year.

7.   **B**   Prohibit means to disallow.

8.   **C**   A shirt, a dress, and a pair of shorts are all articles of clothing.

9.   **A**   Famished means very hungry; arid means very dry.

10. **B**   Biased means taking a position; the opposite is neutral.

11. **A**   A suitcase holds clothes; a briefcase holds papers.

12. **A**   Hinder means to hold back; the opposite is help.

13. **B**   Content means happy or satisfied.

14. **C**   We can diagram this as follows: Rachel > Alice, Richard > Barry. Since we don't know how Rachel and Alice relate to Richard and Barry, we don't know whether Rachel or Richard finished first.

15. **C**   The top of a container is a lid; the top of a house is a roof.

16. **C**   Credible means believable.

17. **B**   Sincere means honest; the opposite is dishonest.

18. **B**   We can diagram this as follows: $I > M > L$. Since Ines is before Marcus, who is before Larry, we know that Larry is not before Ines.

19. **A**   To contaminate means to infect.

20. **C**   We can diagram this as follows: $B > D$, $A > D$, $C > D$. All we know is that Alex and Bink had more balloons than David, but we don't know whether Alex or Bink had more.

21. **D**   Sail, mast, and rudder are all parts of a ship.

22. **D**   Fortunate means lucky.

23. **B** A zoologist studies animals; a botanist studies plants.

24. **A** Apples, peaches, and pears are all kinds of fruit.

25. **A** We can diagram this as follows: $J > B$, $J > E$, $M > J$. Since Mark is taller than John, who is taller than Evelyn, we know that Mark is taller than Evelyn.

26. **B** Water, oil, and vinegar are all types of liquid.

27. **B** Frank means honest.

28. **A** Famine means the lack of food; drought means the lack of water.

29. **C** We can diagram this as follows: $O > J$, $N > J$. All we know is that Olivia and Nancy each ate more than Jennifer, but we don't know whether Olivia or Nancy ate more.

30. **A** A trunk, a branch, and a leaf are all parts of a tree.

31. **C** Immune means not vulnerable to disease; the opposite is vulnerable.

32. **D** Tea, coffee, and water are all things you drink; you eat cereal.

33. **A** Elude means to get away or escape.

34. **A** We can diagram this as follows: $F > J$, $F > N$, $J = M$. Since Frank has seen more than Jonathan, who has seen the same number as Manny, we know that Manny has seen fewer films than Frank.

35. **B** Sole, lace, and heel are all parts of a shoe.

36. **C** To mimic means to imitate.

37. **A** Counterfeit means fake or false; the opposite is genuine.

38. **A** We can diagram this as follows: $K > F > D$, $A > K$. Since Amanda walked farther than Kate, who walked farther than Felix, we know that Amanda walked farther than Felix.

39. **C** Barbaric means rude or uncivilized; the opposite is civilized.

40. **D** Dog, fish, and hamster are all kinds of pets.

41. **C** Conventional means normal; the opposite is strange.

42. **D** To inspect means to examine closely.

43. **A** Varied means different; the opposite is similar.

44. **A** Goat, cow, and horse are all animals that produce milk.

45. **A** Maple is a type of tree; an apple is a type of fruit.

46. **D** To diminish means to reduce.

47. **C** We can diagram this as follows: Mike > Mindy > *W*, Mike > *R*. All we know is that both Mindy and Rochelle read fewer books than Mike. We don't know which of the two read more.

48. **C** Movie, book, and play are all kinds of works that can be fictional.

49. **B** Unbiased means without bias, or neutral.

50. **B** Criticize is the opposite of praise.

51. **B** Mop, broom, and vacuum are all tools used to clean the floor.

52. **B** A bird guides itself with its wings; a fish guides itself with its fins.

53. **C** Permanent means unchanging.

54. **B** We can diagram this as follows: *W* > *S* > *T* > *Z*. Since Wendy has more badges than Terence, who has more than Zack, we know that Wendy does not have fewer than Zack.

55. **A** Serene means calm or peaceful.

56. **C** Enlarge means to grow; the opposite is shrink or reduce.

57. **D** Wind, rain, and snow are all reasons to wear a coat.

58. **A** An hour is a part of the day; a month is a part of the year.

59. **C** Brick, stone, and wood are all materials used to make a house.

60. **B** Authentic means real or genuine.

Quantitative Skills

1. **C** The series goes 2 (× 2) 4 (× 2) 8 (× 2) 16 (× 2) **32**.

2. **D** Each of the figures has two parts out of four shaded.

3. **A** The series goes 6 (+ 9) 15 (+ 9) 24 (+ 9) 33 (+ 9) **42**.

4. **D** $3 \times 5 = 15$. Now try each choice to see which one, if you take 25% of it, gives you 15. $25\% \times 60 = 15$.

5. **D** The series goes 1 (× 3) 3 (× 3) 9 (× 3) 27 (× 3) **81**.

6. **C** Translate each of these: $\frac{40}{100}$ of 80 = 32. $\frac{50}{100}$ of 64 = 32. $\frac{150}{100}$ of 16 = 24.

7. **A** $\frac{1}{4}$ of 24 is 6. What number divided by 3 is 6? 18.

8. **A** The series goes 100 (− 1) 99 (− 2) 97 (− 3) 94 (− 4) **90**.

9. **C** Let's calculate each of the choices: $\frac{1}{4} \times 96 = 24$. $2 \times 48 = 96$. $\frac{1}{2} \times 192 = 96$.

10. **C** The series goes 5 (+ 3) 8 (+ 5) 13 (+ 3) 16 (+ 5) 21 (+ 3) **24**.

11. **B** Let's calculate each of the choices: $32^1 = 32$. $2^5 = 32$. $3^3 = 27$.

12. **B** The series goes 10 (− 3) 7 (+ 1) 8 (− 3) 5 (+ 1) 6 (− 3) **3**.

13. **C** 10% of 40 is the same as $\frac{10}{100} \times 40 = 4$. Now we need to figure out $\frac{4}{5}$ of which number is 4. Try taking $\frac{4}{5}$ of each of the choices until you find the one that makes 4.

14. **C** The series goes 6 (+ 3) 9 (+ 4) 13 (+ 3) 16 (+ 4) 20 (+ 3) **23**.

15. **C** Since (3) has an 8 in the hundredths places, it is the largest number. (2) has an extra digit, and is greater than (1).

16. **A** The series goes 2 (+ 4) 6 (+ 6) 12 (+ 4) 16 (+ 6) 22 (+ 4) **26**.

17. **A** The difference between 80 and 64 is 16. $\frac{1}{4}$ of 16 = 4.

18. **B** Let's calculate these choices: 3(4 + 9) = 39. 12 + 27 = 39. 34 + 9 = 43.

19. **B** $\frac{1}{5}$ of 15 is 3. 18 more than 3 is 21.

20. **B** The perimeter of (A) is 14, the perimeter of (B) is 16, and the perimeter of (C) is 12.

21. **A** Translate this as $\frac{10}{100} \times \frac{20}{100} \times 300 = 6$.

22. **B** The series goes 8 (+ 1) 9 (+ 7) 16 (+ 1) 17 (+ 7) 24 (+ 1) 25 (+ 7) **32**.

23. **B** Let's calculate these choices. For (1), we move the decimal three places to the right to get 3,020. For (2), we move the decimal two places to the right to get 3,200. (3) is 302.

24. **B** Try dividing each number by 7. 51 ÷ 7 = 7 with a remainder of 2.

25. **A** Since *AC* and *FB* are both diameters, they are equal; *ED* is shorter than both of them.

26. **B** The series goes 1 (× 7) 7 | 3 (× 7) 21 | **5** (× 7) 35.

27. **B** *z* is larger than *y*. Since their sum is 180°, *x* must be larger than 90°, and *y* must be less than 90°.

28. **C** (1) = 3.67; (2) = 6.73; and (3) = 7.36.

29. **A** The series goes 2 (× 2) 4 (+ 2) 6 (× 2) 12 (+ 2) 14 (× 2) 28 (+ 2) **30**.

30. **C** Translate 20% of 60: $\frac{20}{100} \times 60 = 12$. What number is 9 times 12? 108.

31. **A** The series goes 9 (− 2) 7 (− 2) 5 (+ 4) 9 (− 2) 7 (− 2) **5** (+ 4) 9.

32. **C** Twice the difference between 15 and 17 is 4. 17 more than 4 is 21.

33. **B** The series goes 9 (+ 11) 20 (+ 11) 31 (+ 11) 42 (+ 11) **53**.

34. **C** Since this is a square, all the sides are equal and smaller than the diagonals.

35. **D** The series goes 7 (× 2) 14 (– 1) 13 (× 2) 26 (– 1) 25 (× 2) **50**.

36. **B** $\frac{1}{11}$ of 121 = 11. To make 11, you need to add 8 and 3.

37. **C** (1) = 16, (2) = 16, and (3) = 32.

38. **C** The series goes 2 (+ 2) 4 (+ 2) 6 (– 2) 4 (+ 2) 6 (+ 2) 8 (– 2) **6** (+ 2) 8 (+ 2) 10.

39. **A** Since they are vertical angles, a = 45°, b = 110°, and c = 25°.

40. **B** The average of 42, 45, and 39 is 42. The difference between 23 and 42 is 19.

41. **D** The product of 8 and 18 is 144. $\frac{1}{4}$ of 144 = 36.

42. **D** Choice (A) has an area of 8; (B) has an area of 8; (C) has an area of 8.

43. **C** The series should go 88 (– 3) 85 (– 2) 83 (– 3) 80 (– 2) 78 (– 3) **75**.

44. **A** (1) = 2, (2) = –2, and (3) = –18.

45. **B** The series goes 49 $\left(\sqrt{\ }\right)$ 7 | 81 $\left(\sqrt{\ }\right)$ **9** | 121 $\left(\sqrt{\ }\right)$ 11.

46. **D** The product of 6 and 3 is 18. 50% more than 18 is 27.

47. **C** 10% of 50 = 5; 20% of 100 = 20. The difference between 5 and 20 is 15.

48. **B** The series goes 6 (+ 2) 8 (– 1) 7 (+ 2) 9 (– 1) **8** (+ 2) 10 (– 1) 9 (+ 2) 11.

49. **C** $\frac{5}{3}$ of 9 = 15. 4 less than 15 is 11.

50. **C** Half the sum of 4, 9, and 11 is 12. 18 more than 12 is 30.

51. **C** The average of 10, 15, and 8 is 11. 2 more than 11 is 13.

52. **B** The series goes 41 (– 30) 11 (+ 41) 52 (– 30) 22 (+ 41) 63 (– 30) **33**.

Reading

Comprehension

1. **A** The passage uses quitting in contrast to playing with his friends. It must therefore mean something like no longer playing with, or leaving.

2. **C** According to the passage, they gathered near the river.

3. **B** The first paragraph states that the narrator is going to take a job while the friends go back to the high school. The narrator is probably around 18 years old.

4. **A** Each paragraph of the passage describes the various friends of the narrator.

5. **B** According to the first paragraph, the narrator will "remember it better" because the narrator is about the leave.

6. **C** The first paragraph says that the author was going "to teach my first country school."

7. **B** The second paragraph says that Otto and Fritz "caught the fat, horned catfish."

8. **B** According to the last sentence, Tip's father worked in a "grocery store."

9. **B** Since the sentence following the mention of the word *generate* discuss the ways in which the eel uses electricity, the word *generate* must mean something like use or make.

10. **A** The author knows a great deal of detail about the electric eel, which is an animal that lives in the sea.

11. **B** The word *current* is right next to the word *electric*, so it must have something to do with electricity.

12. **C** According to the third paragraph, eels use their electricity "to find fish."

13. **B** In the sentence prior to the word *buffer*, we see that it is something that "protects its nervous system."

14. **C** The final sentence of the passage says that it is not certain whether eels use electricity to communicate because "this theory has not yet been proven."

15. **D** Each of these animals is mentioned somewhere in the passage except the horse.

16. **A** The fourth paragraph states that the eel has insulation that "protects its nervous system" from the electricity that it generates. Therefore we can infer that electricity harms the nervous system.

17. **B** The only choice listed that would describe an electric eel is (B).

18. **B** The word *meager* is explained by saying that his salary was so meager that they lived "in an unheated apartment." Evidently he didn't have enough money to afford heat, so the word meager must mean small.

19. **B** The second paragraph says that Pavlov worked on "conditioned reflexes" and showed that they "can be acquired through experience or training."

20. **B** According to the second paragraph, the knee-jerk response is an example of an "innate" reflex.

21. **B** Since the word *innate* is used in the second paragraph in contrast to the word *conditioned*, it must refer to something that is not learned and instead had at birth.

22. **C** The final paragraph says that Skinner was a behaviorist, which was a school of psychology that followed Pavlov's ideas. But we don't know if Skinner was one of Pavlov's students, so (C) is the best choice.

23. **B** In the final paragraph, the author says, "Though behaviorism cannot plausibly explain all of human behavior, it has deepened our understanding...."

24. **D** The second paragraph states that Pavlov worked on "conditioned reflexes" and showed that they "can be acquired through experience or training."

25. **B** The words "bounce up like a ball" are used to describe how Fanny acts when she thinks she sees a mouse.

26. **B** The word *credulous* in the passage is followed immediately by "would believe anything."

27. **B** The final paragraph states that she played the piano and sang.

28. **C** The word *cultivated* is used to describe the "musical gift" of people. Choices (A), (B), and (D) are therefore impossible.

29. **C** According to the first paragraph, "Frank would tell her the most unbelievable and impossible lies" and enjoyed "fooling her."

30. **C** The final sentence of the first paragraph states that "Caesar's historical influence was so great" that these words "are derived from his name."

31. **A** The second sentence says that the Roman Empire was "so large and powerful that no other Western government could be considered its equal."

32. **C** The second paragraph says that Caesar came from a family of politicians, but he "did not simply act in the interests of his family" but rather helped the people.

33. **A** The word *campaigns* is used to describe the Gallic Wars.

34. **C** The fourth paragraph states that "Caesar's popularity and strength began to frighten Pompey."

35. **B** This is stated in the first sentence of the third paragraph.

36. **C** The third paragraph says that *Frankenstein* is "a brilliant work of art."

37. **B** In the third paragraph, the author states that "feminist ideas inherited from her mother" influenced her writing.

38. **C** Choices (A) and (B) are only details of the passage, and (D) is not really discussed.

39. **C** According to the second paragraph, she wrote it at the age of 19. Since she was born in 1797, she must have written it around 1816.

40. **B** The word *calamities* is used to describe events that "included several suicides."

Vocabulary

41. **B**

42. **C**

43. **D**

44. **A**

45. **C**

46. **D**

47. **C**

48. **C**

49. **A**

50. **C**

51. **B**

52. **C**

53. **A**

54. **B**

55. **D**

56. **C**

57. **B**

58. **A**

59. **A**

60. **B**

61. **C**

62. **D**

Mathematics

Mathematical Concepts

1. **B**   First, eliminate choices that have a zero in the tenths place. This leaves (A) and (B). Since (B) has a 1 in the hundredths place, whereas (A) has a 0, (B) is bigger.

2. **C**   The area of a square is length × width. Since this is a square, its length and width are both 5, so the area is 5 × 5 = 25.

3. **D**   Plug in each answer choice until you find one that can be divided by 3, 4, and 5. 30 cannot be divided by 4; 40 cannot be divided by 3; 50 cannot be divided by 3.

4. **A**   Remember that the second place to the right of the decimal is called the hundredths place. Therefore, $\frac{5}{100} = 0.05$, so the sum = 65.05.

5. **C**   Since $60° + a + b = 180°$, $a + b = 120°$.

6. **D**   Remember that when you multiply by 100, you move the decimal point two places to the right: $0.28 \times 100 = 28$. The closest choice is (D).

7. **C**   If we find the factors of 45, they are 1 and 45, 3 and 15, and 5 and 9. Since 9 is not prime, the biggest prime factor is 5.

8. **B**   Percent decrease is calculated by taking $\frac{difference}{original}$. The difference in this case is $40. The original amount of the dress was $160. Therefore, we calculate $\frac{40}{160} = \frac{1}{4} = 25\%$.

9. **A**   When in doubt, write exponents out longhand. $10^3 = 10 \times 10 \times 10$. $10^5 = 10 \times 10 \times 10 \times 10 \times 10$. This makes a total of eight 10s, or 10^8.

10. **C**   Try dividing each choice by 8 until you find the one that cannot be divided evenly.

11. **C**   The volume of his box is $6 \times 8 \times \frac{1}{2} = 24$.

12. **B**   We can make this into a proportion: $\frac{3\ boys}{4\ girls} = \frac{x}{124\ girls}$. If we cross multiply and solve for x, we get $x = 93$ boys.

13. **B**   When in doubt, write out the exponents in longhand. $(4^2)^3$ is the same thing as $4^2 \times 4^2 \times 4^2 = 4 \times 4 \times 4 \times 4 \times 4 \times 4$. There are a total of six 4s, or 4^6.

14. **A**   The product of the digits is $3 \times 6 \times 5 = 90$. The sum of the digits is $3 + 6 + 5 = 14$. $90 - 14 = 76$.

15. **C**   Remember that the tenths place is the first to the right of the decimal. Since the next digit is 4, we round down to 2.8.

16. **B**   Since the squares have an area of 16, their sides must equal 4. The perimeter of the figure covers 6 sides total, so the perimeter is $6 \times 4 = 24$.

17. **B** The angles inside a triangle must add up to 180°. If one of the angles measures 85°, then the other two must measure 180 − 85 = 95°. The only choice that adds up to 95° is (B).

18. **B** $\sqrt{2^2}$ is the same as $\sqrt{4} = 2$.

19. **B** Juan has a total of 17 marbles, and 5 of them are blue. Therefore, $\frac{5}{17}$ of his marbles are blue.

20. **C** You can add only similar roots together, so (C) is the only true statement.

21. **C** The first multiples of 4 are 4, 8, 12, 16, 20, and 24. The first multiples of 6 are 6, 12, 18, and 24. The smallest number that is common to each is 12.

22. **B** Try dividing each choice by 6. 22 ÷ 6 = 3 with a remainder of 4.

23. **A** Try taking a negative even number such as −2 and a positive odd number such as 3, and multiply them to get −6. This number is negative and even.

24. **B** Don't forget to memorize your primes! There are four: 2, 3, 5, and 7.

Problem Solving

25. **B** Use the Bowtie to get a common denominator. $\frac{5}{15} + \frac{6}{13} = \frac{65}{195} + \frac{90}{195} = \frac{155}{195}$ which reduces to $\frac{31}{39}$.

26. **C** To get an average of 48 on four tests, her total score would have to be 48 × 4, or 192. Maxine already has 42 + 45 + 46 = 133 points on the first three tests, so on her fourth she would need 192 − 133 = 59 points.

27. **C** Translate this as $\frac{20}{100} \times \frac{40}{100} \times 500 = 40$.

28. **C** Remember your order of operations! First do parentheses to get 6 − 3(− 2) + 5. Now do multiplication to get 6 + 6 + 5. Now add to get 17.

29. **D** To make this division easier, let's move the decimal point two places to the right. Now we can divide $\frac{2000}{2} = 1,000$.

30. **A** First, we need to find 5% of $25. $\frac{5}{100} \times 25 = \$1.25$. When you take this off the original price, we get $23.75.

31. **D** Let's set up the proportion: $\frac{8 \; miles}{1 \; inch} = \frac{x}{3.5 \; inches}$. Cross-multiply to get $x = 28$ miles.

32. **C** Remember that the places after the decimal point are the tenths and hundredths. So $0.24 = \frac{24}{100}$, which reduces to $\frac{12}{50}$.

33. **C** Let's plug in our own number to make this easier. Let's say that the shirt begins at $100. When the prices is discounted by 20%, it will go down to $80. When it is discounted by another 10%, it will go down to $72. This means that it went from $100 to $72, a discount of 28%.

34. **B** If two numbers have a ratio of 6:9, and the smaller one is actually 18, then we know that we need to multiply the ratio by 3 to get 18:27. The question then asks for the average of these two numbers. The average of 18 and 27 is 22.5.

35. **A** Remember your order of operations! First do parentheses to get $11 + 5 \times 6 \div 3 - (-3)$. Now multiply to get $11 + 30 + 3 - (-3)$. Now we can add and subtract to get 47.

36. **D** The volume of this pool is $4 \times 10 \times 12 = 480$. If it gets filled at 8 cubic feet per minute, it will take $\frac{480}{8} = 60$ minutes to fill.

37. **C** If three hamburgers cost $4.05, then each hamburger costs $1.35. This means that two hamburgers cost $2.70. If two hamburgers and an order of french fries costs $3.55, then an order of fries must cost $3.55 − $2.70 = $0.85.

38. **D** If the ratio of boys to girls is 3:5, that means that for every 8 total students, 3 are boys and 5 are girls. If there are 32 total students, then there are 4 groups of 8 students. This means that there are 12 boys and 20 girls.

39. **D** The area of this circle is πr^2, or 64π. The circumference of this circle is $2\pi r$, or 16π. Therefore, the difference is 48π.

40. **A** To make this problem easier, let's write out the exponents. $4^4 = 4 \times 4 \times 4 \times 4$. Which one of the choices says the same thing? Let's try them. Choice (A) says 16×16, which is the same as $4 \times 4 \times 4 \times 4$.

41. **A** First, let's find how many do attend. $\frac{2}{3} \times 660 = 440$ students. This means that 220 do not attend.

42. **D** If we multiply these two numbers together, we get $6\sqrt{4}$. We can take 4 out of the root to get $6 \times 2 = 12$.

43. **B** To make this easier, let's add the fractions with common denominators together. This gives us $18 + 1 + \frac{3}{6}$. Since $\frac{3}{6}$ is the same as $\frac{1}{2}$, the sum is $19\frac{1}{2}$.

44. **D** Let's begin by subtracting 5 from each side. This gives us $3x = 18$. When we divide 3 from each side, we get $x = 6$.

45. **A** To divide fractions, flip and multiply: $\frac{1}{2} \times \frac{10}{1} = 5$.

46. **D** Since $x = 2$, we know that $2y + 18 = 36$. Now we can solve for y: $2y = 18$, so $y = 9$.

47. **D** The area of this rectangle is the same as length × width, or $15 \times 24 = 360$ ft^2.

48. **B** There is no need to work out the entire problem. Just one term is probably enough to get the right answer. The first terms says $7 \times \frac{1}{100}$. Seven-hundredths means a 7 in the hundredths place, or 0.07. Only (B) has a 7 in the hundredths place.

49.   **A**   By Ballparking, you can probably get this one right. Since 5 pounds would be at least $15, (B), (C), and (D) are all too big. You can also solve by setting up a proportion. $\dfrac{1 \text{ lb.}}{\$3.25} = \dfrac{x}{\$13}$. Cross-multiply to solve for x.

50.   **D**   To make the division easier, move the decimal point one place to the right. Now divide $\dfrac{55}{2} = 27.5$.

51.   **D**   Plug in the answer choices, starting with (A). If Alex is 4 years old, then 4 years ago, he was 0 years old. Does this make him half as old? No. How about (B)? If Alex is 5 years old, then 4 years ago, he was 1. Does this make him half as old? No. How about (C)? If Alex is 6 years old, then 4 years ago, he was 2. Still not half as old. How about (D)? If Alex is 8 years old, then 4 years ago, he was 4. This is half as old as he is now.

52.   **B**   First, change these into ordinary fractions, and then multiply: $\dfrac{11}{2} \times \dfrac{7}{3} = \dfrac{77}{6} \text{ or } 12\dfrac{5}{6}$.

53.   **D**   A wall that is 20 feet by 12 feet has a total area of $20 \times 12 = 240$ square feet. One gallon will cover 2.5 square feet, so divide 240 by 2.5 to see how many gallons we will need.

54.   **B**   Since $y = 5$, we know that $2x^2 + 5 = 55$. If we subtract 5 from each side, we get $2x^2 = 50$. Now we can divide 2 from each side and get $x^2 = 25$, so x could be 5.

55.   **A**   We can multiply these numbers together to get $12\sqrt{36}$. Since $\sqrt{36} = 6$, this becomes $12 \times 6 = 72$.

56.   **D**   Since there are 60 seconds in a minute and 60 minutes in an hour, there are $60 \times 60 = 3{,}600$ seconds in an hour. So in 4 hours there are $4 \times 3{,}600 = 14{,}400$ seconds.

57.   **A**   This problem is best solved by plugging in the answer choices. Let's start with (A). Could there be 62 girls in the group? If there are 62 girls, there are $62 - 24 = 38$ boys. Does this make a total of 100 children? Yes.

58.   **C**   Let's solve for x. First, subtract x from each side to get $-5x - 3 < 2$. Now add 3 to each side and get $-5x < 5$. When we divide each side by -5, we have to change the direction of the sign, so $x > -1$.

59.   **A**   Multiples of 5 and 6 are multiples of 30. How many multiples of 30 are there between 1 and 100? Three: 30, 60, and 90.

60.   **B**   The triangles are formed from two radii, which must be the same length, so the triangle must be isosceles. Since the inside angle is 90°, the other two angles must be 45°.

61.   **A**   We can set up a proportion: $\dfrac{2 \text{ cookies}}{1 \text{ minutes}} = \dfrac{150 \text{ cookies}}{x \text{ minutes}}$. Now we solve for x, which becomes 75 minutes, or 1 hour and 15 minutes.

62. **C** Plug in the answer choices to solve this problem. Start with (A). If Jim is 20 years old, then Carl is 40 and Liz is 15. Does this make Carl 15 years older than Liz? No. Let's try (B). If Jim is 15 years old, then Carl is 30 and Liz is 10. Does this make Carl 15 years older than Liz? No. Let's try (C). If Jim is 10, then Carl is 20 and Liz is 5. Does this make Carl 15 years older than Liz? Yes.

63. **B** If the circumference is 8π and circumference = $2\pi r$, then the radius of the circle must be 4, and the diameter is twice the radius.

64. **A** To divide $8.50 among 5 people, we need to calculate $\dfrac{\$8.50}{5}$. To make it easier to divide, move the decimal points two places to the right: $\dfrac{850}{500} = \$1.70$.

Language

1. **D**

2. **B** Since quick describes the way in which Steve ran around the track, it should be the adverb *quickly*.

3. **B** The correct spelling is parent's.

4. **B** Belgium is a country, which is a singular noun. Therefore, you would use the singular pronoun "it."

5. **A** Names of locations, such as Lake Michigan, should be capitalized.

6. **D**

7. **B** Names of holidays, such as New Year's Eve, should be capitalized.

8. **B** "Whose" is the possessive of "who."

9. **C** A comma should always separate city and state.

10. **C** Names of days of the week, such as Monday, should be capitalized.

11. **D**

12. **C** A comma should follow the word *asked*.

13. **A** Always use a comma in dates. A comma should follow the word Saturday.

14. **A** Since cat is singular, we need the singular pronoun "it".

15. **B** Since the phrase "my friend and me" is the object of a preposition, we use the objective pronoun "me" rather than the subject pronoun "I."

16. **C** Since it is a title accompanied by a proper name, Chief Stanley should be capitalized.

17. **A** "Taken" is the correct past tense verb form.

18. **C** When the subject of a sentence is a group of people, "we" is the correct pronoun.

19. **B** "Is" serves as the main verb in this sentence. The other two sentences are fragments.

20. **B** "Rachel's family" is singular and requires the singular verb form is.

21. **A** In this case we are showing possession, that the dish belongs to the cat, so we need "its".

22. **A** The word *each* is singular and needs the singular verb form *has*.

23. **B** When one person is the subject of the sentence, use the subject pronoun.

24. **A** "Saw" is the correct past tense verb.

25. **D**

26. **A** When counting items, the correct word is *fewer,* not less.

27. **C** The idiom is "as many as" his brother.

28. **A** This question is comparing people and their cookies. If you are unsure, you can read it as "Peter's cookies are better than Steve's cookies."

29. **C** Since the phrase "my sister and me" follows the preposition "between," the objective case is needed.

30. **B** "Heavier" is the comparative form of "heavy."

31. **D**

32. **C** Since Spot belongs to "my friend," friend is possessive, friend's is correct.

33. **D**

34. **D**

35. **A** Since the word *close* describes the way in which the teacher looked at the homework, it should be the adverb *closely.*

36. **A** Since we are counting, the word should be *fewer* not less.

37. **A** "Greatest" is the correct superlative form.

38. **D**

39. **B** The verbs should be parallel. Both should be in the past tense.

40. **A** "Our parents" is plural and requires the plural verb form "help."

Spelling

41. **B** The word *admitted* is misspelled.

42. **D**

43. **C** The word *opportunity* is misspelled.

44. **C** The word *rehearsal* is misspelled.

45. **D**

46. **B** The word *preferred* is misspelled.

47. **A** The word *practices* is misspelled.

48. **B** The word *surprised* is misspelled.

49. **D**

50. **A** The word *mathematics* is misspelled.

Composition

51. **A** Choices (B), (C), and (D) are all in the passive voice.

52. **C** Choices (A) and (B) are awkward; (D) is wordy.

53. **B** Some punctuation is required to avoid a run-on sentence.

54. **B** The sentence to be placed in the paragraph discusses measures that Nightingale proposed. Sentence 4 refers to "These measures," so the sentence should go before sentence 4.

55. **C** The sentence to be placed further discusses ash. Sentence 4 introduces the ash, so the sentence should follow sentence 4.

56. **C** The second phrase contrasts with the first, so an opposite-direction word such as (C) or (D) is needed. Choice (D) doesn't work here, so the answer should be (C).

57. **B** The second phrase is in contrast to the first, so we need an opposite-direction word such as (B).

58. **A** The second phrase gives more information about the first, so we need a same-direction word such as (A).

59. **B** All of the sentences in this paragraph discuss features of rodents, except sentence 3, which discusses people.

60. **C** All of the sentences in this paragraph discuss camels except sentence 4.

NOTES

The Princeton Review®

Completely darken bubbles with a No. 2 pencil. If you make a mistake, be sure to erase mark completely. Erase all stray marks.

1.

YOUR NAME: _____
(Print)   Last   First   M.I.

SIGNATURE: _____   DATE: ___/___/___

HOME ADDRESS: _____
(Print)   Number and Street

_____
City   State   Zip Code

PHONE NO.: _____
(Print)

IMPORTANT: Please fill in these boxes exactly as shown on the back cover of your test book.

2. TEST FORM

6. DATE OF BIRTH

Month	Day	Year
○ JAN		
○ FEB	⓪ ⓪	⓪ ⓪
○ MAR	① ①	① ①
○ APR	② ②	② ②
○ MAY	③ ③	③ ③
○ JUN	④ ④	④ ④
○ JUL	⑤ ⑤	⑤ ⑤
○ AUG	⑥ ⑥	⑥ ⑥
○ SEP	⑦ ⑦	⑦ ⑦
○ OCT	⑧ ⑧	⑧ ⑧
○ NOV	⑨ ⑨	⑨ ⑨
○ DEC		

3. TEST CODE   **4. REGISTRATION NUMBER**

7. SEX
○ MALE
○ FEMALE

The Princeton Review®

5. YOUR NAME

First 4 letters of last name   FIRST INIT   MID INIT

(A B C D E F G H I J K L M N O P Q R S T U V W X Y Z bubbles)

Test ① Start with number 1 for each new section.
If a section has fewer questions than answer spaces, leave the extra answer spaces blank.

Section I—Verbal Skills

1. Ⓐ Ⓑ Ⓒ Ⓓ
2. Ⓐ Ⓑ Ⓒ Ⓓ
3. Ⓐ Ⓑ Ⓒ Ⓓ
4. Ⓐ Ⓑ Ⓒ Ⓓ
5. Ⓐ Ⓑ Ⓒ Ⓓ
6. Ⓐ Ⓑ Ⓒ Ⓓ
7. Ⓐ Ⓑ Ⓒ Ⓓ
8. Ⓐ Ⓑ Ⓒ Ⓓ
9. Ⓐ Ⓑ Ⓒ Ⓓ
10. Ⓐ Ⓑ Ⓒ Ⓓ
11. Ⓐ Ⓑ Ⓒ Ⓓ
12. Ⓐ Ⓑ Ⓒ Ⓓ
13. Ⓐ Ⓑ Ⓒ Ⓓ
14. Ⓐ Ⓑ Ⓒ Ⓓ
15. Ⓐ Ⓑ Ⓒ Ⓓ
16. Ⓐ Ⓑ Ⓒ Ⓓ
17. Ⓐ Ⓑ Ⓒ Ⓓ
18. Ⓐ Ⓑ Ⓒ Ⓓ
19. Ⓐ Ⓑ Ⓒ Ⓓ
20. Ⓐ Ⓑ Ⓒ Ⓓ
21. Ⓐ Ⓑ Ⓒ Ⓓ
22. Ⓐ Ⓑ Ⓒ Ⓓ
23. Ⓐ Ⓑ Ⓒ Ⓓ
24. Ⓐ Ⓑ Ⓒ Ⓓ
25. Ⓐ Ⓑ Ⓒ Ⓓ
26. Ⓐ Ⓑ Ⓒ Ⓓ
27. Ⓐ Ⓑ Ⓒ Ⓓ
28. Ⓐ Ⓑ Ⓒ Ⓓ
29. Ⓐ Ⓑ Ⓒ Ⓓ
30. Ⓐ Ⓑ Ⓒ Ⓓ
31. Ⓐ Ⓑ Ⓒ Ⓓ
32. Ⓐ Ⓑ Ⓒ Ⓓ
33. Ⓐ Ⓑ Ⓒ Ⓓ
34. Ⓐ Ⓑ Ⓒ Ⓓ
35. Ⓐ Ⓑ Ⓒ Ⓓ
36. Ⓐ Ⓑ Ⓒ Ⓓ
37. Ⓐ Ⓑ Ⓒ Ⓓ
38. Ⓐ Ⓑ Ⓒ Ⓓ
39. Ⓐ Ⓑ Ⓒ Ⓓ
40. Ⓐ Ⓑ Ⓒ Ⓓ
41. Ⓐ Ⓑ Ⓒ Ⓓ
42. Ⓐ Ⓑ Ⓒ Ⓓ
43. Ⓐ Ⓑ Ⓒ Ⓓ
44. Ⓐ Ⓑ Ⓒ Ⓓ
45. Ⓐ Ⓑ Ⓒ Ⓓ
46. Ⓐ Ⓑ Ⓒ Ⓓ
47. Ⓐ Ⓑ Ⓒ Ⓓ
48. Ⓐ Ⓑ Ⓒ Ⓓ
49. Ⓐ Ⓑ Ⓒ Ⓓ
50. Ⓐ Ⓑ Ⓒ Ⓓ
51. Ⓐ Ⓑ Ⓒ Ⓓ
52. Ⓐ Ⓑ Ⓒ Ⓓ
53. Ⓐ Ⓑ Ⓒ Ⓓ
54. Ⓐ Ⓑ Ⓒ Ⓓ
55. Ⓐ Ⓑ Ⓒ Ⓓ
56. Ⓐ Ⓑ Ⓒ Ⓓ
57. Ⓐ Ⓑ Ⓒ Ⓓ
58. Ⓐ Ⓑ Ⓒ Ⓓ
59. Ⓐ Ⓑ Ⓒ Ⓓ
60. Ⓐ Ⓑ Ⓒ Ⓓ

Section II—Quantitative Skills

1. Ⓐ Ⓑ Ⓒ Ⓓ
2. Ⓐ Ⓑ Ⓒ Ⓓ
3. Ⓐ Ⓑ Ⓒ Ⓓ
4. Ⓐ Ⓑ Ⓒ Ⓓ
5. Ⓐ Ⓑ Ⓒ Ⓓ
6. Ⓐ Ⓑ Ⓒ Ⓓ
7. Ⓐ Ⓑ Ⓒ Ⓓ
8. Ⓐ Ⓑ Ⓒ Ⓓ
9. Ⓐ Ⓑ Ⓒ Ⓓ
10. Ⓐ Ⓑ Ⓒ Ⓓ
11. Ⓐ Ⓑ Ⓒ Ⓓ
12. Ⓐ Ⓑ Ⓒ Ⓓ
13. Ⓐ Ⓑ Ⓒ Ⓓ
14. Ⓐ Ⓑ Ⓒ Ⓓ
15. Ⓐ Ⓑ Ⓒ Ⓓ
16. Ⓐ Ⓑ Ⓒ Ⓓ
17. Ⓐ Ⓑ Ⓒ Ⓓ
18. Ⓐ Ⓑ Ⓒ Ⓓ
19. Ⓐ Ⓑ Ⓒ Ⓓ
20. Ⓐ Ⓑ Ⓒ Ⓓ
21. Ⓐ Ⓑ Ⓒ Ⓓ
22. Ⓐ Ⓑ Ⓒ Ⓓ
23. Ⓐ Ⓑ Ⓒ Ⓓ
24. Ⓐ Ⓑ Ⓒ Ⓓ
25. Ⓐ Ⓑ Ⓒ Ⓓ
26. Ⓐ Ⓑ Ⓒ Ⓓ
27. Ⓐ Ⓑ Ⓒ Ⓓ
28. Ⓐ Ⓑ Ⓒ Ⓓ
29. Ⓐ Ⓑ Ⓒ Ⓓ
30. Ⓐ Ⓑ Ⓒ Ⓓ
31. Ⓐ Ⓑ Ⓒ Ⓓ
32. Ⓐ Ⓑ Ⓒ Ⓓ
33. Ⓐ Ⓑ Ⓒ Ⓓ
34. Ⓐ Ⓑ Ⓒ Ⓓ
35. Ⓐ Ⓑ Ⓒ Ⓓ
36. Ⓐ Ⓑ Ⓒ Ⓓ
37. Ⓐ Ⓑ Ⓒ Ⓓ
38. Ⓐ Ⓑ Ⓒ Ⓓ
39. Ⓐ Ⓑ Ⓒ Ⓓ
40. Ⓐ Ⓑ Ⓒ Ⓓ
41. Ⓐ Ⓑ Ⓒ Ⓓ
42. Ⓐ Ⓑ Ⓒ Ⓓ
43. Ⓐ Ⓑ Ⓒ Ⓓ
44. Ⓐ Ⓑ Ⓒ Ⓓ
45. Ⓐ Ⓑ Ⓒ Ⓓ
46. Ⓐ Ⓑ Ⓒ Ⓓ
47. Ⓐ Ⓑ Ⓒ Ⓓ
48. Ⓐ Ⓑ Ⓒ Ⓓ
49. Ⓐ Ⓑ Ⓒ Ⓓ
50. Ⓐ Ⓑ Ⓒ Ⓓ
51. Ⓐ Ⓑ Ⓒ Ⓓ
52. Ⓐ Ⓑ Ⓒ Ⓓ

Test ❶ Start with number 1 for each new section.
If a section has fewer questions than answer spaces, leave the extra answer spaces blank.

Section III—Reading

1. Ⓐ Ⓑ Ⓒ Ⓓ
2. Ⓐ Ⓑ Ⓒ Ⓓ
3. Ⓐ Ⓑ Ⓒ Ⓓ
4. Ⓐ Ⓑ Ⓒ Ⓓ
5. Ⓐ Ⓑ Ⓒ Ⓓ
6. Ⓐ Ⓑ Ⓒ Ⓓ
7. Ⓐ Ⓑ Ⓒ Ⓓ
8. Ⓐ Ⓑ Ⓒ Ⓓ
9. Ⓐ Ⓑ Ⓒ Ⓓ
10. Ⓐ Ⓑ Ⓒ Ⓓ
11. Ⓐ Ⓑ Ⓒ Ⓓ
12. Ⓐ Ⓑ Ⓒ Ⓓ
13. Ⓐ Ⓑ Ⓒ Ⓓ
14. Ⓐ Ⓑ Ⓒ Ⓓ
15. Ⓐ Ⓑ Ⓒ Ⓓ
16. Ⓐ Ⓑ Ⓒ Ⓓ
17. Ⓐ Ⓑ Ⓒ Ⓓ
18. Ⓐ Ⓑ Ⓒ Ⓓ
19. Ⓐ Ⓑ Ⓒ Ⓓ
20. Ⓐ Ⓑ Ⓒ Ⓓ
21. Ⓐ Ⓑ Ⓒ Ⓓ
22. Ⓐ Ⓑ Ⓒ Ⓓ
23. Ⓐ Ⓑ Ⓒ Ⓓ
24. Ⓐ Ⓑ Ⓒ Ⓓ
25. Ⓐ Ⓑ Ⓒ Ⓓ
26. Ⓐ Ⓑ Ⓒ Ⓓ
27. Ⓐ Ⓑ Ⓒ Ⓓ
28. Ⓐ Ⓑ Ⓒ Ⓓ
29. Ⓐ Ⓑ Ⓒ Ⓓ
30. Ⓐ Ⓑ Ⓒ Ⓓ
31. Ⓐ Ⓑ Ⓒ Ⓓ

32. Ⓐ Ⓑ Ⓒ Ⓓ
33. Ⓐ Ⓑ Ⓒ Ⓓ
34. Ⓐ Ⓑ Ⓒ Ⓓ
35. Ⓐ Ⓑ Ⓒ Ⓓ
36. Ⓐ Ⓑ Ⓒ Ⓓ
37. Ⓐ Ⓑ Ⓒ Ⓓ
38. Ⓐ Ⓑ Ⓒ Ⓓ
39. Ⓐ Ⓑ Ⓒ Ⓓ
40. Ⓐ Ⓑ Ⓒ Ⓓ
41. Ⓐ Ⓑ Ⓒ Ⓓ
42. Ⓐ Ⓑ Ⓒ Ⓓ
43. Ⓐ Ⓑ Ⓒ Ⓓ
44. Ⓐ Ⓑ Ⓒ Ⓓ
45. Ⓐ Ⓑ Ⓒ Ⓓ
46. Ⓐ Ⓑ Ⓒ Ⓓ
47. Ⓐ Ⓑ Ⓒ Ⓓ
48. Ⓐ Ⓑ Ⓒ Ⓓ
49. Ⓐ Ⓑ Ⓒ Ⓓ
50. Ⓐ Ⓑ Ⓒ Ⓓ
51. Ⓐ Ⓑ Ⓒ Ⓓ
52. Ⓐ Ⓑ Ⓒ Ⓓ
53. Ⓐ Ⓑ Ⓒ Ⓓ
54. Ⓐ Ⓑ Ⓒ Ⓓ
55. Ⓐ Ⓑ Ⓒ Ⓓ
56. Ⓐ Ⓑ Ⓒ Ⓓ
57. Ⓐ Ⓑ Ⓒ Ⓓ
58. Ⓐ Ⓑ Ⓒ Ⓓ
59. Ⓐ Ⓑ Ⓒ Ⓓ
60. Ⓐ Ⓑ Ⓒ Ⓓ
61. Ⓐ Ⓑ Ⓒ Ⓓ
62. Ⓐ Ⓑ Ⓒ Ⓓ

Section IV—Mathematics

1. Ⓐ Ⓑ Ⓒ Ⓓ
2. Ⓐ Ⓑ Ⓒ Ⓓ
3. Ⓐ Ⓑ Ⓒ Ⓓ
4. Ⓐ Ⓑ Ⓒ Ⓓ
5. Ⓐ Ⓑ Ⓒ Ⓓ
6. Ⓐ Ⓑ Ⓒ Ⓓ
7. Ⓐ Ⓑ Ⓒ Ⓓ
8. Ⓐ Ⓑ Ⓒ Ⓓ
9. Ⓐ Ⓑ Ⓒ Ⓓ
10. Ⓐ Ⓑ Ⓒ Ⓓ
11. Ⓐ Ⓑ Ⓒ Ⓓ
12. Ⓐ Ⓑ Ⓒ Ⓓ
13. Ⓐ Ⓑ Ⓒ Ⓓ
14. Ⓐ Ⓑ Ⓒ Ⓓ
15. Ⓐ Ⓑ Ⓒ Ⓓ
16. Ⓐ Ⓑ Ⓒ Ⓓ
17. Ⓐ Ⓑ Ⓒ Ⓓ
18. Ⓐ Ⓑ Ⓒ Ⓓ
19. Ⓐ Ⓑ Ⓒ Ⓓ
20. Ⓐ Ⓑ Ⓒ Ⓓ
21. Ⓐ Ⓑ Ⓒ Ⓓ
22. Ⓐ Ⓑ Ⓒ Ⓓ
23. Ⓐ Ⓑ Ⓒ Ⓓ
24. Ⓐ Ⓑ Ⓒ Ⓓ
25. Ⓐ Ⓑ Ⓒ Ⓓ
26. Ⓐ Ⓑ Ⓒ Ⓓ
27. Ⓐ Ⓑ Ⓒ Ⓓ
28. Ⓐ Ⓑ Ⓒ Ⓓ
29. Ⓐ Ⓑ Ⓒ Ⓓ
30. Ⓐ Ⓑ Ⓒ Ⓓ
31. Ⓐ Ⓑ Ⓒ Ⓓ
32. Ⓐ Ⓑ Ⓒ Ⓓ

33. Ⓐ Ⓑ Ⓒ Ⓓ
34. Ⓐ Ⓑ Ⓒ Ⓓ
35. Ⓐ Ⓑ Ⓒ Ⓓ
36. Ⓐ Ⓑ Ⓒ Ⓓ
37. Ⓐ Ⓑ Ⓒ Ⓓ
38. Ⓐ Ⓑ Ⓒ Ⓓ
39. Ⓐ Ⓑ Ⓒ Ⓓ
40. Ⓐ Ⓑ Ⓒ Ⓓ
41. Ⓐ Ⓑ Ⓒ Ⓓ
42. Ⓐ Ⓑ Ⓒ Ⓓ
43. Ⓐ Ⓑ Ⓒ Ⓓ
44. Ⓐ Ⓑ Ⓒ Ⓓ
45. Ⓐ Ⓑ Ⓒ Ⓓ
46. Ⓐ Ⓑ Ⓒ Ⓓ
47. Ⓐ Ⓑ Ⓒ Ⓓ
48. Ⓐ Ⓑ Ⓒ Ⓓ
49. Ⓐ Ⓑ Ⓒ Ⓓ
50. Ⓐ Ⓑ Ⓒ Ⓓ
51. Ⓐ Ⓑ Ⓒ Ⓓ
52. Ⓐ Ⓑ Ⓒ Ⓓ
53. Ⓐ Ⓑ Ⓒ Ⓓ
54. Ⓐ Ⓑ Ⓒ Ⓓ
55. Ⓐ Ⓑ Ⓒ Ⓓ
56. Ⓐ Ⓑ Ⓒ Ⓓ
57. Ⓐ Ⓑ Ⓒ Ⓓ
58. Ⓐ Ⓑ Ⓒ Ⓓ
59. Ⓐ Ⓑ Ⓒ Ⓓ
60. Ⓐ Ⓑ Ⓒ Ⓓ
61. Ⓐ Ⓑ Ⓒ Ⓓ
62. Ⓐ Ⓑ Ⓒ Ⓓ
63. Ⓐ Ⓑ Ⓒ Ⓓ
64. Ⓐ Ⓑ Ⓒ Ⓓ

Section V—Language Skills

1. Ⓐ Ⓑ Ⓒ Ⓓ
2. Ⓐ Ⓑ Ⓒ Ⓓ
3. Ⓐ Ⓑ Ⓒ Ⓓ
4. Ⓐ Ⓑ Ⓒ Ⓓ
5. Ⓐ Ⓑ Ⓒ Ⓓ
6. Ⓐ Ⓑ Ⓒ Ⓓ
7. Ⓐ Ⓑ Ⓒ Ⓓ
8. Ⓐ Ⓑ Ⓒ Ⓓ
9. Ⓐ Ⓑ Ⓒ Ⓓ
10. Ⓐ Ⓑ Ⓒ Ⓓ
11. Ⓐ Ⓑ Ⓒ Ⓓ
12. Ⓐ Ⓑ Ⓒ Ⓓ
13. Ⓐ Ⓑ Ⓒ Ⓓ
14. Ⓐ Ⓑ Ⓒ Ⓓ
15. Ⓐ Ⓑ Ⓒ Ⓓ

16. Ⓐ Ⓑ Ⓒ Ⓓ
17. Ⓐ Ⓑ Ⓒ Ⓓ
18. Ⓐ Ⓑ Ⓒ Ⓓ
19. Ⓐ Ⓑ Ⓒ Ⓓ
20. Ⓐ Ⓑ Ⓒ Ⓓ
21. Ⓐ Ⓑ Ⓒ Ⓓ
22. Ⓐ Ⓑ Ⓒ Ⓓ
23. Ⓐ Ⓑ Ⓒ Ⓓ
24. Ⓐ Ⓑ Ⓒ Ⓓ
25. Ⓐ Ⓑ Ⓒ Ⓓ
26. Ⓐ Ⓑ Ⓒ Ⓓ
27. Ⓐ Ⓑ Ⓒ Ⓓ
28. Ⓐ Ⓑ Ⓒ Ⓓ
29. Ⓐ Ⓑ Ⓒ Ⓓ
30. Ⓐ Ⓑ Ⓒ Ⓓ

31. Ⓐ Ⓑ Ⓒ Ⓓ
32. Ⓐ Ⓑ Ⓒ Ⓓ
33. Ⓐ Ⓑ Ⓒ Ⓓ
34. Ⓐ Ⓑ Ⓒ Ⓓ
35. Ⓐ Ⓑ Ⓒ Ⓓ
36. Ⓐ Ⓑ Ⓒ Ⓓ
37. Ⓐ Ⓑ Ⓒ Ⓓ
38. Ⓐ Ⓑ Ⓒ Ⓓ
39. Ⓐ Ⓑ Ⓒ Ⓓ
40. Ⓐ Ⓑ Ⓒ Ⓓ
41. Ⓐ Ⓑ Ⓒ Ⓓ
42. Ⓐ Ⓑ Ⓒ Ⓓ
43. Ⓐ Ⓑ Ⓒ Ⓓ
44. Ⓐ Ⓑ Ⓒ Ⓓ
45. Ⓐ Ⓑ Ⓒ Ⓓ

46. Ⓐ Ⓑ Ⓒ Ⓓ
47. Ⓐ Ⓑ Ⓒ Ⓓ
48. Ⓐ Ⓑ Ⓒ Ⓓ
49. Ⓐ Ⓑ Ⓒ Ⓓ
50. Ⓐ Ⓑ Ⓒ Ⓓ
51. Ⓐ Ⓑ Ⓒ Ⓓ
52. Ⓐ Ⓑ Ⓒ Ⓓ
53. Ⓐ Ⓑ Ⓒ Ⓓ
54. Ⓐ Ⓑ Ⓒ Ⓓ
55. Ⓐ Ⓑ Ⓒ Ⓓ
56. Ⓐ Ⓑ Ⓒ Ⓓ
57. Ⓐ Ⓑ Ⓒ Ⓓ
58. Ⓐ Ⓑ Ⓒ Ⓓ
59. Ⓐ Ⓑ Ⓒ Ⓓ
60. Ⓐ Ⓑ Ⓒ Ⓓ

Completely darken bubbles with a No. 2 pencil. If you make a mistake, be sure to erase mark completely. Erase all stray marks.

1.

YOUR NAME: _____
(Print)   Last   First   M.I.

SIGNATURE: _____ DATE: ___ / ___ / ___

HOME ADDRESS: _____
(Print)   Number and Street

_____
City   State   Zip Code

PHONE NO.: _____
(Print)

IMPORTANT: Please fill in these boxes exactly as shown on the back cover of your test book.

2. TEST FORM

_____

6. DATE OF BIRTH

Month	Day	Year
◯ JAN		
◯ FEB	⓪ ⓪	⓪ ⓪
◯ MAR	① ①	① ①
◯ APR	② ②	② ②
◯ MAY	③ ③	③ ③
◯ JUN	④ ④	④
◯ JUL	⑤ ⑤	⑤
◯ AUG	⑥ ⑥	⑥
◯ SEP	⑦ ⑦	⑦
◯ OCT	⑧ ⑧	⑧
◯ NOV	⑨ ⑨	⑨
◯ DEC		

3. TEST CODE   **4. REGISTRATION NUMBER**

⓪ Ⓐ Ⓙ ⓪ ⓪ ⓪ ⓪ ⓪ ⓪ ⓪ ⓪
① Ⓑ Ⓚ ① ① ① ① ① ① ① ①
② Ⓒ Ⓛ ② ② ② ② ② ② ② ②
③ Ⓓ Ⓜ ③ ③ ③ ③ ③ ③ ③ ③
④ Ⓔ Ⓝ ④ ④ ④ ④ ④ ④ ④ ④
⑤ Ⓕ Ⓞ ⑤ ⑤ ⑤ ⑤ ⑤ ⑤ ⑤ ⑤
⑥ Ⓖ Ⓟ ⑥ ⑥ ⑥ ⑥ ⑥ ⑥ ⑥ ⑥
⑦ Ⓗ Ⓠ ⑦ ⑦ ⑦ ⑦ ⑦ ⑦ ⑦ ⑦
⑧ Ⓘ Ⓡ ⑧ ⑧ ⑧ ⑧ ⑧ ⑧ ⑧ ⑧
⑨ ⑨ ⑨ ⑨ ⑨ ⑨ ⑨ ⑨ ⑨

7. SEX
◯ MALE
◯ FEMALE

The Princeton Review®

5. YOUR NAME

First 4 letters of last name				FIRST INIT	MID INIT
Ⓐ	Ⓐ	Ⓐ	Ⓐ	Ⓐ	Ⓐ
Ⓑ	Ⓑ	Ⓑ	Ⓑ	Ⓑ	Ⓑ
Ⓒ	Ⓒ	Ⓒ	Ⓒ	Ⓒ	Ⓒ
Ⓓ	Ⓓ	Ⓓ	Ⓓ	Ⓓ	Ⓓ
Ⓔ	Ⓔ	Ⓔ	Ⓔ	Ⓔ	Ⓔ
Ⓕ	Ⓕ	Ⓕ	Ⓕ	Ⓕ	Ⓕ
Ⓖ	Ⓖ	Ⓖ	Ⓖ	Ⓖ	Ⓖ
Ⓗ	Ⓗ	Ⓗ	Ⓗ	Ⓗ	Ⓗ
Ⓘ	Ⓘ	Ⓘ	Ⓘ	Ⓘ	Ⓘ
Ⓙ	Ⓙ	Ⓙ	Ⓙ	Ⓙ	Ⓙ
Ⓚ	Ⓚ	Ⓚ	Ⓚ	Ⓚ	Ⓚ
Ⓛ	Ⓛ	Ⓛ	Ⓛ	Ⓛ	Ⓛ
Ⓜ	Ⓜ	Ⓜ	Ⓜ	Ⓜ	Ⓜ
Ⓝ	Ⓝ	Ⓝ	Ⓝ	Ⓝ	Ⓝ
Ⓞ	Ⓞ	Ⓞ	Ⓞ	Ⓞ	Ⓞ
Ⓟ	Ⓟ	Ⓟ	Ⓟ	Ⓟ	Ⓟ
Ⓠ	Ⓠ	Ⓠ	Ⓠ	Ⓠ	Ⓠ
Ⓡ	Ⓡ	Ⓡ	Ⓡ	Ⓡ	Ⓡ
Ⓢ	Ⓢ	Ⓢ	Ⓢ	Ⓢ	Ⓢ
Ⓣ	Ⓣ	Ⓣ	Ⓣ	Ⓣ	Ⓣ
Ⓤ	Ⓤ	Ⓤ	Ⓤ	Ⓤ	Ⓤ
Ⓥ	Ⓥ	Ⓥ	Ⓥ	Ⓥ	Ⓥ
Ⓦ	Ⓦ	Ⓦ	Ⓦ	Ⓦ	Ⓦ
Ⓧ	Ⓧ	Ⓧ	Ⓧ	Ⓧ	Ⓧ
Ⓨ	Ⓨ	Ⓨ	Ⓨ	Ⓨ	Ⓨ
Ⓩ	Ⓩ	Ⓩ	Ⓩ	Ⓩ	Ⓩ

Test ② Start with number 1 for each new section.
If a section has fewer questions than answer spaces, leave the extra answer spaces blank.

Section I—Verbal Skills

1. Ⓐ Ⓑ Ⓒ Ⓓ   31. Ⓐ Ⓑ Ⓒ Ⓓ
2. Ⓐ Ⓑ Ⓒ Ⓓ   32. Ⓐ Ⓑ Ⓒ Ⓓ
3. Ⓐ Ⓑ Ⓒ Ⓓ   33. Ⓐ Ⓑ Ⓒ Ⓓ
4. Ⓐ Ⓑ Ⓒ Ⓓ   34. Ⓐ Ⓑ Ⓒ Ⓓ
5. Ⓐ Ⓑ Ⓒ Ⓓ   35. Ⓐ Ⓑ Ⓒ Ⓓ
6. Ⓐ Ⓑ Ⓒ Ⓓ   36. Ⓐ Ⓑ Ⓒ Ⓓ
7. Ⓐ Ⓑ Ⓒ Ⓓ   37. Ⓐ Ⓑ Ⓒ Ⓓ
8. Ⓐ Ⓑ Ⓒ Ⓓ   38. Ⓐ Ⓑ Ⓒ Ⓓ
9. Ⓐ Ⓑ Ⓒ Ⓓ   39. Ⓐ Ⓑ Ⓒ Ⓓ
10. Ⓐ Ⓑ Ⓒ Ⓓ   40. Ⓐ Ⓑ Ⓒ Ⓓ
11. Ⓐ Ⓑ Ⓒ Ⓓ   41. Ⓐ Ⓑ Ⓒ Ⓓ
12. Ⓐ Ⓑ Ⓒ Ⓓ   42. Ⓐ Ⓑ Ⓒ Ⓓ
13. Ⓐ Ⓑ Ⓒ Ⓓ   43. Ⓐ Ⓑ Ⓒ Ⓓ
14. Ⓐ Ⓑ Ⓒ Ⓓ   44. Ⓐ Ⓑ Ⓒ Ⓓ
15. Ⓐ Ⓑ Ⓒ Ⓓ   45. Ⓐ Ⓑ Ⓒ Ⓓ
16. Ⓐ Ⓑ Ⓒ Ⓓ   46. Ⓐ Ⓑ Ⓒ Ⓓ
17. Ⓐ Ⓑ Ⓒ Ⓓ   47. Ⓐ Ⓑ Ⓒ Ⓓ
18. Ⓐ Ⓑ Ⓒ Ⓓ   48. Ⓐ Ⓑ Ⓒ Ⓓ
19. Ⓐ Ⓑ Ⓒ Ⓓ   49. Ⓐ Ⓑ Ⓒ Ⓓ
20. Ⓐ Ⓑ Ⓒ Ⓓ   50. Ⓐ Ⓑ Ⓒ Ⓓ
21. Ⓐ Ⓑ Ⓒ Ⓓ   51. Ⓐ Ⓑ Ⓒ Ⓓ
22. Ⓐ Ⓑ Ⓒ Ⓓ   52. Ⓐ Ⓑ Ⓒ Ⓓ
23. Ⓐ Ⓑ Ⓒ Ⓓ   53. Ⓐ Ⓑ Ⓒ Ⓓ
24. Ⓐ Ⓑ Ⓒ Ⓓ   54. Ⓐ Ⓑ Ⓒ Ⓓ
25. Ⓐ Ⓑ Ⓒ Ⓓ   55. Ⓐ Ⓑ Ⓒ Ⓓ
26. Ⓐ Ⓑ Ⓒ Ⓓ   56. Ⓐ Ⓑ Ⓒ Ⓓ
27. Ⓐ Ⓑ Ⓒ Ⓓ   57. Ⓐ Ⓑ Ⓒ Ⓓ
28. Ⓐ Ⓑ Ⓒ Ⓓ   58. Ⓐ Ⓑ Ⓒ Ⓓ
29. Ⓐ Ⓑ Ⓒ Ⓓ   59. Ⓐ Ⓑ Ⓒ Ⓓ
30. Ⓐ Ⓑ Ⓒ Ⓓ   60. Ⓐ Ⓑ Ⓒ Ⓓ

Section II—Quantitative Skills

1. Ⓐ Ⓑ Ⓒ Ⓓ   27. Ⓐ Ⓑ Ⓒ Ⓓ
2. Ⓐ Ⓑ Ⓒ Ⓓ   28. Ⓐ Ⓑ Ⓒ Ⓓ
3. Ⓐ Ⓑ Ⓒ Ⓓ   29. Ⓐ Ⓑ Ⓒ Ⓓ
4. Ⓐ Ⓑ Ⓒ Ⓓ   30. Ⓐ Ⓑ Ⓒ Ⓓ
5. Ⓐ Ⓑ Ⓒ Ⓓ   31. Ⓐ Ⓑ Ⓒ Ⓓ
6. Ⓐ Ⓑ Ⓒ Ⓓ   32. Ⓐ Ⓑ Ⓒ Ⓓ
7. Ⓐ Ⓑ Ⓒ Ⓓ   33. Ⓐ Ⓑ Ⓒ Ⓓ
8. Ⓐ Ⓑ Ⓒ Ⓓ   34. Ⓐ Ⓑ Ⓒ Ⓓ
9. Ⓐ Ⓑ Ⓒ Ⓓ   35. Ⓐ Ⓑ Ⓒ Ⓓ
10. Ⓐ Ⓑ Ⓒ Ⓓ   36. Ⓐ Ⓑ Ⓒ Ⓓ
11. Ⓐ Ⓑ Ⓒ Ⓓ   37. Ⓐ Ⓑ Ⓒ Ⓓ
12. Ⓐ Ⓑ Ⓒ Ⓓ   38. Ⓐ Ⓑ Ⓒ Ⓓ
13. Ⓐ Ⓑ Ⓒ Ⓓ   39. Ⓐ Ⓑ Ⓒ Ⓓ
14. Ⓐ Ⓑ Ⓒ Ⓓ   40. Ⓐ Ⓑ Ⓒ Ⓓ
15. Ⓐ Ⓑ Ⓒ Ⓓ   41. Ⓐ Ⓑ Ⓒ Ⓓ
16. Ⓐ Ⓑ Ⓒ Ⓓ   42. Ⓐ Ⓑ Ⓒ Ⓓ
17. Ⓐ Ⓑ Ⓒ Ⓓ   43. Ⓐ Ⓑ Ⓒ Ⓓ
18. Ⓐ Ⓑ Ⓒ Ⓓ   44. Ⓐ Ⓑ Ⓒ Ⓓ
19. Ⓐ Ⓑ Ⓒ Ⓓ   45. Ⓐ Ⓑ Ⓒ Ⓓ
20. Ⓐ Ⓑ Ⓒ Ⓓ   46. Ⓐ Ⓑ Ⓒ Ⓓ
21. Ⓐ Ⓑ Ⓒ Ⓓ   47. Ⓐ Ⓑ Ⓒ Ⓓ
22. Ⓐ Ⓑ Ⓒ Ⓓ   48. Ⓐ Ⓑ Ⓒ Ⓓ
23. Ⓐ Ⓑ Ⓒ Ⓓ   49. Ⓐ Ⓑ Ⓒ Ⓓ
24. Ⓐ Ⓑ Ⓒ Ⓓ   50. Ⓐ Ⓑ Ⓒ Ⓓ
25. Ⓐ Ⓑ Ⓒ Ⓓ   51. Ⓐ Ⓑ Ⓒ Ⓓ
26. Ⓐ Ⓑ Ⓒ Ⓓ   52. Ⓐ Ⓑ Ⓒ Ⓓ

Test ② Start with number 1 for each new section.
If a section has fewer questions than answer spaces, leave the extra answer spaces blank.

Section III—Reading

1. (A) (B) (C) (D) 32. (A) (B) (C) (D)
2. (A) (B) (C) (D) 33. (A) (B) (C) (D)
3. (A) (B) (C) (D) 34. (A) (B) (C) (D)
4. (A) (B) (C) (D) 35. (A) (B) (C) (D)
5. (A) (B) (C) (D) 36. (A) (B) (C) (D)
6. (A) (B) (C) (D) 37. (A) (B) (C) (D)
7. (A) (B) (C) (D) 38. (A) (B) (C) (D)
8. (A) (B) (C) (D) 39. (A) (B) (C) (D)
9. (A) (B) (C) (D) 40. (A) (B) (C) (D)
10. (A) (B) (C) (D) 41. (A) (B) (C) (D)
11. (A) (B) (C) (D) 42. (A) (B) (C) (D)
12. (A) (B) (C) (D) 43. (A) (B) (C) (D)
13. (A) (B) (C) (D) 44. (A) (B) (C) (D)
14. (A) (B) (C) (D) 45. (A) (B) (C) (D)
15. (A) (B) (C) (D) 46. (A) (B) (C) (D)
16. (A) (B) (C) (D) 47. (A) (B) (C) (D)
17. (A) (B) (C) (D) 48. (A) (B) (C) (D)
18. (A) (B) (C) (D) 49. (A) (B) (C) (D)
19. (A) (B) (C) (D) 50. (A) (B) (C) (D)
20. (A) (B) (C) (D) 51. (A) (B) (C) (D)
21. (A) (B) (C) (D) 52. (A) (B) (C) (D)
22. (A) (B) (C) (D) 53. (A) (B) (C) (D)
23. (A) (B) (C) (D) 54. (A) (B) (C) (D)
24. (A) (B) (C) (D) 55. (A) (B) (C) (D)
25. (A) (B) (C) (D) 56. (A) (B) (C) (D)
26. (A) (B) (C) (D) 57. (A) (B) (C) (D)
27. (A) (B) (C) (D) 58. (A) (B) (C) (D)
28. (A) (B) (C) (D) 59. (A) (B) (C) (D)
29. (A) (B) (C) (D) 60. (A) (B) (C) (D)
30. (A) (B) (C) (D) 61. (A) (B) (C) (D)
31. (A) (B) (C) (D) 62. (A) (B) (C) (D)

Section IV—Mathematics

1. (A) (B) (C) (D) 33. (A) (B) (C) (D)
2. (A) (B) (C) (D) 34. (A) (B) (C) (D)
3. (A) (B) (C) (D) 35. (A) (B) (C) (D)
4. (A) (B) (C) (D) 36. (A) (B) (C) (D)
5. (A) (B) (C) (D) 37. (A) (B) (C) (D)
6. (A) (B) (C) (D) 38. (A) (B) (C) (D)
7. (A) (B) (C) (D) 39. (A) (B) (C) (D)
8. (A) (B) (C) (D) 40. (A) (B) (C) (D)
9. (A) (B) (C) (D) 41. (A) (B) (C) (D)
10. (A) (B) (C) (D) 42. (A) (B) (C) (D)
11. (A) (B) (C) (D) 43. (A) (B) (C) (D)
12. (A) (B) (C) (D) 44. (A) (B) (C) (D)
13. (A) (B) (C) (D) 45. (A) (B) (C) (D)
14. (A) (B) (C) (D) 46. (A) (B) (C) (D)
15. (A) (B) (C) (D) 47. (A) (B) (C) (D)
16. (A) (B) (C) (D) 48. (A) (B) (C) (D)
17. (A) (B) (C) (D) 49. (A) (B) (C) (D)
18. (A) (B) (C) (D) 50. (A) (B) (C) (D)
19. (A) (B) (C) (D) 51. (A) (B) (C) (D)
20. (A) (B) (C) (D) 52. (A) (B) (C) (D)
21. (A) (B) (C) (D) 53. (A) (B) (C) (D)
22. (A) (B) (C) (D) 54. (A) (B) (C) (D)
23. (A) (B) (C) (D) 55. (A) (B) (C) (D)
24. (A) (B) (C) (D) 56. (A) (B) (C) (D)
25. (A) (B) (C) (D) 57. (A) (B) (C) (D)
26. (A) (B) (C) (D) 58. (A) (B) (C) (D)
27. (A) (B) (C) (D) 59. (A) (B) (C) (D)
28. (A) (B) (C) (D) 60. (A) (B) (C) (D)
29. (A) (B) (C) (D) 61. (A) (B) (C) (D)
30. (A) (B) (C) (D) 62. (A) (B) (C) (D)
31. (A) (B) (C) (D) 63. (A) (B) (C) (D)
32. (A) (B) (C) (D) 64. (A) (B) (C) (D)

Section V—Language Skills

1. (A) (B) (C) (D)   16. (A) (B) (C) (D)   31. (A) (B) (C) (D)   46. (A) (B) (C) (D)
2. (A) (B) (C) (D)   17. (A) (B) (C) (D)   32. (A) (B) (C) (D)   47. (A) (B) (C) (D)
3. (A) (B) (C) (D)   18. (A) (B) (C) (D)   33. (A) (B) (C) (D)   48. (A) (B) (C) (D)
4. (A) (B) (C) (D)   19. (A) (B) (C) (D)   34. (A) (B) (C) (D)   49. (A) (B) (C) (D)
5. (A) (B) (C) (D)   20. (A) (B) (C) (D)   35. (A) (B) (C) (D)   50. (A) (B) (C) (D)
6. (A) (B) (C) (D)   21. (A) (B) (C) (D)   36. (A) (B) (C) (D)   51. (A) (B) (C) (D)
7. (A) (B) (C) (D)   22. (A) (B) (C) (D)   37. (A) (B) (C) (D)   52. (A) (B) (C) (D)
8. (A) (B) (C) (D)   23. (A) (B) (C) (D)   38. (A) (B) (C) (D)   53. (A) (B) (C) (D)
9. (A) (B) (C) (D)   24. (A) (B) (C) (D)   39. (A) (B) (C) (D)   54. (A) (B) (C) (D)
10. (A) (B) (C) (D) 25. (A) (B) (C) (D)   40. (A) (B) (C) (D)   55. (A) (B) (C) (D)
11. (A) (B) (C) (D) 26. (A) (B) (C) (D)   41. (A) (B) (C) (D)   56. (A) (B) (C) (D)
12. (A) (B) (C) (D) 27. (A) (B) (C) (D)   42. (A) (B) (C) (D)   57. (A) (B) (C) (D)
13. (A) (B) (C) (D) 28. (A) (B) (C) (D)   43. (A) (B) (C) (D)   58. (A) (B) (C) (D)
14. (A) (B) (C) (D) 29. (A) (B) (C) (D)   44. (A) (B) (C) (D)   59. (A) (B) (C) (D)
15. (A) (B) (C) (D) 30. (A) (B) (C) (D)   45. (A) (B) (C) (D)   60. (A) (B) (C) (D)

NOTES

NOTES

International Offices Listing

China (Beijing)
1501 Building A,
Disanji Creative Zone,
No.66 West Section of North 4th Ring Road Beijing
Tel: +86-10-62684481/2/3
Email: tprkor01@chol.com
Website: www.tprbeijing.com

China (Shanghai)
1010 Kaixuan Road
Building B, 5/F
Changning District, Shanghai, China 200052
Sara Beattie, Owner: Email: sbeattie@sarabeattie.com
Tel: +86-21-5108-2798
Fax: +86-21-6386-1039
Website: www.princetonreviewshanghai.com

Hong Kong
5th Floor, Yardley Commercial Building
1-6 Connaught Road West, Sheung Wan, Hong Kong
(MTR Exit C)
Sara Beattie, Owner: Email: sbeattie@sarabeattie.com
Tel: +852-2507-9380
Fax: +852-2827-4630
Website: www.princetonreviewhk.com

India (Mumbai)
Score Plus Academy
Office No.15, Fifth Floor
Manek Mahal 90
Veer Nariman Road
Next to Hotel Ambassador
Churchgate, Mumbai 400020
Maharashtra, India
Ritu Kalwani: Email: director@score-plus.com
Tel: + 91 22 22846801 / 39 / 41
Website: www.score-plus.com

India (New Delhi)
South Extension
K-16, Upper Ground Floor
South Extension Part–1,
New Delhi-110049
Aradhana Mahna: aradhana@manyagroup.com
Monisha Banerjee: monisha@manyagroup.com
Ruchi Tomar: ruchi.tomar@manyagroup.com
Rishi Josan: Rishi.josan@manyagroup.com
Vishal Goswamy: vishal.goswamy@manyagroup.com
Tel: +91-11-64501603/ 4, +91-11-65028379
Website: www.manyagroup.com

Lebanon
463 Bliss Street
AlFarra Building - 2nd floor
Ras Beirut
Beirut, Lebanon
Hassan Coudsi: Email: hassan.coudsi@review.com
Tel: +961-1-367-688
Website: www.princetonreviewlebanon.com

Korea
945-25 Young Shin Building
25 Daechi-Dong, Kangnam-gu
Seoul, Korea 135-280
Yong-Hoon Lee: Email: TPRKor01@chollian.net
In-Woo Kim: Email: iwkim@tpr.co.kr
Tel: + 82-2-554-7762
Fax: +82-2-453-9466
Website: www.tpr.co.kr

Kuwait
ScorePlus Learning Center
Salmiyah Block 3, Street 2 Building 14
Post Box: 559, Zip 1306, Safat, Kuwait
Email: infokuwait@score-plus.com
Tel: +965-25-75-48-02 / 8
Fax: +965-25-75-46-02
Website: www.scorepluseducation.com

Malaysia
Sara Beattie MDC Sdn Bhd
Suites 18E & 18F
18th Floor
Gurney Tower, Persiaran Gurney
Penang, Malaysia
Email: tprkl.my@sarabeattie.com
Sara Beattie, Owner: Email: sbeattie@sarabeattie.com
Tel: +604-2104 333
Fax: +604-2104 330
Website: www.princetonreviewKL.com

Mexico
TPR México
Guanajuato No. 242 Piso 1 Interior 1
Col. Roma Norte
México D.F., C.P.06700
registro@princetonreviewmexico.com
Tel: +52-55-5255-4495
+52-55-5255-4440
+52-55-5255-4442
Website: www.princetonreviewmexico.com

Qatar
Score Plus
Office No: 1A, Al Kuwari (Damas)
Building near Merweb Hotel, Al Saad
Post Box: 2408, Doha, Qatar
Email: infoqatar@score-plus.com
Tel: +974 44 36 8580, +974 526 5032
Fax: +974 44 13 1995
Website: www.scorepluseducation.com

Taiwan
The Princeton Review Taiwan
2F, 169 Zhong Xiao East Road, Section 4
Taipei, Taiwan 10690
Lisa Bartle (Owner): lbartle@princetonreview.com.tw
Tel: +886-2-2751-1293
Fax: +886-2-2776-3201
Website: www.PrincetonReview.com.tw

Thailand
The Princeton Review Thailand
Sathorn Nakorn Tower, 28th floor
100 North Sathorn Road
Bangkok, Thailand 10500
Thavida Bijayendrayodhin (Chairman)
Email: thavida@princetonreviewthailand.com
Mitsara Bijayendrayodhin (Managing Director)
Email: mitsara@princetonreviewthailand.com
Tel: +662-636-6770
Fax: +662-636-6776
Website: www.princetonreviewthailand.com

Turkey
Yeni Sülün Sokak No. 28
Levent, Istanbul, 34330, Turkey
Nuri Ozgur: nuri@tprturkey.com
Rona Ozgur: rona@tprturkey.com
Iren Ozgur: iren@tprturkey.com
Tel: +90-212-324-4747
Fax: +90-212-324-3347
Website: www.tprturkey.com

UAE
Emirates Score Plus
Office No: 506, Fifth Floor
Sultan Business Center
Near Lamcy Plaza, 21 Oud Metha Road
Post Box: 44098, Dubai
United Arab Emirates
Hukumat Kalwani: skoreplus@gmail.com
Ritu Kalwani: director@score-plus.com
Email: info@score-plus.com
Tel: +971-4-334-0004
Fax: +971-4-334-0222
Website: www.princetonreviewuae.com

Our International Partners

The Princeton Review also runs courses with a variety of partners in Africa, Asia, Europe, and South America.

Georgia
LEAF American-Georgian Education Center
www.leaf.ge

Mongolia
English Academy of Mongolia
www.nyescm.org

Nigeria
The Know Place
www.knowplace.com.ng

Panama
Academia Interamericana de Panama
http://aip.edu.pa/

Switzerland
Institut Le Rosey
http://www.rosey.ch/

All other inquiries, please email us at
internationalsupport@review.com